W9-BKI-145

Money Shy to Money Sure

Money Shy to Money Sure

A WOMAN'S ROAD MAP TO FINANCIAL WELL-BEING

OLIVIA MELLAN
&
SHERRY CHRISTIE

Walker & Company   New York

This book was written to provide authoritative information. However, it is sold with the understanding that the author and publisher are not herein engaged in rendering legal, accounting, tax, financial planning, or other professional services. Any application of the ideas and suggestions set forth in this book is at the reader's discretion. The author and publisher expressly disclaim any responsibility for any liability, loss, or risk, personal or otherwise, incurred as a consequence of the use or application of the contents of this book.

First published in the United States of America in 2001 by
Walker Publishing Company, Inc.

Published simultaneously in Canada by Fitzhenry and Whiteside,
Markham, Ontario L3R 4T8

Library of Congress Cataloging-in-Publication Data

Mellan, Olivia
    Money shy to money sure : a woman's road map to financial well-being /
Olivia Mellan & Sherry Christie.
    p. cm.
    ISBN 0-8027-1347-5
    1. Women—Finance, Personal. I. Christie, Sherry. II Title.

HG179 .M428 2001
332.024'042—dc21   00-068650

Printed in the United States of America
2   4   6   8   10   9   7   5   3   1

To my husband, Michael, my very first (and favorite!) money mentor; to my son, Aniel, who teaches me some of the most important life lessons; and to all the women who have become money mentors to help other women along the path to money harmony.

—O. M.

To Harry, for his support and understanding, and to the women of my family who helped inspire this book: Betsy, Laura, Dottie, Eula, Carey, Lysa, Abby, Inge, Evelyn, Barb, and, most of all, my mother.

—S. C.

CONTENTS

We're Here to Tell You
That Money Myths
Can Be Overcome

Books, articles, seminars, brochures . . . there's never been a time when women were so passionately encouraged to take charge of their money.

For many women, this spate of information has proved to be the key to financial security and independence. Armed with new knowledge, they've felt confident enough to jump right in and tackle such challenges as refinancing the mortgage, comparison-shopping for a better credit card, and investing for retirement.

If all it took were reading the right books and magazines, many more of us would have joined them. But despite the barrage of financial facts, figures, and advice directed at women since the early nineties, 53 percent of women in a 1999 *Money* magazine poll said they feel "more confused than ever as to the best ways to invest their money." Clearly, some of us haven't found it as easy as others to absorb this information and benefit from it.

To find out why, we talked with hundreds of women around the United States. It seemed that for every financially empowered woman we met, there was another who felt unwilling or unable to take charge of her money. Some said they had avoided becoming proficient with money and investing because they were "never that good in math," or "never had enough money to worry about," or felt "there's plenty of time to take care of that later." Occasionally the response was just "I'll be all right somehow"—as if Sir Galahad would ride up on a white horse to make sure they could continue to buy groceries, live in a decent neighborhood, and obtain quality medical care for the rest of their lives.

As we explored individual women's stories, we found that these attitudes of denial often sprang from self-limiting beliefs and attitudes about how women and men should behave with money. In short, many of these "Money Avoiders" had difficulty addressing financial matters because they were fighting old myths they had absorbed long ago.

This is troubling—and scary. In an era when nine out of ten women will be alone at some point in their lives, ignorance about money and investing isn't bliss. It's a bomb waiting to explode.

For women who believe they can't (or shouldn't) become financially knowledgeable, the best "how-to" information in the world will remain useless unless they can debunk these disabling myths. This is the challenge we've taken on in this book. As a psychotherapist specializing in money conflict resolution and a writer with years of experience in helping people make better money decisions, we feel uniquely suited to the task.

Olivia's story

When I was growing up in the fifties and sixties, I was sure my parents were accurately describing themselves when my mother called herself an early feminist and my dad insisted he was one of the first "male feminists" himself. They were both proud of the fact that I was very good in math and went to an Ivy League college on a full scholarship.

At the time, I didn't see the contradiction between their self-perception and the message I got from them about money. In no uncertain terms, they told me, "You probably won't be too good at dealing with money, honey, but if you're lucky, some man will take care of all that for you."

Many years later, as I was preparing to speak to a group of financial planners about money psychology, I realized I was dreading being asked detailed questions about investing—questions I feared I couldn't answer. I survived this challenge, but it wasn't long before the problem resurfaced while I was looking at a prospectus from an investment firm. My eyes glazed over, and I couldn't make any sense of what I was reading. I knew I needed to learn this information, but it felt as if a fog had descended when I tried to understand it.

Then I began to find out that I wasn't the only one with this problem. In my therapy practice and my workshops, I encountered more and more women who described their feelings about money and investing in similar terms. As they allowed me to explore their attitudes and money histories with them, the same self-defeating beliefs and attitudes emerged time and again.

These misconceptions—I consider them myths—often kept women from taking full charge of their money or providing sensibly for their financial security. On the emotional and spiritual side, these myths also deprived them of the opportunity to feel capable, confident, and serene in reaching what I call "money harmony." When a woman finally began to break free of their harmful influence, all too often it was because a life trauma forced the issue: a divorce, the death of her spouse or partner, or the serious illness of a child.

Looking for more positive ways to inspire women to become financially proficient, I spoke with two of the best-known feminists of our age, Betty Friedan and Gloria Steinem. It was eye-opening to discover that even these role models of independence and empowerment were struggling to fully free themselves from debilitating money myths.

Becoming even more curious, I interviewed other women who are successful in a variety of fields: Katie Couric, the *Today* show anchor; Judy Woodruff of CNN; Faith Prince, the Tony Award–winning Broadway actress; Washington, D.C., congresswoman Eleanor Holmes Norton; Sarah Ban Breathnach (pronounced "ban brannoch"), best-selling author of *Simple Abundance*; Betty Carter, Peggy Papp, Olga Silverstein, and Marianne Walters, codirectors of the Women's Project in Family Therapy; Dr. Jean Houston, codirector of the Foundation for Mind Research; Daria Dolan, who, with her husband, cohosts a popular radio talk show about money; and other women from all walks of life.

Many of the myths I'd identified had profoundly affected even these powerful women. In fact, virtually all of us were on a similar journey toward financial security.

And as I suspected, there were lots of others out there just like us. As Betty Carter observed, "Many women wouldn't be caught dead admitting they believe these myths anymore; but consciously or unconsciously, you bet they do!" Her opinion was decisively confirmed by such experienced financial advisors as Peg Downey and JJ Jamison; Judy Robinett, a businesswoman who has founded many investment clubs; and Grace Weinstein, editor and author of many books on money matters.

Money Shy to Money Sure can be a road map for women who know they need financial expertise yet have been blocked by old beliefs from achieving it. My goal is to help you clear away the obstacles that may be keeping you from enjoying a comfortable relationship with money and investing, and make it possible for you to move from awareness to action—and ultimately to true self-sufficiency and financial security.

Sherry's story

I grew up on air force bases at a time when men were men, and women were "Mrs." This was chafing to my college-educated mother, who joined my father in encouraging the four of us kids to believe we could do anything we set our minds to. Still, for the first several years of my working life, I was a poster child for bag lady fears, with my 401(k) savings totally invested in Guaranteed Investment Contracts.

It was almost by accident that I became financially aware—the result of writing copy for a bank client who believed in educating consumers instead of bribing them with toasters. Back in the mid-eighties, when financial advertising to women was almost non existent, we created a series of IRA ads in women's voices, communicating the message that every woman needs to take charge of her future.

So if you're just starting out on the path to financial knowledge, I understand where you're coming from. It took me years to get up the courage to start investing. Even then, I waded in cautiously, careful not to get in over my head until I was sure nothing was going to grab me and drag me under.

Within ten years, my husband and I were looking at investment account statements that showed our savings had nearly quintupled. Of course, it helped that the stock market's average annual return was double the historical norm during this time. But I'd planned with care, taken prudent risks, and hung in there while the market bounced around, and it felt great to see the results of this determination in black and white.

I want my sister, my sister-in-law, my nieces, and the other women I know to feel proud, confident, and secure when they look at their own financial statements. And I wish I'd known enough, soon enough, to help my widowed mom.

None of us can afford to wait for "someone else" to take care of our money for us, or assume that things will work out somehow. If you'd like to invest sensibly, borrow more wisely, and plan for the future more confidently, join Olivia and me in debunking the money myths that may be holding you back from true financial well-being.

As countless determined women have proved, you really can do anything you set your mind to.

Step by step, we'll help you get more confident about money

For many women, *Money Shy to Money Sure* will be a beginning. For some, it might be an intermediate step. Others will find that this book helps remove the last obstacles to reaching their financial goals. Wherever you stand now, you'll gain competence and confidence as you move toward real harmony with your money.

Once you debunk the myths that are in your way, you may also be surprised to see how much you're enjoying yourself. As Judy Robinett, founder of ten investment clubs, puts it: "Isn't it time to rethink how you feel about money? When you were a kid, you probably didn't think sex sounded like much fun, either!"

ACKNOWLEDGMENTS

There are so many people who contributed to making this book happen, it's hard to include them all. Most of all, I want to thank George Gibson for his faith in us and his positive encouragement and nurturing, and Jackie Johnson for her untiring good judgment and expertise in helping us find the right way to communicate our message.

To keep me motivated, I decided to interview women role models whom I admire from many different walks of life. Thanks to Betty Friedan, Gloria Steinem, Katie Couric, Faith Prince, Sarah Ban Breathnach, Erin Brockovich, Linda Ellerbee, Debbie Reynolds, Michelle Singletary, Megan Rosenfeld, and Judy Woodruff for being sources of inspiration for me in a variety of ways, and for taking the time to talk to me. Thanks also to Congresswomen Eleanor Holmes Norton, Lynn Woolsey, and Lynn Rivers for their unfailing honesty and forthrightness in sharing their journeys to empower other women. I am grateful to Becky Berube, Robin Klee, Katrenka Hunter, and other "hockey wives" for sharing their self-discoveries about money with me.

Thanks to Judy Robinett, Azriela Jaffe, Barbara Stanny, Anne Slepian, May Hunt, Melissa Moss, and Susan Berkley for being models of empowerment and for their valuable insights. Thanks to Judy Jordan and to other professors like Julie Brines and Virginia Sapiro for sharing their perceptions and experience with me.

Thanks to the wonderful therapists who inspired me in writing this book: Harriet Lerner, Betty Carter, Peggy Papp, Olga Silverstein, and Marianne Walters, as well as Ilana Rubenfeld, whose work and creativity I've admired since I was twenty-one. Carol Anderson and Monica McGoldrick were willing to join me with Marianne and Betty on a panel for therapists about Women and Money at the Family Therapy Network symposium, "Shaping the Future of Psychotherapy."

Financial professionals whom I admire are too numerous to mention, but the short list includes Victoria Collins, Gerri Detweiler, Daria Dolan, Peg Downey, Candi Kaplan, Susan Freed, JJ Jamison, Sacha Millstone, Eileen Michaels, Sharon Rich, Dick Vodra, Avis Pohl, Ellie Wotherspoon, Roberta Lee-Driscoll, Alexandra Armstrong, and that brilliant observer who interprets changes in the industry, Bob Veres. Thanks to Karen Gross for her inspirational work in debtor education. Thanks to Bob Clark, who invited me to write for *Investment Advisor* magazine, and to Jamie Green, who makes my work there so satisfying and pleasurable.

Thanks to the dancers and other artists whose journey toward money harmony fascinated me: Sally Nash, Liz Lerman, Michelle Ava, and Nancy Newell, who makes Money Harmony books available in her dance studio!

I gratefully acknowledge Doris Kiser and Katie Van Dyne, who shared their wisdom with us, and all the women who spoke to us anonymously and gave us the benefit of their learnings. I appreciate the generosity of Beth Frishberg and Christine Moore, who invited me to their women's investment clubs, and all other clubs (whether true investment clubs or not) that asked me to visit and share my expertise with them.

Thanks to all the women from my workshops and seminars and attendees of Everywoman's Money Conferences all over the United States who have shared their journeys with me. Thanks also to Jan Black and Jody Temple White for organizing these conferences and the Money School that follows them; through their efforts women enjoy learning about money in the most creative and pleasurable settings. Other wonderful women speakers I met through these conferences made my own speaking career so much more fun: Karen McCall, Paula Monroe, Debbie Owens, Pamela Ayo Yetunde, Sue Vanderlinden and Joan Coulihan, Dee Lee, and Teresa Wilhelmi and Karen Sheridan. Many of these extraordinary women felt like kindred spirits, making my money psychology work much less lonely.

Finally, thanks to my husband, Michael, who supports me in my work and in my writing, and is the most patient money mentor I know; to my son, Aniel, who keeps me honest on all levels; and to Sherry Christie, the best writing partner someone who doesn't like to write books could possibly have. I never thought a work partnership could be this effortless and satisfying.

—OLIVIA MELLAN

Money Shy to Money Sure

The Seven Myths That Can Keep You from Taking Charge of Your Money

Things have changed a lot for women in the last thirty years, especially in the workplace. A number of us hold positions of responsibility and influence. Nearly half of married women contribute at least as much to the family income as their husbands do. (Indeed, one out of five wives now outearns her mate.) Yet many of us are not completely at ease with, or fully in charge of, our money.

Why do so many intelligent, competent women still lack confidence about money and investing? And why does not being proficient with money tend to fill us with so much anxiety and shame that we're unable to move forward?

One woman described the feeling as "like being in a Spanish class and not understanding the language. But I thought it was my fault that I didn't understand it."

Money *is* another language, with a set of concepts and terms of its own. In many families, it's a language that's not taught equally to girls and boys. Even when parents think they're being completely unbiased, some of their spoken and unspoken messages foster insecurity about money matters among their daughters. By the time a girl has grown up, she may be so entrenched in misconceptions that, even with the best will in the world, she can't bring herself to take charge of her money.

Over the past few years, we've spoken with many women whose general competence and clearheadedness seemed to unaccountably desert them when it came to their money. For example, here's how a woman we'll call Claire, a university professor, explained the blind spot in her otherwise very organized approach to life.

My parents were public school teachers, and the emphasis in our family was on being responsible, staying out of debt, and being of service to others. So I did all that for more than twenty years—putting my husband through law school, then supporting myself and my child after the divorce—but I never learned much about investing. I guess it was a cultural thing: "I'm a woman; therefore I'm not supposed to be interested in or good at money-related stuff."

A few months ago I was talking to a former grad school professor whose hobby is investing, and I mentioned that I really needed to reconsider my finances with an eye toward retirement. When I told him that I had no investments or savings accounts, and $75,000 in my checking account, his mouth dropped open. He stared at me and demanded, "What in the world is wrong with you?"

I blurted out angrily, "Dammit, it's not my job to pay attention to all that! It's my husband's job!"

He looked confused and said, "But, Claire, you're divorced."

"Not *that* husband!" I snapped. "I mean my generic husband."

Once I heard myself in all my ridiculousness, I realized I'd better start looking after my finances for myself.

And Claire is doing just that. After buying a book on the basics of personal finance and talking things over with her sister-in-law (who is learning money management a few steps ahead of her), she has begun investing much more aggressively for retirement.

Luckily, it's never too late to start getting more knowledgeable about money. And in many cases, women tend to be very successful once they make the transition to empowerment. To cite just one example, a 1999 study by the National Association of Investors Corporation showed that women-only investment clubs had a lifetime annual earnings rate of 32 percent, versus just 23 percent for men-only clubs. Obviously, women have what it takes to be excellent money managers.

And deep down, many of us know it. Some 94 percent of female respondents told Prudential researchers that women as a group are as capable as men when it comes to understanding money and investing, and 78 percent of us said we'd prefer to be the one in the family who makes the financial decisions.

So what stops so many women like Claire from taking charge of their money? Some of us may just need more financial education. But a great number of us are affected by subtler, deeper money myths ruling our psyche. Many of us never thought of questioning these self-defeating messages, because they were so tightly woven into our view of life.

For example, women are usually raised to cooperate and to share. We learn that a good wife and mother always puts others first and her own needs second. Unlike our brothers, we usually aren't taught to believe that we'll be good with money. In some cases, we're even told that being too financially knowledgeable and assertive will threaten men and drive them away. So when we try to assert our financial competence, we may feel blocked—not because we don't have enough determination or intelligence for the task, but because it seems to clash with our internal scripts in one way or another. These blocks often cause us to act, or fail to act, in ways that imperil our financial security.

For instance, a great many of us (even in this day and age) have fears of losing everything and ending up poverty-stricken, helpless, and homeless, or a burden on our parents or our children.

Obviously, the best remedy for this feeling of insecurity is to become financially secure. But despite our deep fear of poverty, women tend to start saving for retirement much later than men do and put aside only half as much, according to Merrill Lynch and the Federal Reserve Board. And when we do save, we're more likely to choose highly conservative vehicles like CDs (certificates of deposit) and money market accounts, whose low yields can allow inflation to actually shrink our purchasing power.

In short, these self-sabotaging myths influence us to make ourselves poorer—precisely what we fear most!

Seven common money myths seem to prevent many of us from becoming financially confident. Like hailstones, each myth starts with a gritty bit of truth surrounded by traditions, cultural messages, and fears, built up layer upon layer.

- *Myth 1: "Money is too complicated for me to understand."* Many of us fear we will never be able to learn everything about money and investing, but the truth is that not even the savviest financial professional knows it all. In chapter 1, you'll decide what you want your money to do for you, and sort out what you really need to know.

- *Myth 2: "I don't have enough money to do anything with."* Chapter 2 will address this myth with simple, everyday actions that can yield impressive results, regardless of how little money you have initially. You'll also learn no-nonsense ways to find more money to save.

- *Myth 3: "If I take risks with my money, I'll lose everything."* In chapter 3, you'll learn how to tell the real risks from the old bugaboos. We'll show you how to begin a sensible, low-risk investment program to protect your financial security.

- *Myth 4: "I don't have enough time to manage my money."* Though no one has enough time for everything she wants to do, many of us also feel that money management is too tedious and boring to rank high on our "to do" list. We'll address this misconception in chapter 4 and suggest timesaving tricks that can help even the busiest woman put her money to work toward her goals.

- *Myth 5: "It's selfish to put myself first. I'm supposed to take care of everybody else."* You'll learn in chapter 5 how to look after your loved ones without neglecting yourself. We'll help you draw the line between giving and overgiving, and explore ways to take care of yourself *and* your family financially.

- *Myth 6: "If I take charge of my money, I'll antagonize others and might end up alone."* The fear that it's unfeminine to be authoritative about money often keeps even single women from claiming their financial power. In chapter 6, you'll discover how to change your role with a partner, parent(s), children, or boss in gentle but assertive ways that will ultimately lead to better communication and stronger relationships.

Finally, the most harmful myth of all:

- *Myth 7: "Someone else should be taking care of all this for me."* Many women won't admit it out loud, but our probing into attitudes and behaviors showed that this old belief is hard to shake. In chapter 7, you'll learn ways to debunk it once and for all, empowering you to move toward the serenity that comes from taking good care of yourself . . . financially and in other ways.

Why are these myths are so dangerous? Because in real life, failing to become financially knowledgeable is just about the biggest risk you can take. If you've been hesitant to learn about taking charge of your money, the following scary statistics should bring the urgency home to you.

- *You're virtually certain to be on your own at some point.* Money skills are essential for all women, not just those who never marry. Today, half of new marriages fail. Nearly one in five women between the ages of forty-five and fifty-four is now divorced and facing the possibility of starting retirement alone. Of the women in this group who are still married now, seven in ten will eventually outlive their husbands by as much as fifteen to twenty years, according to AARP.

- *Women's longer life span means you'll need a bigger nest egg than most men.* Women can expect to live five to seven years longer than men born the same year. This means that to retire comfortably at age sixty-five, a single man earning $50,000 needs to have saved only $11,390 by age thirty-five, whereas a thirty-five-year-old single woman with the same income should have saved $55,180, according to Merrill Lynch. Worse yet, since women typically earn only 75 percent as much as men and are in the workforce three to five years less, women tend to retire with lower Social Security and pension benefits. To close the gap, we women need to save all we can—and invest intelligently to make our money grow faster.

- *Workers are increasingly responsible for their own retirement security.* Pension plans that provided a fixed monthly check were a safety net for earlier generations, but today's workers are more likely to be offered a do-it-yourself savings plan. Employees of small companies, part-timers, and self-employed workers are often completely on their own. Overwhelmed by this responsibility, some women who could save for the future do nothing. Others, unsure about "risky" investment choices, put their money in safe but low-earning investments, where it hasn't a hope of growing into the sizable nest egg they'll need for a secure future.

Clearly, there's a great deal at stake for a lot of women . . . single and married, of all ages, incomes, and ethnic backgrounds. As you'll see, even well-known public figures are struggling with the same issues.

But you *can* overcome these money myths. In this book, you'll learn how to protect your financial security—and create a sense of financial well-being—with simple action plans that get results.

This doesn't mean you'll never again have money problems. But as you gain more confidence, you'll find it easier to take them in stride. As Washington, D.C., author and fund-raiser Georgette Mosbacher cautioned after a devastating divorce: "You don't know what life has in store for you, so you must be prepared. Regardless of what comes along, you can buy yourself time to look at the options."

In the following chapters, we'll introduce you to more women like Georgette who have succeeded in taking charge of their "moneylives," as you learn to debunk myths that make you act against your own best interests. Although some of these seven myths may seem to apply to you more than others, take time to read about them all so we can help you build your financial expertise chapter by chapter.

You'll find practical help and encouragement as you follow the steps and do the exercises we've provided. And once you've confronted the beliefs that may have been holding you back, you'll begin to enjoy the process of becoming financially self-confident. You'll face the future with greater assurance and optimism, as you move toward the financial serenity that is your birthright.

Where are you starting from?

Before you begin tackling the seven money myths, take a few moments to answer these questions. The results will give you a benchmark to measure your progress.

1. When it comes to balancing my checkbook:
    a. I just don't do it.
    b. I put it off as long as possible because I'm afraid I'll make mistakes.
    c. I can never find the time, so I just trust my partner or the bank to get it right.
    d. It's important to me to know how much money I have, so I balance it regularly.

2. When it comes to paying bills:
   a. I often have to juggle payments but am never sure what my priorities should be.
   b. The process makes me so anxious that I procrastinate and sometimes pay bills late.
   c. I don't know anything about it; my partner pays all the bills.
   d. I usually budget well enough so that there's money on hand to pay the bills on time.

3. When it comes to doing taxes:
   a. I guesstimate and overpay so I don't have to get into all that arithmetic.
   b. I'm always late pulling my records together for my partner or accountant.
   c. I delegate the task to someone else and hope that person won't make mistakes.
   d. I either prepare my own return or carefully check the work if someone else does it.

4. As far as investing for my retirement is concerned:
   a. I put a little money aside now and then, and hope for the best.
   b. There are so many other priorities that I haven't been able to save any money yet.
   c. I trust somebody else (spouse, employer, or both) to take care of it for me.
   d. I have a regular investment plan and am reasonably confident I'm in good shape financially.

5. Whenever I think about negotiating a raise or a discount on a purchase:
   a. I'm just not assertive enough to confront anyone about money.
   b. I'll give it a try but will back off if I meet opposition.
   c. I end up compromising to make sure the other person feels satisfied and happy.
   d. I negotiate hard for what I think is right.

6. If I were to negotiate for a new car:
   a. I'd probably pay the asking price even if I thought someone more assertive would get a better deal.
   b. I'd take the loan or lease the dealer recommends; the dealer knows what's best.
   c. Since I get flustered making money decisions, I'd bring along my partner or a friend.
   d. I'd do research, decide how much I'd be willing to pay, and stick to my limit.

7. When I consider reading a personal-finance magazine like *Money*:
   a. I dismiss the idea quickly and choose something else I enjoy reading.
   b. I usually find it tedious and boring and decide to come back to it later.
   c. I know it will make me feel dense, so I'd rather ask a friend or family member for advice.
   d. I read it and use whatever information fits my own financial circumstances.

8. When I need to talk to a banker or insurance agent:
   a. Even when I'm confused, I sit there nodding as if I understand every word.
   b. I put it off if possible and try to get the information I need from a friend.
   c. I'm afraid I won't understand, so I try to have someone else come with me to talk to the expert.
   d. I ask questions, and repeat them if necessary, until I'm sure I understand.

9. If a friend recommended a mutual fund, I would:
   a. Shrug it off, since I don't have any idea how to invest in mutual funds.
   b. Send for more information but probably never get around to wading through it.
   c. Take my friend's advice and invest in it right away.
   d. Find out whether the fund suits my investment strategy, then make a decision.

10. If I were counseled to consult a financial advisor:
    a. I wouldn't do it because I'd be too afraid of getting ripped off.
    b. I'd never pursue it—it's too hard to figure out whom I could trust.
    c. I'd ask a friend or relative and go with his or her recommendation.
    d. I'd make a checklist and interview several candidates to find someone competent and aligned with my goals.

To evaluate your answers, add up the number of *a*'s, *b*'s, *c*'s, and *d*'s, and see where your heaviest concentration is.

- *If you have mostly a's, you're a Money Avoider.* You need to challenge your belief that money is tedious and boring, or that you just can't understand it. In starting to educate yourself about money, you'll gradually build up confidence in your own abilities and judgment.
- *If you have mostly b's, you're a Money Procrastinator.* To reclaim your money power, you'll want to concentrate on getting past the myths that you don't have enough time to learn about money, or that it will be too complicated and unpleasant.
- *If you have mostly c's, you're a Money Dependent.* Although you're willing to ask others for help instead of totally avoiding money matters, you're surrendering your financial well-being to others (a partner, friend, or financial advisor) without knowing enough to be sure you're in good hands. You need to sharpen your financial skills so you can be more confident about your own expertise and judgment.
- *If you have mostly d's, you're already on your way to becoming a Money Maven.* (We hope that after you read this book, you will all be Money Mavens!) Keep working to hone your skills—not just to improve your own well-being but to become a better money mentor for other women who aren't as far along in the journey as you are.

How to begin improving your moneylife

When you debunk a money myth and begin adopting positive new habits, make a point of rewarding yourself. In fact, why not start right now?

What's the first step you need to take to get better at managing your money? It doesn't have to be a big step. For example, you might decide to track your spending better by keeping your checkbook up to date. Think about how it would help you financially, emotionally, in a relationship with a partner, or any other way.

How will you reward yourself for taking this first step? You could make time for a favorite activity, call a friend for lunch, or treat yourself to a movie or concert.

Once you've done it, notice how you feel. Proud of yourself? Nervous? Or at ease.

Now begin integrating this new action into your life. You've taken another step in taking charge of your moneylife!

CHAPTER ONE

Myth 1:
"Money Is Too Complicated for Me to Understand"

*I am living proof that you can understand money, because
nobody thought it was more complicated than I did. If I can
do it, anyone can!*
>   —DARIA DOLAN, *cohost of* The Dolans,
>   *a national personal-finance radio program*

* * *

"I was so stupid about money that I didn't know I needed to do any
more than pay my bills on time, balance my checkbook, and save a
few dollars," says this energetic brunette. A theater arts major from
Long Island, New York, she became a flight attendant in order to see
the world, then got married at twenty-four.

Today, you may know Daria Dolan as one of the nation's most ar-
ticulate and visible women on the subject of money and investing.
Cohost with her husband, Ken, of *The Dolans* syndicated radio call-in
show, she's a frequent guest on TV news shows and coauthor of three
financial books, including *Sams Teach Yourself e-Personal Finance Today.*

What inspired her to change from someone to whom higher
money matters were a mystery into an expert who now feels at home
discussing asset allocation, junk bonds, and risk-return ratios in front
of a national audience? Here's what Daria told us.

Growing up, I was always told that if I picked up a pool cue I should
lose, but I've always been competitive as hell.

When I met Ken, he was working for a Wall Street firm and dealt
with money all day long. When we got married, I had some money

and no bills, while he was three thousand dollars in debt, so I decided that as the better money manager I would be the one to pay the bills and balance the checkbook.

Fifteen years into our marriage, Ken came home and said he wanted to leave Wall Street to become a talk-show host, with a 70 percent cut in pay. I was acting in theater at the time, and I figured I'd better get serious about making some money to fill the gap. To this day, I don't know what made me say, "Well, I guess I'll have to become a stockbroker."

To get her broker's license, Daria studied investments seven days a week during three months of training. "God knows I never had a modicum of interest in the topic," she says, "but I found I had a facility to understand how this stuff worked." After a year as a broker, she joined Ken's show as an on-air money consultant. In 1986, they formally became a team . . . and the rest is history.

Like Daria Dolan, many intelligent women grew up expecting that the mysteries of money would be a closed book. Yet thousands of women around the country have proved that the notion that money is "too complicated to understand" is just a myth. When it comes to investing, for example (the topic many of us mean when we say "money is too complicated"), women often beat men, hands down.

- The National Association of Investors Corporation reports that women-only investment clubs earned nearly 10 percent more than men-only clubs in 1999 (and almost 5 percent more than coed clubs). It's important to note that many of these club members are ordinary working women, homemakers, and retirees who taught themselves—and each other—the fundamentals of investing.
- There are successful women investors in the big leagues, too. An analysis of more than 2,500 mutual funds for *Money* magazine showed that over the three years ending August 31, 1997, women fund managers posted better investment returns than male managers in most important fund categories, including U.S. diversified stocks, international stocks, taxable bonds, municipal bonds, and hybrid stock/bond funds.
- This investment savvy is beginning to percolate into homes around the country. Thirty percent of women in a June 2000 *Wall*

Street Journal/NBC News poll said they alone make the decisions about buying mutual funds and stocks for their households.

> **Brains have no sex.**
> —MURIEL SIEBERT, *first woman member of the New York Stock Exchange*

Many of us know more about investing than we suppose

As many women can testify, understanding money is like getting comfortable with a foreign language. The way to begin feeling at home with money is the same way you'd learn Spanish or French: by relating it to what you already know. With this in mind, many of the basics of investing may not seem so foreign after all.

Investing in stock is similar to buying a house. You can understand the principle behind investing in stock if you've ever owned a house and sold it for a profit. When you buy stock, you become an owner of a company. (Actually, you share ownership with other investors—the reason why stockholders are often called *shareholders.*) You hope that when you sell your stock, it will be worth more than you paid, letting you pocket a profit. Many stocks also have an advantage that home ownership can't match: They pay dividends, giving you a share of the company's profits every quarter. *When you think of stocks, think "I own."*

Investing in bonds is similar to putting money in a CD. If you've ever earned interest on a certificate of deposit, you understand the principle behind investing in a bond. You're loaning your money for a certain period of time to a company, government unit, or even the U.S. Treasury. The debtor gives you its "bond" (as in "my word is my bond"), promising to pay you a fixed rate of interest and return your principal at a certain point in the future. (Despite this promise, however, bonds are not federally insured like CDs.) *When you think of bonds, think "I am owed."*

As for the stock and bond markets, imagine them as two auction desks in a big tent full of investors who are ready to buy if the price is right. Some investors focus on stocks because they want their money to grow. Other investors need steady income, so they concentrate mainly on finding the best bond deals. Many others—professional money managers, day traders, speculators—try to keep an eye on both desks so they can jump into what's hot and out of what's not.

On the stock side, the action is pretty straightforward. There's usually lots of demand for the stock of companies with rosy prospects, so investors tend to bid up the price. By contrast, the stock of a company on the skids becomes cheaper—the Wall Street equivalent of a fire sale. Prices may change constantly during the course of a day, according to what buyers are willing to pay.

The bond market is driven by demand, too. When a company, state, or city decides to raise money by floating a new bond issue, it has to pay an interest rate attractive enough to entice investors without bankrupting itself. If the bond is viewed as relatively risky, the issuer has to pay a higher rate to reward investors for taking on the extra risk. That's why supersafe Treasury bills, backed by the U.S. government, pay investors less than high-yield corporate bonds, whose greater risk is evidenced in their nickname, "junk bonds."

Stripped of its jargon, the Great and Powerful World of Investing is really just a glorified bargain barn. In fact, women's experience as smart shoppers tends to make them excellent investors. As fund manager Loretta Morris puts it, once women begin educating themselves about money, "they make careful decisions, gathering all the information they can. They tend to be more thorough." Knowing how to choose efficiently, recognize bargains, and learn from past mistakes is a priceless advantage.

But what if the whole idea of investing, comparing interest rates on loans, doing your taxes, or balancing your checkbook makes your palms get sweaty or your heart race?

For women with math anxiety, help may be right around the corner

If you get physically anxious about dealing with numbers, this feeling probably goes back to your school days. Despite the years since then, old memories of frustration and discouragement still have the power to influence your adult attitude toward dealing with money.

According to a 1997 study by the Dreyfus Corporation, women who had math anxiety as girls are likely to be more risk-averse, more fearful of making investment decisions, and less financially prepared for retirement.

> **I felt so stupid about money. I couldn't look at numbers without instantly feeling like falling asleep or crying.**
> —ANNE SLEPIAN, *cofounder of* More Than Money, *a journal that explores issues of wealth and values*

Why is math anxiety so much more common in women than in men? Research shows that boys don't find math any easier than girls do, but they often have more confidence in their ability to learn it. Even today, when teachers and parents are united in stressing this subject's importance, many girls don't feel they can master math . . . or money matters. For example, in a survey of junior high and high school students by Liberty Financial, girls were only half as likely as boys to consider themselves "very knowledgeable" about money and investments—even though the study showed little real difference in knowledge levels!

Some teachers are trying innovative ways to make girls more comfortable with mathematical concepts. *Ms.* magazine founder Gloria Steinem mentioned that Sheila Tobias (author of *Overcoming Math Anxiety*) had helped her see that there are "many different paths to math, not one right way to do it" or learn about it. For example, Tobias suggests reading about the lives of great mathematicians as a way of getting into their ideas.

Another fresh thinker is Dr. Galeet Westreich, who teaches "dancing mathematics" to young girls, encouraging them to experience geometry by creating an array of shapes in different planes with their bodies. Westreich says research has shown that kinesthetically oriented young women improve tremendously in their grasp of geometric and other mathematical skills after using creative learning techniques like these.

> **I believe that more creativity needs to come into
> our attitudes about our relationship with money.
> Money to me is energy, a fascinating resource that
> brings me freedom and security. I've been surprised
> at how much fun I've had learning about it.**
> —CAROLYN CONGER, Ph.D., consultant and workshop leader
> in psychological growth and healing

But what about you? If you're determined to take charge of your money now, how can you get past math anxiety created in your youth?

To begin with, try to put aside math-associated feelings of shame, dislike, and anxiety that may have sunk their roots into your tender adolescent self-esteem. Remind yourself that math is just another language. Maybe you don't know yet how to say what you want in this language, but you can learn.

So the first step is developing a new attitude. Try to remember the confidence and joy with which you approached your favorite subject (whatever it was) early in your education. That excited new learner is still somewhere inside you, looking forward to the pleasure of making numbers dance.

Now here's the good news: You don't need to know advanced math to manage your money well. As Washington, D.C., financial planner Susan Freed told us, "It doesn't get more complicated than addition, subtraction, multiplication, and percentages."

So forget about geometry, calculus, or any of that college stuff. A shopper who knows how to figure 20 percent off a regular price, multiply the cost of new shoes by three kids, or add sales tax to a planned purchase has virtually all the know-how she needs to manage her money.

Once you feel confident that you have what it takes to understand money concepts, you'll find they're far less complicated than you feared.

But what if you simply can't attain that level of confidence—perhaps because you did miss some of the fundamentals, or you've just felt insecure about math for so long? Here are some possible solutions:

- Look for an adult math class offered through a nearby community college or university continuing education program. Encourage a buddy to sign up with you (or make a friend in the class) so you can compare notes and cheer each other on.
- Ask a financially proficient female friend to mentor you as you restore your knowledge and confidence (perhaps bartering your skills in another area for hers).
- If you'd prefer to work with a partner at your own level, enlist a female friend or relative and coach each other with the aid of a self-help guide. (For our suggestions see the Appendix.)
- Find a simple money or math task you can do, and drink in the feeling of confidence that comes from completing it. Then use that confidence as a springboard to take on a harder math or money assignment.

Change Your Inner Critic into a Cheerleader

If you run into a money or math concept you find difficult, practice "self-talk" as you tackle it. First, acknowledge the negative thoughts and feelings that run through your head. Then counter with positive thoughts and emotions.

At the beginning, you may benefit from doing this as a written exercise. Use the left-hand side of your page for negative self-talk and the right-hand side for positive thoughts. When you make progress, write yourself a congratulatory note ("Way to go!"), ideally in a different color of ink.

If you find you're beating yourself up with negative talk, focus on encouraging messages ("I know I can understand this. . . . How else could I approach it?"). Remind yourself of difficult things you've mastered in the past. ("This can't be more difficult than CPR!") If you're feeling physical anxiety symptoms, close your eyes and draw ten deep slow breaths all the way down to the bottom of your lungs while you relax every muscle.

By writing down your anxieties and blocks, then countering them with positive affirmations, you'll remind yourself that debunking this myth starts with a change of attitude. You'll be surprised at how powerful it can feel simply to change the way you talk to yourself.

Managing money isn't rocket science

Money is a tool we can use to build what we want out of life: security, pleasure, comfort, prestige, power, freedom, loyalty, even love (or so we may hope). Once we get past old money messages, math anxiety, and whatever else may be in the way, it's easy to see that this tool itself is actually pretty simple. We can lend money or borrow it, save it or spend it, invest wisely or speculate wildly, grow it or blow it. In the course of a lifetime, we'll probably do all these things.

Sometimes we avoid learning how to build what we want with our money because we wrongly feel we don't deserve much in life. But in many cases, the problem is simply that we don't know what we want. To use this tool effectively in our complicated lives, we need a plan. Here's how to put one together.

> **I used to think money management was about numbers, just tedious and boring. But actually it's about fascinating issues—our core values, how our relationships work, and what's most important in our lives.**
>
> —ANNE SLEPIAN, *cofounder of* More Than Money, *a journal that explores issues of wealth and values*

STEP 1: WHAT DO YOU WANT MONEY FOR?

Setting goals may sound like a big commitment, especially to someone who feels her future is constantly subject to change. But without goals, we tend to forget what our priorities are. We buy things that don't really matter and pass up choices that do—like a dieter who falls for a mouth-watering chocolate cake in the bakery, only to wish later that she'd spent her money in the supermarket produce section instead.

Without goals, we may also be swept into the wrong decisions by someone else who *does* have an agenda—a partner, parents, boss, kids, financial advisor, or maybe a shrewd marketer.

Women need to be good at understanding their priorities, setting goals for both the short and long term, and mapping out a way to reach their objectives.

—GRACE WEINSTEIN, *financial editor, author, and consultant*

For example, let's say you've squirreled away $3,000 with no particular purpose in mind. Your brother, whose ambition in life is to open an electric-car recharging depot, begs you for a loan to start his business. Since you don't have the money earmarked for anything else, you agree. Unfortunately, there are only two electric autos in the whole county, so your brother soon goes broke, leaving you with nothing to show for your savings but a $3,000 bad-debt write-off and a strained family relationship.

If you'd been saving that money for a specific reason, wouldn't you have been a bit more reluctant to hand it over? In other words, a goal can not only help make your innermost dreams come true but also validate your financial choices—an important advantage for women raised to defer to the wants and needs of others.

Many of us have some general idea of what we want to achieve in life. But motivational experts tell us that when we write down dreams and wishes on paper, they become much more powerful. Simply crystallizing them into words emphasizes their validity and their importance. And once they're written down, you can review the list regularly to reinforce your determination and make sure you're on the right track.

We recommend starting this process with some blank sheets of paper in front of you. Take a few deep breaths and imagine yourself in a relaxed setting (on the beach, in a Japanese garden . . . whatever works for you). Ask yourself: If I could do or have anything I really want, what would it be? Let your most deeply felt dreams, longings, and desires surface.

First, consider the short term. What secret or not-so-secret dreams would you like to see come true within the next five years? In what ways would you like to improve your financial well-being? How about other nonfinancial goals that would enrich your life? For example, would you like to:

- Learn how to invest more confidently?
- Increase your retirement savings substantially?
- Get out of debt?
- Buy a first home, move up to a more comfortable place, or get a vacation home?
- Start your own business?
- Establish a college fund for a child?
- Learn a musical instrument, a new language, or a craft?
- Travel somewhere you've always wanted to go?

At the top of a blank page, write "Here's what I really want to do during the next five years" and then write down your goals and dreams for that time frame. There can be any number of them, and they can be in any order.

Next, think about what you would like to do (or enjoy) in ten or twenty years. Is there another kind of work you'd rather be doing? Where would you like to be living? What will your relationship be with your family? Contemplate your future after age sixty or sixty-five, or after you stop working full-time. (Although we often refer to these as "retirement" years, they might—with a good financial foundation—actually be years of joyful creativity or a nourishing blend of work and play.) For example, would you want to:

- Spend summers in the North and winters in the South?
- Be able to travel whenever and wherever you wish?
- Make sure your parents get the care they may need?
- Build a sailboat and go cruising in the Caribbean?
- Retire early, move to the Riviera, and paint?
- Help pay for your grandchildren's education?
- Keep working, either as a consultant or in a completely different line of work?

Head another blank page with "Here's what I really want to do in the long term," and write down how you envision the rest of your life.

A dream has to be something that's truly important to you—not just a temporary whim. To find out which of your desires are really abiding, try writing another dreams list a week from now, and do a third list in two weeks. (Don't look at the old list or lists when you write the new one.) After comparing the three attempts, you should be able to create a "final" list that reflects what's truly important to you.

Even then, of course, it won't really be final, because life doesn't always turn out the way we want it to. You may fall madly in love and marry (or remarry). You may become a new mom when you'd thought your childbearing years were over. You may lose your partner. You may decide to follow an independent path instead of settling into a long-term relationship. And, we hope, you'll reach some of your short-term goals and want to choose new ones. So feel free to update your list whenever appropriate.

If you're in an intimate relationship with a partner who's also done this goal-setting exercise, you'll want to take the extra step of getting together to compare and discuss your lists. Once you've identified the dreams and goals you can both get behind, create a single list of shared goals. (Remember: Don't give up on a dream that's really important to you!)

To Clarify Your Dreams, Try Writing the Story of Your Life

If you have trouble identifying your dreams and goals, it can help to write a fantasy obituary for yourself. Start with your "ideal" demise. (For example, you may hope to pass away peacefully in bed at age 125, surrounded by your loved ones.) Write the obituary as if you had accomplished everything you want to do, traveled to all the places you'd like to see, done all the things you want to be remembered for, and so forth. This exercise, which may sound somber at first, has actually been a positive, energizing experience for workshop participants and therapy clients who have tried it. They love what they discover about themselves, and it helps infuse their goals with passion and zest for life.

By the way, it's fine to keep money for mutual goals in a joint account if you wish. But in this age of divorce, we believe it's prudent to keep funds for personal goals (like a financially secure retirement) separate from jointly held money.

We know that insisting on separate accounts may make you feel like Hard-hearted Hannah. But your wise Uncle Sam already stipulates that you can receive tax breaks on retirement savings only if they are held in your own name. Follow this lead, and your assets will be better protected from predators and creditors than they would be in a joint account.

STEP 2: TURN YOUR GOALS INTO FINANCIAL TARGETS

For each of the goals you identified in step 1, you need to ask yourself: What financial resources (or abilities) would it take to make this goal a reality? Write down your answers to this question, being as specific as possible. (You may need to do a little research to make sure you set realistic targets.) For example:

> *My goal: To keep my small business growing without worries about fluctuating cash flow.*
> *My financial target: To save $10,000 to cover my living and operating expenses for three months.*

> *My goal: To travel somewhere exciting every fall.*
> *My financial target: To earn an extra $3,000 for travel by making and selling ten quilts a year as a sideline business.*

> *My goal: Keeping up my current lifestyle in retirement.*
> *My financial target: To create enough wealth to generate income of $60,000 a year from age sixty-five until I'm ninety.*

No matter what else you want to achieve, we strongly suggest you put these two "musts" high on your list: (1) a fund for financial emergencies; and (2) financial independence and security in your sixties, seventies, eighties, nineties, and beyond. "A financially secure future" should head every woman's list of long-term goals, as we'll discuss more fully in chapter 5. Meanwhile, an emergency fund can rescue you if your income fluctuates a lot or if you get budget-busting bills. And having this cash reserve will take away a lot of the tension every jobholder feels in today's downsized, merger-prone work environment.

Your emergency fund should be big enough to cover at least one month's living expenses. If you're especially worried about losing your job, a minimum of two months' worth would be better. And if a job search in your situation might take longer, three months' worth of living expenses would give you a better cushion.

Claiming Your Goals If Your Partner Is the Breadwinner

When you have your own source of income, it's easier to feel entitled to your own aspirations. But if your spouse is the only wage earner in the family, you may feel as though you're not allowed to have your own goals and dreams.

You need to challenge this common misperception. Ask your partner to join you in writing down his own dreams. Then find a time to sit down and share your respective lists. And let him know that you consider it vitally important to fund a financial plan that will give you more confidence about your future security.

If you're staying home and raising children, we recommend that you and your partner set a salary for this absolutely vital service you're providing to your family. This will give you a stronger sense of the value of your work at home, as well as your right to decide how to spend—or save—your money.

STEP 3: START MAKING YOUR DREAMS AND GOALS
PART OF YOUR LIFE

Now it's time to begin turning your goals list into an actual plan. Select a financial goal that you'll focus on (for now) from your short-term list and another from your long-term list. If you have a hard time choosing, begin with establishing or building up a cash cushion for emergencies and a fund for your retirement years.

- Think of one step you could take this week to move toward your short-term goal, and write it down—even if you're not quite sure yet how to accomplish it.
- What step could you take to get started toward your long-term goal? (Even though achieving this goal may be many years or even decades away, it will be easier to reach your destination if you focus on it and start working toward it now.)
- To reinforce your commitment to these goals, share your list with your partner, a close friend, or a money mentor. Together,

brainstorm ideas that could help you accomplish the steps you propose to take toward these goals. One successful saver told us, "All during the holiday shopping season, I carried a picture of a girl in a cap and gown on top of my credit cards. It really worked—I thought about my daughter's college fund and didn't overspend on gifts the way I did the year before."

- When you take these important first steps, reward yourself by doing something you really enjoy.

"Educating myself about money has really empowered me": a success story

Pamela, a single woman in her late forties, grew up sheltered from financial adversity. But once she recognized the need to become more knowledgeable about money, she found herself fascinated by what she learned. Here's what Pamela told us.

I didn't start learning about money until I was forty-one, after my grandmother was diagnosed with Alzheimer's. My parents were struggling financially, so I felt it was up to me to come up with funds for her care. My father and mother had never talked about money, and I had no idea how to manage it or make it grow. I used to think that "yield" was a liberated stop sign!

The way I started was by going on-line to the CompuServe Investors Forum, where I sort of lurked around to learn all I could about investing. I also read the *Wall Street Journal* and *Barron's* and books about investing. I really became fascinated by the whole business. First I learned about stocks, then bonds; then I tried to get at what Congress was doing; then I tried to understand what [Federal Reserve Board chairman] Alan Greenspan was saying; and so on.

I didn't realize how far I had come until the Dow hit 4000 in February 1995 and my uncle took a lot of money out of the stock market. That didn't make sense to me, so I kept following my own investment philosophy. While he was expecting the market to go down, I invested more heavily, and I made some significant gains.

I consult now and then with a stockbroker our family has used for years, but I make sure I know what I want. For example, I'll call him and say, "I'm looking for an investment that yields 7¾ percent," and he tries to find what I want.

I used to think that money was too complicated for me to understand. But even though I never finished college, I feel that educating myself about money has really empowered me. I like the idea that I'm making responsible decisions to help take care of my grandmother, my parents, and myself.

Where to find help and support

As Pamela's story suggests, learning about money can be easier if you feel you're in a safe place—"somewhere I can ask questions without feeling stupid," as more than one woman said to us. Here are some suggestions.

FIND A "MONEY MENTOR" YOU TRUST

Coaching by someone who cares can help you overcome old messages that money is something you can't or don't want to understand. For example, Anne Slepian told us she grew up "absorbing a societal message that concern about money was a prison." From an upper-middle-class family, she had little financial guidance from her parents. ("My parents didn't believe in balancing their checkbooks," she said. "There was always enough, so why bother?") When her mate, Christopher Mogil, inherited wealth shortly after their relationship began, she was very willing to let him manage their money.

Her avoidance, however, prompted her loving partner to keep coaxing her into becoming more involved with their finances. "My portfolio statement just arrived," he would tell Anne cheerfully. "Come on, just take five minutes to look it over with me." When Anne reluctantly agreed, he would go over the statement with her, then invite her to tell him a couple of things she had learned from it. Finally, he would ask, "What's one thing you'd like to have explained?"

Today, Anne is grateful that "Christopher has been a wonderfully patient coach."

If your partner manages the money now, explain that you'd like to be more involved in your finances. For example:

- *Review account statements together.* Discuss what and where your assets are, how your portfolio is allocated, considerations in buying or selling (or in making deposits or withdrawals), and why these particular accounts or investments were chosen.

- *Share financial decision making.* When it seems appropriate to make a change—for instance, to sell an investment, transfer a balance to a lower-rate credit card, or look for cheaper auto insurance—your partner should explain the reasons why, and show you how to do it.
- *Consult with your financial advisors jointly.* Be sure you both understand and agree with the choices made.
- *Take turns managing your money.* Every other month, for example, the two of you might trade the jobs of maintaining the checkbook and paying the bills.

Of course, mates sometimes aren't suited to be good money mentors. If your partner isn't as knowledgeable, open, or patient as Anne's, try to find a friend who is willing to mentor you in your journey toward empowerment.

WORK WITH OTHER WOMEN WHO WANT TO LEARN

Now in her fifties with two grown children, Christine Moore had always left investment decisions to her husband, despite his encouragement to become more involved. She says, "I guess I thought that learning about investing in detail might be too complicated for me—until I saw the Beardstown Ladies interviewed on TV, started reading about them, and got all fired up." At her next get-together with a group of friends who met regularly for conversation and a good meal, she started a discussion about a recent PBS special on the Beardstown Ladies' Investment Club.

"We decided to buy their book and set up a finance club," Christine says. Now thirteen women strong, they've become the Gourmet Investment Club of Virginia. She adds: "Our three goals are education, social interaction, and financial success, in that order. We're always learning, we're having fun, and we've made some real good friends!"

If you have friends who are willing to help you learn—or learn along with you—start a weekly or monthly study group. Like the Gourmet Investment Club, you can combine food and finance, or whatever makes the gathering enjoyable as well as educational. (In chapter 4, you'll find out more about investing with a group.)

How to Talk to Bankers, Brokers, and Other Money Professionals

The language of money is filled with jargon. But when you're dealing with financial professionals, you can get by just fine in plain English. Simply explain your goals.

For example, you might say: "I'm forty now, and I want to have income of $60,000 a year from age sixty-five to age ninety-five. Help me figure out how to do that." Or: "I want to pay off this $4,500 credit-card balance in two years. How much should I pay each month to accomplish that?" A real pro's eyes will light up at this challenge, and he or she will reach for a calculator or computer keyboard.

(If this individual isn't responsive, or makes you feel dense or incompetent, stop right there and find someone else. More on this in chapter 4.)

One day you may feel expert enough to say something like: "I think my portfolio is overweighted in domestic stocks. I'd like to diversify into an international stock fund that doesn't have too much emerging-markets exposure."

But to start out with, it's fine to just state your goal and ask your advisor to explain how the strategy he or she is recommending will help you get where you want to go. As one woman explained, "It's the same thing as knowing what you want your house to look like, without having to be the architect or the electrician."

If there's anything in the explanation you don't understand or feel uneasy about, say so. Ask your financial professional to write a plain-English summary of the recommended course of action. Keep asking questions until you understand fully. Then take time to think it over, or if you feel comfortable with the proposal, go ahead with it.

READ MAGAZINES AND BOOKS ABOUT PERSONAL FINANCE

To see how other people use money to get where they want to go, start with the human-interest stories in personal-finance magazines like *Money, Kiplinger's,* and *SmartMoney.* As you become more aware of the role money plays in the destiny of companies and on the national and international scene, you may want to explore the dramatic tales of betrayal, greed, ambition, and skulduggery in such business publications as the *Wall Street Journal* and *Fortune*. Don't feel you have to pore over them cover to cover; just read what interests you.

To help yourself make better money decisions, one of the smartest investments you can make is a good financial reference book. Use it whenever you encounter a new concept or need to clarify something you've already learned. For a selection of the best resource books we've found, see the appendix.

> **Remember, you don't have to take it all on at once. Carve out one area at a time that you want to know more about, and start to educate yourself in this one area.**
>
> —*GRACE WEINSTEIN, financial editor, author, and consultant*

Exercise:
Turn information into knowledge

To practice turning financial facts into knowledge you can use, read the following article about Individual Retirement Accounts (IRAs). (Note that the figures mentioned reflect tax law as of year-end 2000.) Then write down at least three questions about how this information might apply to your own financial situation.

IRAs: NOW YOU CAN CHOOSE REGULAR OR ROTH
Among the provisions of the new tax law was a real gem for women wanting to boost their retirement savings: the Roth IRA. Here's a brief rundown on the Roth, plus tips on other IRA changes effective in 1998:

- *What's the difference between a Roth IRA and a traditional deductible IRA?* With a deductible IRA, you deduct your contributions, then pay the deferred income tax when you withdraw the money.

With a Roth IRA, you owe no tax at all at withdrawal. Instead, you pay tax upfront on your annual contributions, while everything you earn is tax-free. (In both cases, there may be an IRS penalty for making withdrawals before age 59$^{1}/_{2}$.)

- *Is a Roth IRA always a better deal?* Tax experts say you may actually earn more with a deductible IRA, provided you invest your annual tax savings and are in a lower tax bracket in retirement. But the fact is that most people spend their savings, and it's impossible to predict tax law changes—so a Roth IRA is worth serious consideration by anyone who qualifies.
- *Is it easy to qualify for a Roth IRA?* You can contribute up to $2,000 per year to a Roth IRA if your joint Adjusted Gross Income (AGI) is $150,000 or less ($95,000 or less for individuals). Contribution limits shrink for joint AGIs between $150,000 and $160,000 ($95,000 to $110,000 for individuals), then phase out completely.
- *How does that compare to qualifying for a deductible IRA?* No matter how much you earn, you can have a deductible IRA if you're not eligible for an employer-sponsored retirement plan.

  Even if you are covered by an employer plan, you can still fully or partially deduct your contribution to a regular IRA if your income meets certain limits. For the 2001 tax year, these limits are $62,000 for joint filers and $32,000 for individuals. These limits will increase in steps over the next several years.
- *Are nonworking wives getting more help?* Yes! You can deduct a full IRA contribution even if your husband has a retirement plan through his employer, as long as your joint AGI is under $150,000.
- *What if my AGI is too high to qualify for either a deductible IRA or a Roth IRA?* You can still contribute to a nondeductible IRA, which requires you to pay tax on your earnings at withdrawal.
- *Can I have more than one kind of IRA?* Yes, but the total of your IRA contributions can't exceed $2,000 a year.
- *Can I convert my existing regular IRAs into Roth IRAs?* If your joint or individual AGI is $100,000 or less, you can roll

over existing deductible or nondeductible IRAs into a Roth by paying the taxes you've deferred to date.

Even if you're already contributing the limit to a 401(k) or other employer-sponsored plan, we recommend taking advantage of this opportunity to plump up your retirement nest egg. After all, underestimating the cost of a comfortable retirement is a mistake you might have a long, long time to regret.

Now find out the answers to the three questions you've thought of, and write them down. In this case, if you don't prepare your own taxes, you might ask your accountant or tax advisor or your partner. Sources of answers to other kinds of questions might include your banker, an investment company representative, your insurance agent, or a money mentor you trust, perhaps your partner or a friend.

Once you have the answers, take any action that's called for. In this example, you might decide to look into converting your existing IRA to a Roth IRA. Your action might be to talk to a financial professional at the institution where you have your IRA. Ask him or her to calculate whether converting to a Roth IRA would make sense for you.

Last, reward yourself with some pleasurable experience to mark your new progress. With common sense, confidence, and some defined dreams to pursue, the world of money should already feel much less intimidating.

Where are you now?

If you haven't yet taken all of our suggested steps to debunk the myth that "money is too complicated for me to understand," here's a reminder of what you need to do before moving on to the next chapter.

1. Know the basic difference between stocks and bonds, and familiarize yourself with the idea of investing as a process where your smart shopping skills are very valuable.
2. To overcome math anxiety, work on changing negative feelings that may have carried over into your attitude toward money. If you need more support to boost your confidence, ask a friend to coach you or seek out a math course for adults.

3. As the first step in learning how to build what you want with your money, establish goals for the next five years and for the longer term. If you're not sure what your goals are, try writing the ideal story of your life from birth to death.
4. As the second step, set dollar amounts next to your goals so you can transform them into financial targets. Be sure to include an emergency cash reserve and a retirement fund among your priorities. If you're in a committed relationship, discuss your goals with your partner and invite your partner to do the same with you.
5. As the third step, focus on moving toward one of your short-term goals and one of your long-term goals this week. Share your list with someone supportive. Reward yourself for taking action toward your goals.
6. Find a partner or other money mentor who's willing to serve as your coach, or a group of women who can help you glean more money-management knowledge.
7. Start reading a personal-finance magazine, and buy a good reference book.
8. In talking with a financial professional, describe your goals. Ask questions until you're sure you understand. If you don't feel respected or supported, find someone else.

Congratulations! We hope you're beginning to find that learning about money stimulates your curiosity—and that acting on your new knowledge makes you feel more confident and in control of your life.

CHAPTER TWO

Myth 2:
"I Don't Have Enough Money
to Do Anything with"

*I always figured that when I made more money, then I would
invest, or pay down my debts, or whatever. I finally realized
that no matter how much money I made, it was never
enough. I had to change my attitude.*
—GERRI DETWEILER, *credit consultant and author*

* * *

"Not enough money" is often given as the reason that we can't save
more. In a 1998 SunAmerica survey, 61 percent of women felt that after paying bills they had little or no money available to save for retirement, compared to only 53 percent of men. This feeling of
powerlessness is particularly strong among minority women: 69 percent of Hispanic women and 75 percent of African-American women
said they didn't have money left over to save after paying bills.

And there are clearly a number of real-world obstacles that keep
women from having money to put aside for the future:

- Women tend to outnumber men in low-paying "pink collar"
  jobs such as clerks, nurses, and tellers.
- Even in comparable jobs, many women are still paid less than
  men (the gap is initially narrow but widens with age, averaging
  about three-quarters of men's pay).
- Wives who stay home to raise children often find that with
  only one household income, it's extremely difficult to save after
  paying all the bills.

- Single working mothers have an even tougher challenge after paying for child care.

Yet many women manage to turn even modest incomes into solid financial security. Among them are the "minimum-wage wealthy" who make the news every now and then—the hardworking cleaning woman or post office clerk who somehow accumulates hundreds of thousands of dollars on a meager income. How do they do it?

Financial advisor Dick Vodra has created a button he wears when he's speaking to groups. The top half of the button says "Everyone has enough money" and the bottom half says "No one has enough money." Vodra, a Certified Financial Planner with Legacy Advisors in McLean, Virginia, suggests that it's not really your pocketbook that determines which of these statements is true. It's your priorities—and the daily choices you make.

Chances are, you've got what it takes

In a 1999 *Money* magazine survey, nearly two-thirds of women said they would have to have $1 million or more to "feel rich." If you think a million dollars is way out of reach, take a few minutes to answer these questions:

1. What's your monthly after-tax income? $ _____
2. How many years before you plan to retire?   _____ years
3. Multiply by 12 to get months till retirement: _____ months
4. How much income will you have earned
   by then? (Multiply your answer to no. 1
   by your answer to no. 3) $ _____

For example, suppose your monthly after-tax income is $3,000. If you want to stop working in twenty years, that's 240 months (20 x 12). By that time, you'll have earned $3,000 x 240, or $720,000! Add in twenty years' worth of compound interest (and potential raises), and you could easily be looking at well over $1 million.

In a survey they did for their best-selling book, *The Millionaire Next Door*, Thomas J. Stanley and William D. Danko discovered that 80 percent of American millionaires created their own wealth. They report that the typical self-made millionaire "is a compulsive saver and investor," with a spouse who's a "planner and meticulous budgeter."

While compulsiveness in any form isn't necessarily good, the important thing is that these people focused on saving their money instead of spending it. In fact, most of these households invested at least 15 percent of their income every year.

Where and how they invested was important, of course (a topic to be addressed in chapter 3). But what really made the difference in their success was that they faithfully saved money that could then be put away to grow. Stanley and Danko conclude that the three words that best characterized these do-it-yourself millionaires were *frugal, frugal, frugal*. Many of them even clipped supermarket coupons!

Enough money . . . or not enough money?

As Dick Vodra's button implies, the difference is what you do with what you have. If you insist on buying whatever your heart desires right away, as so many people do, you could be a multimillionaire and still not have "enough" money. On the other hand, if you know you can't have everything you want the instant you want it, and instead make it a priority to save for the important things you'll need in the future, you're likely to feel satisfied and in control—and much closer to financial well-being.

Unfortunately, many of us—men as well as women—are influenced by money messages and traumas from childhood that keep us from learning how to delay gratification and save for the future. For example, consider the story of a forty-seven-year-old woman we'll call Lisa, who just couldn't hang on to her money. Anything in her wallet had to be quickly spent, and she lived from paycheck to paycheck. But Lisa told us she hadn't always been a compulsive spender:

> When I was four or five, I used to save all my money carefully in a big piggy bank that sat in my room. I would look at that piggy bank getting heavier and heavier, and feel excited about all the money I had saved.
>
> One day my mother came in when I wasn't there, took my piggy bank away and broke it open, and took all my money. She not only didn't pay me back, she never even apologized, and she made me

feel like a baby for crying hysterically when I saw my piggy bank was gone. I know I made a vow that from then on I would spend my money as quickly as I could, so no one could ever again get their hands on it and take it away from me.

Though Lisa was a successful salesperson and entrepreneur, she couldn't save a dime until she had done some hard work in healing the wounds of that traumatized little girl. At first, she gave many "reasons" for not being able to save—and a lot of them sounded plausible. She did have to put a daughter through college, pay for half of her son's bar mitzvah, and keep up the house she had lived in since her divorce some years earlier.

But with help, she was able to sell the house and move to a smaller, more appropriate, and much less expensive place; consult a financial planner; and begin saving more money for her retirement. Now she absorbs financial books, seminars, and tapes, trying to learn all she can about making her money work harder for her. Recently she said: "I can't believe I once thought getting a 2 percent return on my 401(k) meant I was taking care of myself. What planet was I living on, anyway?"

As her financial knowledge has slowly but steadily grown, Lisa is more and more grounded and calm about her future. She reported, "I feel better about myself, and less desperate about whether or not I ever remarry." Her courage in deciding to take on her money demons in her late forties began a process that turned her life around.

As you consider your own attitudes about saving, take some time reviewing your childhood and growing-up years to see if you're being influenced by events or attitudes from people you looked up to. Did someone once tell you, "You shouldn't have to worry about money, honey"? Or, "I hope you don't grow up a skinflint (or spendthrift) like your mother (or father)"?

As you've learned, one of the best ways to counteract negative messages that limit you is to write down positive ones. For example, tell yourself, "Saving money doesn't mean I'm turning into a miser; it means I'm planning prudently for the future."

Once you identify the money messages you've received, you'll be free to choose the ones that truly reflect your mature self and your goals and values as an adult.

Are you spending what you could be saving?

Many women find it harder to save because of the many inducements to spend, spend, spend. In our success-oriented society, there's a lot of pressure to appear as prosperous as the Joneses next door, with their pool behind the house, Ford Explorer in the driveway, and personal entertainment center in the den. This encourages us to buy whatever we "need" right now and finance it with a bigger mortgage, bigger car payments, bigger home equity lines, and bigger credit-card bills.

> **Look at your checkbook stubs to see what they reveal about your statement of values. I suspect that many of us are still spending more on our outsides than on our insides, and more on the present than on the future.**
> —GLORIA STEINEM,
> *author and women's rights pioneer*

Also, spending often equals love and caring in today's relationships, notes Martha Moyer, LCSW, a psychotherapist and workshop leader in Torrance, California, who specializes in money issues. "This leads to family situations in which women are bought. 'I won't be home for the next three weeks, dear. How many sweaters do you want?'" she says. "Many women are compensating for the lack of men in their lives by shopping and spending without a clue to their future," whether or not they're in a relationship.

No wonder so many of us are struggling to keep up with our debts, instead of putting money away for what's truly important! But it doesn't have to be this way. With a little creative planning and organizing, you'll see that you probably do have enough money . . . money you can begin putting aside to reach your long-term goals.

If you want to save more, the logical first step is to figure out where your money's been going.

Most of us don't have a very good idea of where our dollars go. They seem to disappear no matter how hard we try to hold on to them. Whether we shop at the warehouse club or the gourmet deli, buy clothes at the resale shop or a designer boutique, it ends up being the same struggle to pay bills every month.

That's why it's a good idea to track expenses (and savings) with personal-finance software such as Quicken or Microsoft Money. Many women say that the time they spend entering this data makes them feel pleasurably in control of their moneylife for the first time.

At the touch of a few keys, you can quickly see whether you're spending a lot more in a certain category than you did last year, or tally the current value of your savings and investments (a definite morale booster). Christine Stolba, director of economic projects for the Independent Women's Forum, a public policy group, told us, "It's heartening to see the increased use of personal computers in homes. Now almost any woman can buy and use Quicken, and educate herself in ways that weren't available ten years ago."

If you're not a computer person, write down your expenditures for two or three months to get an approximate idea of where your money goes. The simplest way is to jot down every purchase or bill payment in a small notebook you carry with you. (Some women find keeping this notebook in the car works best for them.)

If you faithfully enter every check you write in this monthly spending diary, you're apt to find that one big item seems to hog every spare dollar you earn. It's (uh-oh) debt.

Credit-card debt was a major problem for Gerri Detweiler, author of *Slash Your Debt: Save Money and Secure Your Future* and *Invest in Yourself: Six Secrets to a Rich Life*. Now education advisor to the nonprofit Myvesta.org, she used to be an overspender.

I always had a vision that I would either get a great job and earn a lot of money, or marry someone who had a lot of money. Did it happen? Not really.

Moving from southwest Michigan to D.C. around college age, I found it was much more expensive to get by. I spent money on friends and entertainment when I didn't really have it, just closed my eyes and pulled out the credit card, thinking, "Someday I'm gonna strike it rich and it'll be okay."

I racked up a lot of debt. By the time I was twenty-six, I had seven credit cards and ten thousand dollars of debt, and wasn't making a lot of money even though I had two jobs. When I became executive director of Bankcard Holders of America, I was terrified—literally panic-stricken that I had this job and was supposed to help people with their credit, but had all this debt. I felt a real sense of failure.

Around age twenty-seven or twenty-eight I finally wised up and got out of debt. I sold my Mustang convertible and got a used Toyota Tercel, started taking lunches to work, got books from the library instead of buying them, and tracked every expense. At the same time I took on freelance work to bring in more income, and sold my first book.

It took me a couple of years to get out of debt. Although it was hard, it wasn't as hard as I thought it would be, and I felt so good about it. And every other paycheck, I was able to save!

In 1993, I went out on my own. I had money saved, so I could do it. I started a retirement account, buying no-load mutual funds. I'm not at all a conservative investor; all my retirement money is in the stock market.

Believe me, I'm the last person who wants to sit down and master financial stuff. I grew up with the feeling that I was in a fog when it came to money. But now I can pick up a fund prospectus and know something about it, and it feels really good. My basic feeling is, "If I can do this, anyone can do it!" [Sound familiar?]

You may recognize yourself in Gerri Detweiler's description of how easily she got overloaded with debt. With enticements to spend surrounding us morning, noon, and night, most of us are still too quick to pull out the credit cards or checkbook.

When overspending becomes compulsive, we tend to make purchases without asking ourselves, "Do I really need this?" or "Can I afford it right now?" We give ourselves what sound like good excuses: "I work so hard; I deserve this," "I'm not extravagant; it's on sale," or "He'd love to have this; I know he'd buy it himself if he were here."

But despite the rationales, there's a definite problem when (a) we can't really afford something we really want, and (b) we refuse to put off spending until we *can* afford it. Denying ourselves makes us feel deprived, upset, and angry.

As a result, even though we may really want to save money, we just can't seem to stop spending. So every month it's the same old struggle to make ends meet, and we live constantly on the edge of financial disaster.

If this sounds familiar, consider following these five steps.

1. Identify "slippery places" that tempt you to overspend—certain malls and stores, for example—as well as "points of temptation" such as payday, after a fight with your partner, or when you feel bored, fat, or neglected. Strategize ways to prevent or cope with the urge to splurge, perhaps enlisting the help of a friend who's not an overspender.

2. Sensitize yourself by recording your emotions in your spending diary. Comment on each expenditure as you record it. For instance, "Good buy!" or "What a waste!" or "I already have tons of these." If it's a big purchase, figure out how many hours you'll have to work to replace the money. Was it worth it?

3. Ask at your library or nearest bookstore for *Overcoming Overspending: A Winning Plan for Spenders and Their Partners*. In this book, we outline a strategy for regaining your financial sanity and solvency. Another good reference is Colette Dowling's *Maxing Out: How Women Sabotage Their Financial Security*.

4. Find the nearest Debtors Anonymous chapter. This free twelve-step program has helped chronic overspenders turn their destructive spending behavior around.

5. If you feel you need more help to win the battle, seek a therapist who's comfortable dealing with money problems. (In later chapters we'll suggest how to find one)

Successful saving is a state of mind

Saving comes easier to some women than others. For example, you probably have little difficulty putting money aside if you have a Planner personality. Planners tend to be disciplined, feel in control of their lives, and know how much they need to save.

By contrast, saving is a real chore if you're a Spender. You're hooked on immediate gratification and find it hard to cut back on spending. Spenders need to think of spending less and saving more as a way of making sure there will be money to spend in later years. Even so, you may need to trick yourself into saving (read on for ideas).

Another group of women are Avoiders, who refuse to think about saving to protect their financial security. Like Spenders, Avoiders may rationalize that they'll have time later to worry about saving, or perhaps hope vaguely that someone else will solve the problem for them (a partner, an employer, the government, or their parents via an inheritance). If you're an Avoider, it's important to recognize that you'll almost certainly be alone at some point in your life. Don't wait for a crisis to force you to wake up and take charge of your own financial security.

Another large segment of the population is what we might call Strugglers. Though they may know the importance of saving, they feel they're barely able to keep afloat financially and don't have any money to save.

If you're a Struggler, a self-aware Spender, or a reformed Avoider, the key to savings success may be a financial plan. Why? Because generic saving doesn't work—at least not compared to the immediate temptation to spend your money on something. If you simply try to save what's left at the end of the month, you'll find there's never anything left by the time the bills are paid.

By focusing on what you're saving for, you'll be able to get there faster. In fact, families with a financial plan tend to save about twice as much as families in the same income bracket who don't have a plan, according to a 1997 survey by the Consumer Federation of America.

Planning is so important! Don't just dream of being financially successful—plan on it! And keep learning. You'll get there!

—ERIN BROCKOVICH, a pollution-fighting crusader who directs environmental research at a Los Angeles law firm

---

Fortunately, your journey has already gotten off on the right foot. In chapter 1, you set goals and estimated how much you'll need to save each month to reach them.

If you're a gratification-focused Spender, it may be especially important to have a savings goal you can eagerly anticipate. Let's say you decide to go to Europe in three years. The trip will cost $5,000. If you don't have personal-finance software that can calculate how much to save per month, just divide 5,000 by 36 (it works out to about $139 a month). If you save this amount faithfully, you'll get your $5,000— plus the interest your savings will have earned.

When it comes to your biggest and most important goal, financial security in retirement, we believe you should save at least 10 percent of your gross income. If 10 percent is beyond your means right now, start with as much as you can afford and raise the amount by 1 percent a year.

In short, the million-dollar secret of successful savers is really quite simple: Just write down your goals and how much you'll save each month to get there. Now you have a plan.

You may already have more money than you think

How much money do you have in savings accounts or CDs, in investments, or in your 401(k), IRA, or Keogh? How much equity do you have in your home? (In other words, how much would you keep if you sold it for its market value, after paying off what's left of the mortgage and/or home equity loan?)

If you've been in the dark about all this, hoping your employer or your partner was looking out for your future financial security, now's the time to find out what kind of position you're really in. It will take a little detective work—you'll need to locate your latest account statements—but the answers may reassure you that your savings plan is starting from a solid base. In fact, you may find you're already well on the way toward your goals.

Here's what you need to find out:

What You Own

Cash in checking:	$ _____
Cash in savings:	$ _____
Market value of home and/or other real estate owned:	$ _____
Vested interest in retirement accounts:	$ _____
Nonretirement investments:	$ _____
Net worth of business(es) owned:	$ _____
Market value of vehicles and other personal property:	$ _____
Money owed you by others:	$ _____
Life insurance cash value:	$ _____
Your total assets:	$ _____

If you have no savings or investments and don't own a home, the first item on your goal list should be to put money aside for financial emergencies. Once you've saved enough to cover one to three months' worth of living expenses, you'll feel a tremendous sense of financial freedom—allowing you to move on to the fun stuff on your list.

Now add up your debts to see how the totals compare. You may need to call the mortgage company to find out your current balance. Just use last year's tax bill to estimate this year's taxes (unless your circumstances are radically different this year).

What You Owe

Principal left on mortgage:	$ _____
Amount owed on home equity line/loan:	$ _____
Amount owed on other loans:	$ _____
Amount owed on credit cards:	$ _____
Alimony owed (if appropriate):	$ _____
Taxes owed for the current year:	$ _____
Your total liabilities:	$ _____

Calculating your net worth

Your total assets:	$ _____
Minus your total liabilities:	$ _____
Your net worth:	$ _____

If you own more than you owe, that's good—you have a positive net worth. If your debt outweighs your savings, you're in a much less secure position. Either way, by determining where you stand now, you've begun to blow away the fog that keeps you from taking full charge of your money.

To save or pay off debt, that is the question

If you're like many women, it's just plain hard for you to focus on saving money when you owe money. Aside from the difficulty of finding anything to save after paying the bills, you may believe you'll feel more financially secure if you clean up all your debt before you start putting money in the bank. And on a rational level, it just makes sense to pay off a 17 percent credit card before you put a penny into a 3¹/₂ percent savings account.

Irrational as it may seem, we beg to differ. If you don't have an emergency cash reserve or any retirement savings, it's important to scrape up some money—even if it's only $25 or $50 a month to start with—and begin to make it grow, no matter what other debts are hanging over your head.

At the same time, you do need to take charge of the debt that's dominating your financial life. The first step is to determine how much of it is "good debt" and how much is "bad debt." Just like HDL and LDL cholesterol, there are some types of debt that are basically okay for your financial health and others that you want to reduce as quickly as possible.

It's all about your choices.
You're going to spend your money one way or another.
The problem is that people don't see it as a choice
and just let the money dribble away.
—PEG DOWNEY, CFP (Certified Financial Planner),
financial advisor in Silver Spring, Maryland

"Good debt" is debt connected with an investment that's likely to gain value. Some examples are a mortgage (your home value may increase, and you save the expense of rent in the meantime), student loans (an investment that can pay off in enhanced earning power later), or a business loan (if intended to finance greater efficiency or growth). All three types of loans have tax advantages, indicating that Uncle Sam recognizes their contribution to strengthening the fabric of society.

"Bad debt" is debt connected with things that lose value. Loans for cars, boats, and RVs; financing on refrigerators, mobile homes, and wall-to-wall carpet; and credit-card balances for vacations, clothes,

dinners out, or a new computer are some examples. That's not to say
you should never borrow to buy items that depreciate. It simply
means you should get rid of this "bad debt" as fast as you can, especially since it's ordinarily not tax deductible and has a higher interest rate.

If you calculated your net worth in the previous section, figure out
how much of your debt is the "good" kind and how much is the
"bad" kind.

Good debt: $ _____   Bad debt: $ _____

*If you have a lot of bad debt at relatively high interest rates, see if you
might qualify for a debt consolidation loan from your bank.* These install-
ment loans have a fixed interest rate and fixed monthly payments,
both of which are likely to be lower than what you're now paying. Be
sure to compare the total interest on a consolidation loan with what
you'd pay on your current debts, to make sure you'll come out ahead.
(Caution: If you haven't yet conquered overspending, debt consolidation can be dangerous, encouraging you to rack up new debt on paid-
off credit cards.)

Whether you get a debt consolidation loan or just hack away at
your existing loans, you'll need to decide on the maximum amount
you can afford to put toward savings and debt repayment every
month. Then parcel it out to your creditors and your savings account
50/50, 40/60, 60/40, or in whatever other ratio you're comfortable
with. Pay off the highest-rate debt first. When you've knocked the balances on your "bad debt" down to zero, start paying into your savings
account the amount you'd been sending your creditors.

*If your debt is mostly good debt, you probably shouldn't sacrifice your sav-
ings to prepay it.* In most cases, prepaying your mortgage should be at
the bottom of the priority list, since this ultimate "good debt" is apt
to be the cheapest loan you have. For instance, a 7.5 percent mortgage
actually costs someone in the 28 percent tax bracket only 5.4 percent,
because the interest is deductible. In other words, if you put your savings into prepaying this loan, you'd "earn" only 5.4 percent on your
money. By investing your money elsewhere, you could conceivably
earn enough to pay off your mortgage and have money left over.

But like every rule, this one has exceptions. For example, if you want to have the mortgage paid off by the time you retire, go for it—as long as prepayment won't put a crimp in your retirement saving. (Remember, if you miscalculate and need money later for living expenses, it'll be a lot easier to get it out of a retirement account than out of the house.) Also, note our suggestion on page 50 about refinancing if rates have dropped a percentage point or more since you got your mortgage.

SPECIAL TIPS ON PAYING DOWN CREDIT CARDS

If you're swamped with this kind of debt, there are three things you should do.

First, switch your balance to the lowest-rate credit card you can find. If you pay $200 a month on a credit card with an interest rate of 17 percent, wiping out a $5,000 balance can cost you almost $1,400 in interest and take thirty-two months. By switching to a 9.9 percent card with a fixed rate and paying the same $200 a month, you'd be clear in twenty-nine months and pay under $675 in interest. That means you can start adding $200 a month to your savings program three months sooner. (When you find a better deal, call your own card issuer first and ask if it will match the terms. Card issuers' acquisition costs can run between $75 and $140 per account, so there's a good chance they'll try to hold on to an existing account, according to RAM Research, a card-industry tracking group.) Be sure to close your old credit-card accounts in writing and destroy the cards.

Second, put your new credit card away and use it only in an emergency. If necessary, lock it in a safe deposit box.

Third, make sure you repay more each month than the minimum required. Otherwise you'll pay a fortune in interest over time—money you could have been using to fund your other goals. For example, if you make minimum monthly payments of 2 percent on a 17 percent credit card, it will take *forty years* to pay off a balance of $5,000, and cost you a total of $16,304. But by paying just $50 more than the minimum every month, you'd have the card balance paid off in a little more than six years—and save $8,701 in interest.

In the meantime, it's a good idea to resolve never again to charge more than you can pay off each month. Better yet, switch to a debit card for all but big-ticket emergencies—and be sure to track debit-card usage in your check register, so you don't spend money you don't have.

THE PROS AND CONS OF
HOME EQUITY LOANS AND CREDIT LINES

Home equity borrowing may be "good debt" (e.g., when used for home improvements or college costs), "okay debt" (e.g., when used as a tax-advantaged substitute for a car loan or debt consolidation), or "bad debt" (e.g., when used for Christmas shopping).

In its favor are several "pros": Home equity loans are cheaper than most other ways to borrow. You can use the money for anything, even if it's unrelated to your home. The interest is usually tax deductible. And a home equity credit line is convenient; you can usually write an equity line check, use a credit card linked to your line, or transfer funds by phone.

But there are also a number of "cons": They're a riskier way to borrow because your home serves as collateral. You may have to pay closing costs to get one. And they're abused by some lenders, who charge excessive fees and/or high rates, or who encourage homeowners to borrow as much as 125 percent of the equity in their homes. For example, if your home's current appraised value is $100,000 and you owe $60,000 on your mortgage, you have $40,000 in actual home equity. But a 125 percent equity loan would give you $65,000 in cash ($125,000 minus $60,000). The problem: If you have to sell your home, you will owe the mortgage company and the home equity lender a total of $125,000—$25,000 more than a buyer would be likely to pay you.

If you already have a home equity loan or credit line, check with other lenders in your area to make sure the interest rate you're being charged is competitive. If it's not, look for a lender who'll let you refinance it at a better rate with no closing costs.

If you're a homeowner who doesn't have a home equity credit line, you should consider applying for one—even if you never plan to use it. (*Disregard this advice if you're an overspender.*) In a pinch, your line of credit can be used as an emergency reserve. If you can obtain a credit line of $10,000 or more free of closing costs or annual fees, it's a cheap and easy way to give yourself a financial safety net. You won't owe any interest, of course, unless you use the available credit.

Once you've taken stock of your monthly spending needs, figured out how you're going to handle your debt, and decided how much you'll save, put together a monthly spending plan. A simple budget note-book (available at office supply stores) may be all you need. Or if you'd prefer step-by-step assistance in developing a monthly budget that will help you squeeze savings out of your income, try Judy Lawrence's *The Budget Kit* (see appendix for details).

After you've followed your plan for a few months, you'll get a feel for how well you're doing on the grocery bills and know without looking at the budget book whether you can afford to spring for those new shoes or an elegant dinner out.

> **I had a friend tell me that she just didn't have enough money to save. I said, "Do you have ten dollars a week to spare? How about twenty?" How much you start with isn't as important as starting and keeping going.**
> —JJ JAMISON, *a CFP in Colorado Springs*

Four time-tested ways to make even small sums grow

Regardless of how much or how little money you have, it's crucial to get yourself in the habit of putting money aside. Even if it's just $5 a week, you'll find you don't really miss it, and you'll start to discover the feeling of being in control. Better yet, you'll discover that over the course of ten, twenty, or thirty years, even small amounts can make a huge difference.

To make this happen, you need to consider saving as an obligation, not a choice. Make it a budget item, like your rent or mortgage and your utilities. And follow these four basic principles, which can make the challenge a lot easier:

1. *Start now, even if you can't save a lot.* Let compound interest do the hard work for you. In twenty years, for instance, compound interest at 7 percent a year can transform $3,000 into more than $11,600. Except for some Christmas Club accounts, compound interest is a feature of all bank savings accounts, including CDs.

Mutual funds and most stocks allow automatic reinvestment of dividends, which makes compounding possible.

Compounding also means that the sooner you start, the less money you'll need to put aside to reach your goal. For example, if you're twenty-five years from retirement, $1,000 invested at a 7 percent rate of return will grow to $5,427. But if you wait a year to start saving, you'd have to put in $1,070—7 percent more!—to reach the same total by retirement age. So don't postpone your savings program because you think you can't possibly put aside enough to make a difference. Saving a little now could mean you won't need to save a lot more later.

The Power of Compound Interest

It's said that when Albert Einstein was asked to choose mankind's greatest invention, he answered, "Compound interest."

According to a calculation by GE Capital, if Christopher Columbus had invested $1 at 5 percent simple interest back in 1492, that $1 would have grown by now to just $26.20. (Simple interest is calculated each year on the principal only.) By contrast, if Chris had invested the same dollar at 5 percent compound interest (which is calculated on the principal plus the interest previously earned), it would have grown to a breathtaking $48 billion.

---

2. *Put your savings program on autopilot.* If you don't, you'll have to decide every month whether to save or spend—and guess which one will win?

If you're fortunate enough to qualify for a 401(k) or similar payroll-deduction plan, you've struck gold. Since your savings contribution is deducted before your paycheck is cut, you never get a chance to spend the money—making this an ideal way for freewheeling Spenders and don't-bother-me Avoiders to save. Saving pretax dollars is also the best way for Strugglers to get more bang for each buck. But since most withdrawals before age 59 1/2 trigger tax penalties, use this strategy chiefly for your retirement savings.

To build an emergency fund and save for other shorter-term needs, ask your employer to deduct your savings contribution automatically from your paycheck and send it to your account at a bank, credit union, or mutual fund company. Can't get payroll deduction? Arrange with your bank to have savings taken automatically from your checking account.

3. *Take every opportunity to get free money.* If your employer offers to match savings you contribute to your retirement plan (often dollar for dollar or fifty cents on the dollar, up to a certain percentage of your pay), try to go for every penny you can. In addition, if you take advantage of Uncle Sam's generosity in letting you defer tax on income you park in a deductible IRA, 401(k), or similar plan, be sure to put the money you'd otherwise have had to pay the IRS into savings. For example, a $2,000 tax-deductible IRA contribution will save you $300 a year in taxes if you're in the 15 percent bracket, or $560 if you're in the 28 percent bracket. Don't spend your savings—save it!

4. *Keep the tax man away from your money while it's growing.* It's a fact of financial life: The more tax you pay, the less money you have left to save. And if you keep having to raid your existing savings to pay the IRS every year, you'll lose a lot of the benefit of compounding.

Unfortunately, there aren't many ways to avoid taxes on non-retirement savings. One of them, investing in municipal bonds, will be discussed in the next chapter. For your retirement money, the solution is an employer savings plan like a 401(k), SIMPLE, 403(b), 457 plan, SEP-IRA, or Keogh; or a tax-deductible IRA if you don't have access to an employer plan. The reason: You won't have to pay tax on your money in these accounts until you withdraw it. This means it can grow much faster than comparable savings that are tapped to pay taxes every year.

Frankly, you just can't beat employer plans for value when it comes to saving for your long-term financial security.

How to find money you didn't think you had

If you'd like to jump-start your savings program, try the following ideas.

1. *Don't overpay the IRS.* One of the most expensive ways to save is to have too much tax withheld from your paycheck. In 1999, the average refund was a whopping $1,550.

If you take advantage of child-care or education tax credits or open a deductible IRA without changing your withholding, you could overpay by an extra $300 to $400 or more. Although you can ask for this money back at the end of the year, Uncle Sam doesn't pay interest. In fact, with an annual inflation rate of 3 percent, a dollar you overpay will be worth only ninety-seven cents when you get it back. It's a better idea to fine-tune your W-4 to come as close as you can to your true tax liability, then save or invest the difference through payroll deduction.

2. *Don't keep money idling in the bank.* To avoid monthly service fees, your bank may require a minimum checking-account balance of as much as $1,000, which may (if you're lucky) pay an underwhelming 1½ percent in interest. Find a fee-free account, and you could invest that $1,000 instead.

If you want to stick with the same financial institution, you might get a better deal by consolidating more of your business there. For example, most big banks provide free interest-paying checking (and checks) to customers with a significant balance in deposit accounts, loans, credit cards, and/or investments. If you prefer to bank à la carte, community banks and credit unions in your area are more likely than big banks to offer free interest-bearing checking with no fees. (This is also a good way to simplify your financial life, as you'll see in chapter 4.)

Also, be alert for nickel-and-dime banking charges that can wipe out your savings gains without being noticed. For instance, if you get cash once a week at an ATM your bank or credit union doesn't own, you'll typically pay fees and surcharges of $2 or more per withdrawal, or over $100 a year—more than you'd earn from a $2,000 CD paying 5 percent. The solution: change your habits . . . or your bank.

3. *Refinance your mortgage and invest the savings.* Low mortgage interest rates can give you a great opportunity to free up hundreds of dollars a month by refinancing. For example, let's say you've already paid off $5,000 of the $85,000 you owe on your thirty-year fixed-rate mortgage at 9.5 percent. By refinancing the remaining $80,000 with a twenty-five-year mortgage at 7 percent, you could lower your monthly payment from $715 to $565. After recouping your refinancing costs, you'd have $150 a month to invest elsewhere. To explore "what-ifs" yourself, try the

interactive refinancing calculators at www.kiplinger.com or www.hsh.com. (Personal-finance software often has a built-in refinancing calculator, too.)

4. *Explore cheaper health and life insurance and invest the difference.* If you and your spouse both have family health insurance through separate employers, you may be paying significantly more but getting only a minor increase in benefits. Your company benefits administrator should be able to help you decide whether the less generous policy is really worth the extra premium. If you drop it, funnel the monthly payroll deduction into an investment account instead.

If you have individual coverage through a traditional indemnity plan and don't want to switch to cheaper managed care, there's one way to save big without losing your free choice of providers—by increasing your deductible and your copayment. Protect yourself by investing the money you save each month in an easily accessible account, where it can keep earning interest if not needed for medical bills.

For the self-employed, there's an even better alternative: a Medical Savings Account the whole family can use for medical expenses, including prescriptions, eyeglasses, dental care, and other needs not usually covered by health insurance. Contributions are tax deductible, and money not used can be rolled over to continue compounding for you. Your MSA must be paired with a high-deductible (i.e., relatively cheap) insurance policy that serves as a safety net. Ask your bank, broker, or insurance agent for details, or go on-line to the Council for Affordable Health Web site (www.cahi.org).

If you bought term life insurance a while ago, you may be able to bank several hundred dollars a year by replacing it with a less expensive policy. Making this possible are national insurance clearinghouses accessible by phone or computer. Quotes you request by phone (try Quotesmith, 1-800-431-1147, or MasterQuote, 1-800-337-5433) come to you by mail, while on-line quotes are instant and don't require you to identify yourself. Start with www.quotesmith.com, whose huge database includes insurer credit ratings. You may find different leads at www.insuremarket.com and www.quickquote.com.

5. *Drop insurance you don't need.* Don't stint on paying for good ba-

sic health, homeowners, and auto insurance, or on life insurance if you have children. But buying life insurance on a child is a waste, unless your kid is a movie star or a world-class athlete whose income your family depends on. Credit life insurance on mortgages, credit cards, and other loans (usually sold through the lender) is a high-priced way to pay off the balance if you die or become disabled. Unless you're in poor health and can't get regular life insurance, it will probably cost less to buy a term life insurance policy, whose payout can be used for any purpose. Specialty disease insurance, such as a policy that pays if you get cancer, is a gamble with relatively little likelihood of a payoff. Again, if you cancel any of these high-cost coverages, put the money you save into savings.

6. *Salt away all your "found money."* Use it to bump up your retirement savings contribution or automatic savings transfer. Inheritances, bonuses, raises, or lottery payouts (lucky you!) can all be socked into savings right away.

Consider the Cost of Money Before You Spend

The next time you're tempted to spend $20 on a CD you may not like or a toy your child doesn't really need, consider this: You may have to earn nearly $37 to replace it! To be precise, after taking into account federal income tax at 28 percent, state income tax at 6 percent, local income tax at 1 percent, and Social Security/Medicare tax at 7.65 percent, you'd have to earn $36.97 to replace the $21.20 (including 6 percent sales tax) that you spent. That's one expensive CD! If you make a habit of considering the replacement cost of money before you spend it, you may find it's easier to cut back on discretionary purchases and save more.

Find lower-cost solutions
to reward yourself and others

When you track your spending, you may soon see a pattern of little expenditures that add up to big bucks. Could you save $25 a week or more by bringing lunch to work, giving up that costly coffee, or going longer between perms or manicures?

We often forget to count gifts as spending. But they are—so don't overlook the presents for parents, partner, or siblings; the clothes and toys you buy for your kids or your nieces and nephews; even the $3.50 birthday cards you grab for your hairdresser or cubicle-mate at work. For many of us, these purchases trigger a form of do-it-yourself emotional blackmail ("I can't say no to this; it would make my child/nephew/colleague feel I don't care, and I couldn't stand that!").

Develop new self-talk that helps you feel good about expressing your appreciation in nonmonetary ways. For example, tell yourself, "These flowers from my garden are a more personal way to say thank you, and choosing to give this kind of gift helps protect my financial well-being."

When you put your mind to it, there are plenty of ways to reduce your spending on discretionary items: clothing, CDs, books, videos, and other gifts for yourself or others. Every week, try to brainstorm a low-cost or no-cost alternative that lets you reward yourself or show others your love or affection.

Finding wiser ways to express your caring will enhance your feelings of self-worth, as well as pay financial dividends. You're giving what you have to give and what you can truly afford, not just something that makes you look good right now (and possibly feel bad later on).

If your children are your weak spot, it's important to set an example by saying no sometimes so that you can put money aside. Otherwise, you may unwittingly encourage them to become habitual overspenders like so many Americans today. What's more, if your overspending on them leaves you financially unprepared for the future, they may end up having to support you when they're older. This burden could hurt much more than having to forgo $150 shoes or a designer prom dress today. In other words, saying no at times to your children, kindly but firmly, may be the best gift you can give them.

(Sometimes kids will even acknowledge this, making your job easier. A corporate executive told us that after the tears and wailing that followed her firm explanation of why she wouldn't buy the expensive sneakers her daughter craved, she overheard the girl defend her lack of fancy footwear to a friend: "It's really ridiculous—I can't believe how much money they want for something you outgrow so quickly!")

At first, cutting back on expenditures this way may seem like serious deprivation. (We hear you, Spenders!) To counter this, review your goals list every day to remember what you're saving for. Find a picture that reminds you of your primary goal, and keep your enthusiasm high by carrying it in your pocketbook—ideally, in your wallet on top of your credit cards. Looking at a postcard of a beach in Tahiti or a magazine photo of a youngster in a cap and gown will remind you why you're choosing not to buy that designer sweater right now.

Most important, when you save money by not spending it, *save it*. In other words, don't expect it to be waiting patiently in your checking account at the end of the month—because, trust us, it won't be. Take the $3 you were about to blow on a mocha latte, or the $35 you almost spent on a videogame your son doesn't really need, and immediately put it in an envelope marked "Savings." (If you don't have the cash on hand, write a check.) At the end of the month, plunk it all in a savings account or money market fund.

But don't stop there. Deposit little checks—rebates, dividends, expense checks—instead of cashing them. Empty your pockets into a piggy bank every night. In your check register, round up every debit and round down every credit to the nearest dollar, then transfer this accumulated cash (along with your piggy-bank proceeds) into savings once a month. You'll probably never miss this small stuff, and it could boost your savings by $150 or more a year . . . just one more way you can start right now to make greater strides toward your goals.

When You Adopt Better Money Habits, Reward Yourself

When you put your gift giving on a budget, or refinance your mortgage to free up savings, think about rewarding yourself for your new behavior in ways that don't cost a lot of money or undermine your success. A visit to your favorite museum? A nature hike with your best friend? How about two hours a week on an "artist's date" with yourself? Julia Cameron suggests the latter in The Artist's Way *as a method of anchoring yourself in your own creativity and self-esteem. Just don't celebrate your progress by spending your savings!*

As you see your money beginning to mount up, a wonderful thing will happen. Your feelings of sacrifice and deprivation will start to fade, replaced by pride and satisfaction in taking charge of your own financial security. As you begin to feel more in control of your life and more positive about the future, you'll find it easier and easier to keep saving toward your goals.

If you can't spend less, maybe you can earn more

After you've looked at your income and your outgo, you may decide there's no way to stretch your paycheck one more millimeter. In this case, the solution could be to make more money instead of trying to spend less.

To begin exploring ways to earn more, consider things you enjoy doing or favorite places you're rarely able to visit. Is there some way to take on part-time or weekend work doing something you like, preferably somewhere you love? For example, if you like to make jewelry as a hobby and enjoy being with people, you might seek part-time work at your favorite arts and crafts supply store or in an art gallery. (Spenders beware: Don't choose a place that tempts you to spend all your new income on the merchandise.)

The reason we suggest starting with your passions, interests, and hobbies is that when you're doing something you love, or are in a place you enjoy, part-time work won't become drudgery. The goal is to maximize your income in as fulfilling and enjoyable a way as you can. If you take on a job that bores or depresses you, you could end up sabotaging your own attempts to generate income, or become so stressed that the financial benefit just doesn't seem worth it.

If this avenue of brainstorming doesn't pay off, explore how you could use your skills to generate more income. For instance, if you're a computer whiz, could you troubleshoot for small businesses in your area? A good cook might moonlight as a personal chef—taking an afternoon or a few evenings to prepare meals for busy couples to stash in the freezer. Who knows, a microbusiness might even become more profitable than your full-time job—as well as being a good way to generate income in retirement later on.

Are you already working too hard to consider a second job? Perhaps you need to lobby for a raise.

Interestingly, almost every woman we surveyed for this book said that in negotiating for more pay, she would seek a "win-win" outcome for herself and her boss. That's very generous (and win-win solutions are certainly desirable wherever possible), but your first priority should be getting paid at a level that reflects your value to the company. Don't expect the boss to reward you for the great job you're doing unless you approach her (or him) directly and toot your own horn a little. (More about this in chapter 6.)

Without exaggerating your contribution or abilities, you should be willing to spell out why you deserve the compensation you're asking for. When you present your arguments firmly and clearly, without any emotional dramatics, your boss should be favorably impressed by your businesslike attitude. If you don't receive a pay increase afterward or a really good explanation of why you're not getting one, that may be your cue to start looking for a better-paying job elsewhere.

Consider the smartest ways to stash your cash

By stashing your savings in "safe" places with limited potential for compound growth, you may unwittingly shortchange yourself.

For relatively short-term goals, there are several choices, all with pros and cons. Which of these options are you comfortable with?

- *The cookie jar.* It's convenient. But money doesn't grow just by snuggling up to other money. Be sure to empty your cookie jar at least once a month and tote the contents off to a place that will pay you interest on your deposit.
- *Savings accounts.* These accounts typically pay only 2 to 3 percent interest, which means you could sock away money till the cows come home and still not do much better than you would with a cookie jar. Savings accounts are best used for getting started or for parking money you'll need in the next few months. If you qualify to join a credit union, or if there's a savings bank or savings-and-loan association near you, you'll probably find its savings account interest rates more attractive than a big bank's.

  Pass up any savings account with fees you can't avoid. Skip Christmas Club accounts, which pay little or no interest, and passbook accounts, which don't pay much more. At most smaller banks, the best value is a statement savings account. Larger banks may offer a money market account insured by the Federal Deposit Insurance Corporation (FDIC), which can be a super deal if its rate mirrors the current average yield of money market mutual funds. Be sure to ask, though—because at some financial institutions, "money market" accounts simply mimic the ups and downs of current money market fund yields, while paying you much less.

- *Certificates of deposit.* CDs are safe, no question about it. You know what interest rate you're going to earn, and you can be sure of getting all your money back, thanks to FDIC insurance. But you generally can't make withdrawals before maturity without incurring a penalty, which means you could forfeit interest (sometimes even part of your principal) if you have to get cash out in an emergency. And if you lock up your money in a CD with a long term, you'll be stuck on the sidelines if interest rates increase.

  CDs can make a lot of sense for savers in two kinds of situations:

  1. You've accumulated or inherited a chunk of money that you plan to use at a certain point during the next two or three years and need to keep safe until then. For example, if you're anticipating your teen's first college tuition payment, or buying a house when your apartment lease expires, you can purchase a CD with an appropriate maturity date and not have to worry about a thing. But if your goal is more than a few years away, a CD probably isn't the best choice. That's because over longer periods, its modest earnings can be badly eroded by inflation, leaving you with little or no real increase in your purchasing power.

  2. You have a diversified portfolio of investments, chosen to guard against a broad spectrum of risks. Your stable-value investments (including CDs) help cushion your portfolio against market fluctuations, while your growth investments (stocks and/or stock mutual funds) help protect you from losing buying power to inflation and taxes.

     You may not have that diversified portfolio yet—but don't be concerned. In the next chapter, we'll address ways to put your money to work toward longer-term goals.

- *U.S. savings bonds.* Think of these as Uncle Sam's CDs. Backed by the U.S. Treasury, they're a very safe investment. Savings bonds make good gifts for children because they typically cost only half of their eventual face value and don't mature for a long time. (Currently, Series EE bonds reach face value in eighteen years.) However, their low-powered interest rates limit their appeal for grown-ups who need growth.

* *Money market mutual funds.* Money market funds pay a higher return than savings accounts and give you easier access to your cash than CDs (you can often write checks on your account). You'll find them only at mutual fund companies like the Vanguard Group or Fidelity Investments, or at brokerages like Charles Schwab or Merrill Lynch.

  When you purchase shares in a money market fund, your money is pooled with cash sent in by other investors and invested by a professional money manager in short-term Treasury bills, CDs, and other securities of high credit quality. This low-risk investment approach makes money market funds almost as safe as money in the bank—so safe that many households use them as the primary place to stash their short-term savings.

  Unlike other mutual funds whose shares bounce around in value every day, money market funds try to maintain a constant share price of $1. For example, if you invest $100, you own 100 shares. If those shares earn interest at 5 percent, in a year you'd own 105 shares worth $105, and so on.

  You should be aware, though, that money market funds aren't FDIC insured. Fund companies don't guarantee them, either. This means that if the fund invests poorly, its share price might go down below $1 (known as "breaking the buck"). However, the importance of investors' trust in the stability and integrity of money market funds is so widely accepted that on the very few occasions when a particular fund has lost money, the fund company has voluntarily stepped in with extra cash to make sure investors aren't hurt.

When you're just getting your saving program off the ground, don't agonize too much over which of these alternatives to choose. If the easiest way for you to save is to put $25 in a cookie jar every week, just do it. Then, as your savings start to build, look around to see if there's a better place for your money to grow—perhaps a high-yielding savings account, CD, or money market fund.

Remember, these choices are essentially for money needed in the short term or for a long-term savings program that's just getting off the ground. Once you've accumulated $1,000 or so toward a long-term goal like retirement, you'll want to consider investing it—a topic we'll explore more fully in the next chapter.

> **Almost any investment is okay to start with.**
> **Success isn't really determined by**
> **investment behavior, but by investor behavior—**
> **whether or not you get started and keep going.**
> —DICK VODRA, *a CFP in McLean, Virginia*

From bankruptcy to financial independence: a success story

Raised in a wealthy family, Samantha grew up having every material advantage she could have wished for. For example, while her classmates walked to high school, she drove a convertible. But this comfortable life changed drastically when she was eighteen, after her father's business partner absconded with the firm's money. Her father was forced to declare bankruptcy, both of their homes were sold, and Samantha discovered that her newly impoverished family could no longer afford to send her to college.

Recovering from this financial (and psychological) shock, she found two jobs at school to pay for her tuition, took out student loans to cover the rest, and finished all four years of college. Not long afterward came another blow: She was diagnosed with breast cancer. Samantha says this difficult period taught her several important lessons: "For the first time in my life I learned how to live frugally, and to value what was most important—personal relationships, friendships, self-esteem—the things money can't buy."

During her health crisis, she met her future husband, Mike, who supported her through her treatment and recovery. Marrying just as he launched his own accounting business, they moved from pricey New York City to Washington State, where the cost of living was lower. The change in Samantha's outlook on life was reinforced by *Your Money or Your Life*, by Joe Dominguez and Vicki Robin, a book that showed her she could choose to save and invest no matter how little she made. Another influence was Amy Dacyczyn's *The Tightwad Gazette* (although Samantha admits, "I don't go to yard sales and do everything she suggests—I find ways that work for me").

The result is that with a job that pays $28,000, Samantha has been able to save $700 a month while Mike works on paying off his business start-up debt. She reads voraciously about money and investing, and has begun investing in the stock market.

How does she manage to find so much money to put aside? Here's a clue: When her car died recently, she and Mike decided to see how long they could go with just one vehicle. Samantha says: "He drives me to work in the mornings, and I run home at night—I'm a runner, and I need the exercise anyway. It kills two birds with one stone! My friends think I'm a little nuts, but I love being frugal and creative about money."

Her financial philosophy of life is simple: "I know the secret is living below my means, no matter how much money I have, and letting the money I put aside work for me to achieve my longer-term goals. My husband and I discuss our future plans avidly; we totally share decision making. My parents can't believe how I've turned out, considering the lavish lifestyle I grew up with. I think they're in awe of how I've evolved."

Samantha didn't have to read *The Millionaire Next Door* to learn the secret of living below her means. What motivated her to change was life lessons—the inspiring books she read, and the health crisis that helped her learn that "what's truly important are quality relationships, not having the best of everything or keeping up with the Joneses." This wise young woman is a reminder that no matter how we are raised, we always have the choice of dealing with our money in a way that reflects our own values and integrity.

> **I think it's not really financial security
> we want, but financial serenity.
> And that has nothing to do with how much money
> we have. It's the feeling of truly having enough.
> That's the difference between security and serenity.**
> —SARAH BAN BREATHNACH, *author of* Simple Abundance

Where are you now?

You're well on your way to debunking the myth that "I don't have enough money to do anything with" if you've taken the steps recommended in this chapter.

1. Encourage yourself by estimating how much you'll earn by the time you retire.
2. Think about whether childhood "money messages" or seductive societal cues have been discouraging you from saving. If so, write a list of positive messages that counter the old negative scripts.
3. Track your expenses to see where your money's going. Include notes on how you feel about your expenditures.
4. Know your strengths and weaknesses as a saver, by determining whether you're a Planner, a Spender, an Avoider, or a Struggler. Work on creating a plan focused on your goals.
5. Review how much you should be saving to reach your goals.
6. Pay off debt as efficiently as possible. If you have a spending compulsion, get help.
7. Take advantage of four ways to make your money multiply.
   - Start now, even if you can't save a lot.
   - Put your savings program on autopilot.
   - Take every opportunity to get free money.
   - Keep the tax man away from your money while it's growing.
8. Look for ways to cut back on unnecessary expenditures, then put that money into savings. Reward yourself for changing your habits.
9. See if you can generate more income to boost your savings— by taking on additional work that's enjoyable and satisfying or getting a raise at your current job.
10. Choose the best place for your money to grow in the short term.
11. Get ready to learn more about investing as a way to help you reach longer-term goals.

Do you have enough money . . . or not enough money? It really depends on how you feel about it and what you do with it. If you focus on your goals, make a plan to achieve them, and start saving, you'll feel a greater sense of pride, happiness, and confidence—the confidence of being truly in control of your moneylife as you work toward the financial serenity we all seek.

Myth 3:
"If I Take Risks with My Money, I'll Lose Everything"

Women often worry about the risks of investing. But the real risk is that you'll outlive your money.
—PEG DOWNEY, CFP, *a fee-only financial planner in Silver Spring, Maryland*

* * *

"I had been taught by both sides of my family that 'if you put money in the stock market, you'll lose everything,'" says Judy Robinett. "Then I started working for a Fortune 500 company with a 401(k) employer match and stock options, and I was given a window on a world I had never seen. I said to my mother incredulously, 'These people go to Hawaii once a year!' Then several friends told me, 'You ought to buy stocks,' and a lightbulb kind of went on."

Now CEO of Medical Discoveries, a publicly traded biotechnology company, this Twin Falls, Idaho, businesswoman has founded ten investment clubs for women. She told us more about how she learned to get comfortable with the risks of investing.

I can still remember an article I read that said, "Dealing with money is just a skill; it's nothing you are born with." So I made a commitment to start learning. I had been getting the *Wall Street Journal*, but I always used to toss Section C. Can you believe it? A manager at an international corporation—and I was throwing out the Money and Investing section!

At that point, I quit throwing it in the trash. I found a great article about no-load mutual fund investing for the fainthearted investor—I still give it to people I teach about money.

Even so, it was hard for me. I was so frightened, so sure I was going to lose everything. But I put in fifty dollars a month. Sometimes the fund would go up, sometimes down . . . but after two years, I noticed that regardless of it going up and down, I was making money.

Then I got brave and started buying stock. I found out about investment clubs and joined one of them.

This was a ten-year process, and all the time I was waiting for the ax to fall. Half the people on the news would say, "Get out of the market. The sky is falling!" I learned not to listen to them, just to keep putting the money in.

Since then, I've founded many investment clubs and coached a number of women about money. I take this very seriously. I believe that one of the reasons I'm here is to teach others about financial independence.

Many women were brought up to distrust the stock market, just as Judy Robinett was. Whether or not our parents or other influences warned us away from investing, we're instinctively reluctant to put our money at risk.

Even women who have begun investing tend to be more risk-averse than men. In a 1998 Investment Company Institute study of mutual fund shareholders, some 20 percent of women who were their household's sole financial decision maker said they wanted to take little or no risk, compared to only 9 percent of male decision makers.

For many of us, this financial caution has its roots in a deep fear of losing everything and ending up penniless and alone. Bag lady fears trouble even wealthy women. In fact, heiresses are especially vulnerable, worrying that their inheritance may vanish as unexpectedly as it appeared. Successful working women aren't immune, either. As TV anchorperson Katie Couric told Olivia, "I'm a hoarder, and I do have bag lady fears—especially working in television, which is such an unpredictable business."

Whether we're aware of it or not, this fear of being helpless and poverty-stricken drives many of our decisions. It prompts us to seek the safest possible places to stash our money, even though we often pay for this apparent security in poor financial returns.

Investing too conservatively is the biggest mistake women investors make, according to financial advisor and psychologist Dr. Victoria Collins, author of *InvestBeyond.com: A New Way of Investing in Today's Changing Markets*. Says Collins, "Women need to take the risk to achieve the returns needed to fund their own retirement."

Fear of financial risk can affect us in other ways, too. At work, for example, we may hesitate to ask for the compensation we're worth, for fear that making waves will cost us our job in the next cutback. And how many women stay in a bad marriage because they fear they won't be able to support themselves?

> ## It's the rooster that does the crowing, but the hen that delivers the goods!
> —Ann Richards, *former Texas governor*

By learning to recognize when financial risk is appropriate and acceptable, we can give ourselves a better opportunity to reach our important long-term goals. In fact, once women begin to invest, our innate prudence often works to our advantage. For instance:

- Women are more likely to be "buy-and-hold" investors who don't incur the risks—and costs—of moving their money around in hope of anticipating the market's next move. On average, women trade only two-thirds as often as men do, according to research by University of California–Davis economists.
- Our more conservative investment outlook tends to pay off. The same study found that women earned 1.4 percent more a year than men did, when returns were adjusted for risk. In other words, men didn't earn the higher returns needed to compensate for investing in riskier securities.
- Women are less likely to put their nest egg in the same basket with their paycheck by overloading a 401(k) account with their

own company's stock, according to another study by benefits consultants Watson Wyatt & Co. "Women seem to act somewhat more independently and I'd say somewhat more rationally," concludes Sylvester J. Schieber, one of the authors of this study.

For both men and women, extreme risk taking may be as hazardous to their wealth as total risk avoidance. The ideal investor is somewhere in the middle. Where do you fit right now?

What feels really risky to you?

Assess your general attitude toward risk with this six-question quiz.

1. Your longtime job pays well with good benefits, but it bores you. Suddenly a pal calls to offer you an exciting, creative position at a brand-new start-up company. The new job pays less and has no benefits; but if the company succeeds, you could end up earning much more money than you're now making. What do you do?
   a. I'd stay put—being bored beats being jobless if the new company goes under.
   b. I'd review the business plan, interview the owners, and weigh costs and benefits carefully before I decide.
   c. I'd jump at the chance to do more fulfilling work and help a new company grow.
2. You've just started dating a wonderful guy. He seems to be the man of your dreams, except for his passion for technical rock climbing. For weeks, he's been coaxing you to go climbing with him on your vacation. You say:
   a. "Thanks, but I'll pass. It's a little too scary for me."
   b. "Tell me more about what might happen. I need to know what I'd be getting into."
   c. "Sure, that sounds really exciting!"
3. After answering a question correctly on a game show, you're told you can choose any of the following prizes. Which one do you pick?
   a. $1,000 in cash.
   b. A choice of two doors with a 50 percent chance of winning $2,500.

      c. A spin of the wheel with a 25 percent chance of winning $5,000.

4. You've inherited $100,000 from a wealthy relative and decide to let it grow until you can afford to retire on it. Where do you invest the money?

      a. In something I won't have to worry about, like a jumbo CD or a Treasury bond.

      b. In a "lifestyle" fund that automatically selects a good blend of investments for my time frame.

      c. In tech stocks, high-yield bonds, and anything else that might pay off in a big way.

5. You haven't saved nearly enough for your teenager's college education. Your husband wants to give the money you do have to a broker friend, who says he has a "can't-miss" scheme to triple it in six months. You say:

      a. "I wouldn't sleep a wink if this money was anywhere but in U.S. savings bonds."

      b. "Whoa! This sounds pretty risky. Let's sit down with the broker and talk about it."

      c. "Sure, it's worth taking a chance if it means we can send Algernon to Harvard."

6. Your well-off friend is eager to visit Israel, and offers to pay your way if you'll accompany her. Knowing the Mideast's political tensions and risks, you say:

      a. "I wish I could see the Holy Land with you, but it just sounds too dangerous. What would my kids do if anything happened to me?"

      b. "It's a wonderful offer, and I'd love to go with you. But before I say yes for sure, let's talk about how we could plan to make this a safe trip."

      c. "Hey, life is full of danger—I could get run over by a bus tomorrow. When do we start packing?"

- *If your answers are mostly a's, you're a Risk Avoider.* Your strong sense of personal responsibility leads you to resist putting your security at risk. In some instances, this makes good sense; but by avoiding *all* risks, you may miss valuable opportunities to stretch yourself personally and financially.
- *If your answers are mostly b's, you're a Risk Manager.* Good for you!

You believe in taking intelligent risks to get what you want, and are willing to do your homework to sort out the good from the bad and the ugly.

- *If your answers are mostly c's, you're a High Risk Taker.* To your credit, you believe in living life to the fullest. However, you may be so attracted by the thrill of the ride that you don't fully think through what the outcome might be.

Even if you're willing to accept a fair amount of risk on the personal side, you may still be a Risk Avoider where your finances are concerned. This chapter will focus on helping Risk Avoiders begin investing with confidence. Our goal is to help you move more toward the middle as a prudent, patient Risk Manager—without going to the extremes of a High Risk Taker.

> **For women, the greatest risk is not to invest.**
> —*ELLIE WOTHERSPOON, a financial advisor in Washington, D.C.*

Getting over "bag lady" fears and other bugaboos

To begin transforming fear of loss into a healthier attitude toward risk taking, imagine how you'd cope if your worst fears came true.

By envisioning this worst-case scenario, you become desensitized to the paralyzing effects of your fear. This in turn can allow you to develop the necessary emotional distance and sense of humor to brainstorm ways to solve the problem if it ever arises, and combat the anxiety that may plague you now.

Some women have been helped by attending workshops in which the leader dresses up as a bag lady and encourages participants to join her in acting out their fears. But there's an easy, wonderfully therapeutic exercise you can try on your own to address your nightmares about being impoverished and abandoned.

Simply take time to imagine in detail what might happen if you lost your money. Write down your thoughts or dictate them into a tape recorder.

1. *How would it happen?* Do you envision the stock market crashing the day after you invest your life savings? Are you concerned that your husband or your investment advisor might make unwise financial decisions or even embezzle your money? No matter what you imagine happening, is it likely to occur?
2. *How would it affect your life?* Would you lose your home? Your job? Your friends? How would it affect your family?
3. *How could you cope with it?* If you were left with nothing, what would you do? Who could help you? What kind of living arrangement could you find? What kind of work could you get? Who could lend you some money to get back on your feet? Which friends and family members would stand by you?

By walking through the fear as you write down or record your solutions to the crisis you've dreaded, you'll discover that the possibility of ending up penniless is infinitesimally small, and that you have many options if the worst actually should happen. This realization will help give you the courage to put your fears behind you and act more assertively with your money.

> **You bet I'll be a bag lady!**
> **I'll have a bag from Neiman-Marcus**
> **in one hand, and one from Saks**
> **in the other!**
> —JJ JAMISON, *a CFP in Colorado Springs*

The difference between saving and investing

If you're used to putting savings in the bank, you may wonder whether it would be wiser to save or to invest in order to reach a particular goal.

- As a rule, save money that must be kept absolutely safe, especially if it may be needed within the next year or two. Places to save include savings accounts, certificates of deposit, and money market funds.
- If you have more time before you'll need to use the money, invest, in such areas as mutual funds, stocks, and bonds.

Savings Accounts, CDs	Investments
Potential return: low to moderate	Potential return: nil to high
Little opportunity to grow buying power	Good opportunity to grow buying power
Rate of return often guaranteed	Rate of return usually not guaranteed
Return of principal guaranteed	Return of principal not guaranteed
FDIC-insured up to $100,000	Not FDIC-insured

With women's paychecks typically much smaller than men's, it can be hard to justify taking financial risks. Why consider putting your precious savings into investments whose value fluctuates from day to day?

This price volatility is the risk that's usually associated with investing. But the truth is that unless you sell an investment when the price is down, you haven't really lost a penny. If it has good long-term potential, you should eventually come out ahead despite temporary fluctuations in value. *This focus on the long term is the difference between an investor and a trader.*

A preference for financial liquidity may also make us resist investing. In our genes are generations of thrifty housewives who hoarded cash in the mattress or under the floorboards (at least figuratively), where it would be easy to grab in case of need.

Even women who are smart, well-educated, and financially independent still fall into this way of thinking. Just in case they may need their money at the drop of a hat, they want to keep it close by and totally safe. One of the most extreme cases in our interviews was a woman we'll call Danielle, who earned close to $100,000 a year as a computer systems engineer. On that handsome salary, she'd been able to build up a nest egg of nearly $60,000—which she kept in a savings account paying less than 3 percent a year.

This forty-two-year-old woman knew she was shortchanging her own future by passing up investments that could have helped her savings grow substantially. But she was afraid that if she needed cash, she wouldn't be able to sell her investments quickly and might lose a lot of money if the market happened to be down.

There's a kernel of truth here. Although you can place a "sell" order in moments by phoning your financial advisor or going on-line to your investment company's Web site, it may take from one to ten days to get a check in the mail. But when was the last time you had an emergency so dire that a week's delay in raising cash would have devastated you?

Most women would say "Never." And once you actually own shares of stock or a mutual fund, this concern will dissolve as you realize that your invested money remains yours. That's important, because keeping long-term money in a short-term account is like hitching a racehorse to a donkey cart.

After you clearly define your goals and know what you're saving for, it won't seem necessary to keep all your money on hand "just in case." You'll be able to decide how much you really need to keep in a savings account or money market fund for near-term needs, while moving longer-term savings into investments where they'll have a chance to earn more for you.

Anyone with years ahead of her has little to fear from short-term ups and downs. Most women face a far more dangerous risk: that they'll outlive their savings.

Many advisors say that women should base their financial planning on living to age ninety. This is a tremendous challenge, considering that we typically receive smaller Social Security and pension benefits than men, putting even more pressure on our ability to save. Worse yet, the money we do manage to put aside must fight off two deadly threats: inflation and taxes.

Remember when you could buy a candy bar for a nickel? And a new Mustang convertible cost only $3,600? What's happened since then is inflation. Over the past seventy years, every dollar you owned on January 1 would typically have been worth only ninety-seven cents by the following December 31. And while inflation is busily shrinking your buying power, federal, state, and local taxes eat up fifteen to fifty cents or more (depending on your tax rate) of every dollar your savings earn.

In short, if your savings don't stay ahead of inflation and taxes, you'd be better off stockpiling cans of tuna fish instead of money—because a dollar you put in the bank today will buy less than a dollar's worth of stuff when you need to spend it.

For example, suppose you want to retire in ten years. Assuming that inflation increases at 3 percent a year, a bag of groceries that costs $40 today will ring up at nearly $54 in ten years. Will you be able to afford it?

If you put $40 today into a CD earning 5.25 percent, ten years from now you'd have about $67. This would allow you to buy a $54 bag of groceries with close to $13 left over. However, you'd owe more than $10 in taxes (at a combined federal and state income tax rate of 38 percent) . . . leaving you with a grand total of less than $3. That's not much of an increase in buying power after tying up your money for ten years.

But suppose your $40 earns 11 percent a year (close to the average annual rate of return of the stock market). After ten years, you'd have more than $113, or nearly $86 after taxes. After buying the bag of groceries, you'd still have close to $32 to spend! At the higher rate of return, you haven't just kept pace with inflation; you've significantly increased your purchasing power. That can make a big difference to your financial security.

In the long run, "supersafe" savings struggle to keep up with inflation and taxes. For such long-term goals as retirement or a child's college education, it's essential to learn how to manage the risks of investing, so you can take advantage of its potentially greater rewards.

How other women
overcame their fear of investment risk

A forty-eight-year-old divorcée we'll call Gail told us: "For me, it was a real risk to put most of my money in the market versus in the bank. It's taken me a long time to get over the belief that stock market investing creates great risks and that one will surely die in the poorhouse."

The crisis that helped this woman get mobilized was her divorce. She saw clearly that after twenty-five years of marriage, her money hadn't grown much after having been parked in low-risk or "no-risk" savings accounts, CDs, and savings bonds.

"After the divorce I had half the money but no real gains, and no retirement plan because of our frequent moves," Gail said. "I had to find a way to make my money grow before I retired—or could even plan to retire." With sound investment advice from a broker who encouraged her to read books about money, she turned her financial future around. "Now, twenty-one years later, I have a portfolio of $250,000 and growing," she reported. "I feel so good about myself for having taken charge in this way!"

Some of the women we talked to were motivated to begin investing by their own fears, especially if they had seen loved ones grapple with poverty. For example, Carolyn overcame her fear of risk after "seeing my mother struggle to live on minimal Social Security benefits."

For Ruth, the motivation was "realizing how poor an investment a savings account is, and wanting to have more money!"

Kelly was spurred by "realizing that I was getting near retirement age, now that the kids are grown. It scared me, really woke me up."

Other women began investing for positive reasons:

"Wanting to be independent," Brenda said.

Mary Ellen was encouraged by having "knowledge, confidence, my own paycheck."

Said Kim, "I have the confidence now that it's all right to mess up. I can survive it."

Amy's motivation was "finding that little losses generally rebound into big growth."

Maggie's commitment was reinforced by "earning money from my own investment strategy. Successful investing is an 'upper'!"

And Fran told us, "My investment club really motivated the shift." (More about this in the next chapter.)

> **I really believe that
> women can make the
> best long-term investors.**
>
> —ELLIE WOTHERSPOON,
> *a financial advisor in Washington, D.C.*

Learning to become more of a Risk Manager

Nobody likes to lose money. That's why investments whose rewards are chancy have to offer investors the potential to earn more.

In general, the more risk you're willing to take, the higher your possible return. For example, you have the opportunity to earn far more with stocks, in which your money is at risk, than with Treasury bonds, which are backed by the U.S. government.

The Three Building Blocks of an Investment Plan

- Stocks (also known as equities)
- Bonds
- Short-term investments, also known as cash (highly safe and accessible investments of any kind, including interest-bearing checking accounts, CDs, savings accounts)

For a woman starting with only a fraction of the wealth she needs to safeguard her security and reach her other goals, there's proved to be no better way to grow money over the long run than to invest in stocks. For example, according to Roberta Lee-Driscoll, a Certified Financial Planner in Honolulu, if you had $10,000 at the start of 1970:

- By the end of 1999, it would have had to grow to over $44,600 to represent the same buying power (that's the impact of inflation).
- Investing in the "safety" of three-month certificates of deposit during this period would have given you only $48,400 after taxes—barely keeping up with inflation. (This assumes you're in the 28 percent tax bracket.)
- If you'd invested in a broad portfolio of U.S. stocks (represented in this example by the S&P 500 Stock Index), your money would have grown to over $347,000 after taxes, or $469,000 in a tax-deferred retirement plan.

Adjusting for thirty years of inflation and taxes, each dollar you'd put into CDs would have been worth less than $1.09. Invested in stocks, each dollar would have been worth almost $8!

Although there's no assurance that this performance will be repeated in the future, over the past seventy-plus years the greater rewards of "risky" stock investments have made a big difference in helping millions of investors achieve their goals and dreams. "Women need to have some of their money in safe places, but much of it has to be invested for this kind of long-term growth," says Lee-Driscoll.

> **Learn to embrace calculated risks.**
> **Enjoy that huge gray area, where little**
> **is black and white.**
> **Without uncertainty there are no choices,**
> **no ability to build a magnificent future.**
>
> —*JUDY ROBINETT, entrepreneur*
> *and women's financial coach*

We've all heard stories of investors leaping out of windows after being bankrupted by the 1929 stock market crash. Could that happen again?

Economists never say "never." But assuming you spread your money into several different investments, you're unlikely to lose it all unless one of two things happens:

1. Through some economic cataclysm, the securities you've invested in become totally worthless. The stock of GE, IBM, Microsoft, Coca-Cola . . . municipal bonds issued by states and cities all over the country . . . bonds backed by homeowners repaying their mortgages . . . even bonds backed by the U.S. Treasury . . . all would have to tank in order for investors to be totally wiped out. To put it mildly, the odds are against this scenario. On the contrary, at the start of the twenty-first century, the United States is widely viewed as having the strongest and most efficient economy in the world.

2. Or the United States would have to plunge into such a deep recession that stock values took a swan dive and people went broke. In 1929, many so-called investors were really speculators who overpaid for investments, gambling that prices would continue to soar. Many had borrowed heavily against their current stock holdings to buy more high-flying stocks. When the value of their collateral began to tumble and their brokers demanded payment on these "margin loans," many speculators were forced deeply into debt to come up with more cash. Others were driven into bankruptcy. If they hadn't been overextended, many more of these unfortunate folks might have been able to hunker down and wait for the market to recover. These days, this scenario is less likely because so much of the market is owned by long-term investors.

Feeling a little more optimistic? These two amazing-but-true findings may improve your outlook even more:

1. *The longer you hold stock, the less likely you are to lose even a penny.* "If you'd held the stocks in the S&P 500 over any fifteen-year period since 1928, you would never have lost money before taxes, and you would almost always have kept ahead of inflation, too," says Dick Vodra, CFP, a planner in McLean, Virginia. "Your investment would have had time to recover from crashes, wars, and other events, if you had the discipline to stay with it." Although some five- and ten-year periods since 1928 have been painful and discouraging, investors have bounced back even from those. Vodra says, "The good news is that the average returns for broadly diversified stock accounts or mutual funds usually keep ahead of both inflation and taxes."

2. *Even if you start investing in stocks at the worst time, you're apt to do better than if you hadn't started at all.* "Don't bother trying to pick the best time to invest your money," recommends Honolulu planner Roberta Lee-Driscoll. "Investors who add money to their accounts regularly have done well, while those who try to time the market seem to miss out on much of the long-term growth. One study shows that people who are unfortunate enough to invest on the 'worst' day of the year, when prices hit

their yearly high, do almost as well over time as those who invest on the 'best' day—and both have done much better than people who keep all their money in CDs and money market accounts." Using one large mutual fund as an example, she points out that adding money each year from 1980 through 1999 would have produced a 16.2 percent return for an "unlucky" timer and 17.6 percent for a "lucky" timer. By contrast, someone who stayed out of the stock market entirely would have earned only 6.27 percent in three-month CDs.

Of course, this doesn't mean that Wall Street has turned into Easy Street for stock market investors. Lee-Driscoll cautions, "One of the hardest jobs for a financial planner is to convince our clients—and, often, to remember ourselves—that the next ten years may not look anything like the last ten years. But with a balanced, diversified portfolio and patience, an investor's money should grow faster than inflation, even after fees and taxes. I would advise investors not to expect more than that— but to enjoy it if it happens!"

> **The Two Kinds of Financial Risk**
>
> **1. The risk of losing money if you act.**
> **2. The risk of losing money if you *don't* act.**

Can you reduce risk by leaving decisions to an advisor or broker?

If you simply hand over your money and let someone else make all the investment decisions, you may be adding to your risk, not reducing it—as "Carrie" and her mother found.

After Carrie's father died unexpectedly, her mother entrusted their money to a broker she knew. Unfortunately for the struggling young widow, he favored risky investments such as junk bonds and gold mines, which lost thousands of dollars before he sold them.

Later, Carrie herself inherited $30,000 from another relative. Determined to avoid her mother's mistake, she took the money to a stockbroker recommended by a friend. Within a year or so, she was horrified to see on her brokerage statement that the value of her portfolio had plummeted.

The broker explained that it was a bad time for the market, and that many other people were in the same boat. But Carrie's faith in investing—and in financial advisors—was shattered. Yanking the remains of her inheritance out of the brokerage account, she refused from then on to trust anyone else with her money or to take any risk whatsoever with it. She now keeps her savings of close to $15,000 in a checking account. And although she knows she should try to get over her fear of financial risk, she is still paralyzed by the shock of having seen her money disappear in the market, just as her mother's did.

Unfortunately, Carrie's mother didn't realize that junk bonds and gold mines are among the riskiest kinds of investments, best suited to wealthy investors who can afford to lose their stake. Had she taken time to educate herself, she'd have been better able to protect her financial security by insisting on more suitable choices for her needs, such as blue-chip stocks or government bonds.

And despite her good intentions, Carrie repeated this mistake. She gave her money blindly to someone else to invest, without knowing whether the choices made by the broker were too risky for her. When the market fell, she panicked and immediately withdrew her remaining funds. Had she left her investments in place, she would almost certainly have seen their value rise again as the market recovered from its slump.

It's dangerous for a woman to be totally in the dark about how her money is being managed. If her advisor (or partner or parent) fails to safeguard her financial security as a result of incompetence or deception, divorce or death, her blissful ignorance can become a poverty-stricken nightmare.

Keep educating yourself, with the help of a knowledgeable friend who has no stake in your financial affairs. Ask this money mentor to oversee your portfolio until you get up to speed. You might even consider setting up a personal "board of directors" to counsel you, as financial planner Susan Freed suggests. Just remember that the ultimate responsibility for money decisions isn't theirs—it's yours.

The three secrets of successful investors

There are three simple ways to reduce the risk of investing in stocks (or other securities) while improving your returns.

1. *Start as soon as possible.* No matter what your goals are, the key to reaching them is to start *now*. When you start early, the magic of compounding turns time into money for you. The ability to piggyback your earnings onto your original investment and earn even more on this new amount, year after year, can double, triple, or quadruple your nest egg—or even more, depending on how soon you start and what your rate of return is.

   Waiting even a year to invest can cost you a lot of money. Here's an example provided by financial advisor Peg Downey: Suppose you and your friend Mary Smith both decide to start IRAs. You make $2,000 contributions at the very beginning of every year, on January 1, while Mary always waits till the very end of every year. Over the next twenty years, each of you contributes a grand total of $40,000. If you both earn a hypothetical rate of return of 10 percent a year, your IRA would grow to $114,550, while Mary would have only $102,318. Waiting a year cost her $12,232!

   Even if you're already on the shady side of thirty, forty, or fifty, the message is clear: The sooner you start investing, the more extra money you may earn for long-term goals like a comfortable retirement. Compounding makes the difference.

2. *Invest steadily through market ups and downs.* Even the pros can't time market swings successfully. By jumping in and out of the market, you risk having to sell at a low price, missing sudden rallies that can more than make up for lost ground, and then having to buy at high prices to get back in.

   If you stay invested, you'll find that temporary fluctuations usually cancel each other out, allowing you to benefit from longer-term upward trends. In fact, you can make market volatility pay off by investing the same amount regularly in additional mutual fund or stock shares. By buying more shares when prices are low and fewer shares at high prices, you'll reduce your average cost per share. Of course, this technique, known as *dollar-cost averaging,* doesn't guarantee a profit if you sell in a down market.

3. *Diversify your investments.* By spreading your money over a variety
of investments chosen with your goals in mind, you can shrink
your risk without losing the opportunity to earn long-term rewards. For example, owning several different stocks cushions the
impact of a decline in any individual security, while giving you
the chance to benefit from income or growth generated by any
of them. That's the whole idea behind mutual funds . . . a great
way to get your investment program growing.

Mutual funds: an easy way to reduce market risk

Although you may want to diversify later into owning individual
stocks or bonds as your investment balance grows, a risk-averse
woman will find much broader protection from market fluctuations
by starting out with a few selected mutual funds.

When you buy shares in a mutual fund, you're joining other investors in pooling money that a professional money manager invests for
you in individual stocks, bonds, and/or cash alternatives. Depending
on the market value of the securities owned by the fund, the value of
your fund investment will rise and fall from day to day. (You'll find
the current price per share—the Net Asset Value, or NAV—reported in
most daily newspapers and on the Internet.) If your shares gain value
over the long haul, you should be able to sell at a profit.

In addition, you receive a portion of any interest and dividends
generated by securities the fund owns. These earnings may be sent to
you or automatically reinvested. If you're investing for long-term
goals, always choose reinvestment.

Here's why nearly one out of two U.S. households owns mutual
funds today:

- *A professional investor does most of the hard work.* In return for paying a share of the annual operating expenses (generally less than
  1.5 percent of the amount you've invested), you benefit from the
  fund manager's investment analysis, securities selection, and portfolio management . . . whether you own one fund share or 1,000.
- *You can own some of the best investments in the world at an affordable price.* A fund investment of as little as $25 will typically buy
  you a stake in 30 to 300 carefully selected stocks, bonds, or other

investments—a diverse portfolio that might cost thousands of dollars if you were to buy the individual securities yourself.

- *There's less risk because a fund has its eggs in lots of baskets.* By owning dozens or hundreds of individual securities, the fund has some protection in case a few of them don't perform well. Some funds are more narrowly focused—on stock of companies in a particular industry, for example—while others are more diversified.
- *It's easy to buy and sell anytime.* To turn your investment quickly into cash or move your money into a different fund, all you have to do is contact the fund company or your investment advisor.

> **I used to shy away from investing.**
> **Now I'm enjoying it. As I've learned**
> **more over a period of several years,**
> **my confidence has increased.**
> —*Participant in a women's investment seminar*

To put together an investment portfolio of your own, first get to know the five major kinds of mutual funds. Like the major food groups, each can help you in a different way.

1. *Growth funds* try to increase your purchasing power. As you might expect, these funds typically hold stocks. If you're investing for growth, you can be reasonably well diversified without leaving this category, since there are almost as many kinds of growth funds as Baskin-Robbins has flavors. Many buy exclusively U.S. companies, while international funds invest only abroad and global funds invest anywhere in the world.

   Some funds specialize in larger companies, often household names, with high market capitalizations; others in mid-cap or small-cap firms. They may differ in investment approach, too, focusing on buying promising stock at bargain prices (value investing) or on buying stock whose earnings are increasing (momentum or growth investing). Sector funds concentrate on a particular industry segment, such as technology or utilities.

2. *Growth-and-income funds* try to provide some income while growing your long-term buying power. These funds usually invest in dividend-paying stocks. Some may also hold bonds. A growth-and-income fund's typically greater stability may make it a good first choice for a conservative new investor, although it probably won't earn as much as the average growth fund in the long run.

3. *Income funds* try to provide income while protecting the principal you've invested. These funds may specialize in interest-paying government bonds, corporate bonds, or a mix of government and corporate obligations. You might want to invest in an income fund if you rely on investment income to pay your living expenses, or if you want to reduce short-term risk in a growth-oriented portfolio (in this case, instead of spending the income, you'd instruct the fund company to automatically reinvest it for you).

4. *Tax-exempt income funds* try to provide tax-free income while protecting your principal. These funds hold municipal bonds, issued by states, municipalities, and their agencies to pay for public works or general obligations. When interest paid by these bond issuers is passed on to you, it's usually exempt from federal income tax (and from state and local income tax too, if you live in the state where the bonds were issued). However, you *will* owe tax on profit earned when the fund manager sells bonds.

    Tax-exempt municipal bonds pay investors less than taxable bonds. But if you're in a high tax bracket, you may actually pocket more money than you would after paying tax on the income from a taxable bond fund.

5. *Money market funds* try to ensure a high level of investment safety, with some protection of purchasing power. These funds typically invest in bank CDs and very secure government, corporate, and/or municipal bonds. They're an excellent place to park money you may need soon. As a longer-term investment, they can also (in moderation) help diversify a growth portfolio.

At any given time, at least one of these major market categories is hurting, others are chugging along, and one is usually booming. To reduce the risk that your portfolio will be hit hard if a particular cate-

Take Risk-Return Charts with a Grain of Salt

In investment company literature, you'll often see a chart like this one, showing which types of funds are more volatile than others. The riskiest: emerging growth (including new technologies as well as new overseas economies) and high-yield junk bonds. But don't choose all your investments from the safer end of the spectrum. You'll end up with a low-powered portfolio that may fall short of your goals—a huge risk for a woman.

Lower return potential/less market risk

Money market
U.S. government bond
Municipal (tax-exempt) bond
High-quality taxable bond
Balanced (stocks and bonds)
Growth and income
Large-company growth
Midsize company growth
Small-company growth
Emerging growth
High-yield bond

Higher return potential/more market risk

gory is in the doghouse, and increase the chances of doing well no matter what, you should plan to diversify your portfolio by investing in two, three, or more kinds of funds that tend to respond differently to market conditions.

It's important to understand this key concept, because neophyte investors sometimes believe that diversification simply means "different investments." You may own a government bond fund from Fund Family A and another government bond fund from Fund Family B, but that doesn't make you diversified. *Diversified investments behave in different ways.* Some examples are government bonds and blue-chip stocks, or large-company and small-company growth funds.

Developing an investment strategy and deciding where to put your money

So how do you put this information together? You've already taken the first step: After preparing your list of dreams and goals that are five years or more away, you know why you want to invest.

These goals will help determine what mix of investments is most suitable for you. Now it's time to figure out that mix, in a long-term master plan known as your asset allocation strategy.

We've talked about the benefits of diversification—dividing your money among several funds with different objectives. This helps balance out the strengths and weaknesses of different investments, improving the chance that your portfolio will stay on track toward your goals, no matter what the market does.

Your asset allocation strategy is an outline for how you'll diversify your portfolio. It might prescribe, for example, that you'll keep 35 percent of your assets in large-company growth, 25 percent in small-company growth, 15 percent in international growth, 15 percent in diversified income, and 10 percent in short-term investments.

Along with helping to improve your returns, an asset allocation strategy can reduce market risk. Since no single type of investment performs well in all kinds of market conditions, spreading your money into different investment classes and categories may allow you to offset temporary losses in one area with gains in another.

To improve your chances of success, decide on your strategy and stick to it. Since your asset allocation strategy will be designed with your particular goals in mind, including how much time you have and how much risk you can afford to take, you should make a commitment to stay with it unless your goals or financial situation change drastically. Many financial advisors believe that more than 90 percent of the variations in portfolio performance may depend on this strategy, while the specific securities you choose—and when you buy and sell them—will affect your return by less than 10 percent.

In other words, you needn't have a Ph.D. in economics to be a successful investor. Just start with a good plan, make prudent choices, and don't worry about short-term ups and downs.

How much will you earn with a particular strategy? It's easy to look back and see what a certain portfolio did in the past, but the best anyone can do is make an educated guess about what it will do in the future. As Princeton University economist Burton Malkiel, author of *A Random Walk Down Wall Street*, said, "The stock market has no memory." After all, the risk of investing is that nobody knows for sure what will happen.

However, it's possible to get an idea of how much difference an asset allocation strategy can make. According to Victoria Collins, a fee-only Certified Financial Planner in Irvine, California, and the author of *InvestBeyond.com: A New Look at Investing in Today's Changing Markets*, an investor would have experienced the following results using various strategies from 1970 through 2000.

SAMPLE ASSET ALLOCATION RETURNS, 1970–2000*

Growth	Moderate Growth	Conservative	Very Conservative
80% stocks	60% stocks	40% stocks	0% stocks
15% bonds	30% bonds	45% bonds	40% bonds
5% short-term	10% short-term	15% short-term	60% short-term
Average annual return:			
24.25%	9.58%	7.38%	2.2%
Largest one-year gain:			
33.36%	9.83%	8.61%	6.88%
Largest one-year loss:			
−20.23%	−4.80%	−2.87%	0.05%

* In these calculations, stocks are represented by the S&P 500 index. Bond returns from 1970 through 1998 are from Ibbotson, *SBBI Yearbook: Stocks, Bonds, Bills, and Inflation*. For the years 1999 and 2000, bonds are represented by Lehman Bros. Bond Index using 50 percent intermediate-term U.S. government bonds and 50 percent long-term corporate bonds. Cash equivalent returns for the years 1970 through 1998 are from Ibbotson, and for 1999 and 2000 from 6-month T-bill returns.

During this period, growth investors would have earned ten times as much as very conservative investors. Very conservative investors enjoyed lower market risk (they didn't have any one-year losses during this 31-year period, compared to the growth portfolio's largest loss of −20.23 percent), but they paid for it by earning only 2.2 percent a year, while growth investors earned more than 24 percent a year.

If your answers to questions about risk suggest that you're a Risk

Avoider, an investment consultant might recommend a relatively conservative asset allocation strategy for you. That may not be so dangerous if the reason you're investing is to buy a house or put a child through college, since you can always compensate for lethargic investment growth by making a smaller down payment or applying for scholarships. But when you're investing for retirement, you need to be prepared to accept whatever reasonable risk it takes to reach your goals within the time you have available. Otherwise, you may end up having to reduce your standard of living as you grow older, or keep working—not because you love it, but because you have to. (In chapter 5, we'll provide more guidelines on how to grow your retirement nest egg.)

WHAT'S YOUR ASSET ALLOCATION NOW—
AND WHAT SHOULD IT BE?

Take a few minutes to assess what your portfolio currently looks like. You may already have investments you've chosen, inherited, or been awarded in a divorce settlement. Or perhaps you have savings you've faithfully been stashing in a 401(k) or other company retirement plan, CDs, or a savings account. If so, you can figure out your current asset allocation in about fifteen minutes with a pencil and paper, a calculator, and your most recent account statements.

Using this worksheet as a model, write down how much you have invested in each category:

MY PORTFOLIO

	Nonretirement savings/investments	+ Retirement savings	= TOTAL
Savings account(s)	$_____		$_____
CDs (1–12 month maturity)	$_____		$_____
CDs (13–60 month maturity)	$_____		$_____
Guaranteed Investment Contracts (GICs)		$_____	$_____
Money market funds	$_____	+ $_____	= $_____
Bonds or income funds	$_____	+ $_____	= $_____
Stocks or growth funds	$_____	+ $_____	= $_____

Total portfolio value:　$_____

Some tips:

- Any mutual fund that calls itself an "equity" or "capital appreciation" fund belongs in the "Stocks or growth funds" category.
- If you own a hybrid fund ("balanced," "growth-and-income," "equity income," or "asset allocation," for example), put down half your balance in "Bonds or income funds" and the other half in "Stocks or growth funds." (This is just an approximation; you can find out a more accurate ratio by checking the fund's latest annual report.)
- Include in "Savings accounts" any other cash you've set aside (for example, in your checking account) but don't plan to spend.

To figure out your asset allocation, first determine how much you have in short-term investments, bonds, and stocks. Then divide each subtotal by your total portfolio value.

MY ASSET ALLOCATION

Short-term

Savings account(s)	$_____		
CDs (1–12 month maturity)	$_____		
Money market funds	$_____		
Total short-term	$_____		
divided by total portfolio value of	$_____	=	_____ %

For example, let's say Susan Jones, a thirty-year-old meter reader for the electric company, has a portfolio worth $7,500. Her short-term investments include $300 in a savings account, $1,500 in a 12-month CD, and no money market investments, adding up to $1,800. Short-term investments are thus 1800/7500ths of her portfolio, or 24 percent.

Bonds

CDs (13–60 month maturity)	$_____		
GICs	$_____		
Bonds or income funds	$_____		
Total bonds	$_____		
divided by total portfolio value of	$_____	=	_____ %

To continue the example, let's say Susan doesn't own any CDs with maturities of more than a year, but she does have $2,700 invested in a fixed-income (Guaranteed Investment Contract) option offered through her 401(k) plan. She also has $3,000 worth of shares in a growth-and-income mutual fund left her by her aunt, half of which she's counting in this category. The total income component of her portfolio thus is 2700 + 1500, or $4,200, which is 56 percent of her total portfolio value.

Stocks

Stocks or growth funds $_____

divided by total portfolio value of $_____ = _____%

Here's where Susan would include the other $1,500 from the growth-and-income fund. Let's assume she doesn't own any other growth funds or stocks, so the total stock component of her portfolio is 1500/7500ths, or 20 percent.

Your own percentages should add up to 100 percent, as they do in Susan's case:

Stocks	20 percent
Bonds	56 percent
Short-term	24 percent
Total	100 percent

Looking back at the sample asset allocation returns on page 85, you can see that Susan's allocation is closest to the "Conservative" model, which earned an average of 7.38 percent a year in the 31 years between 1970 and 2000. Although there's no way to know if similar returns will result in the future, this asset allocation may not be aggressive enough for a woman who needs to make serious strides in protecting her financial independence.

Compare your own asset allocation to the models. Do you think you're where you should be? If not, do you need to be more aggressive?

The following sample allocations are suggested by financial planner Victoria Collins. Since you're likely to be investing for both a

> **The only thing anyone can guarantee you about the stock market is that tomorrow it will be different than it was today. Bulls see the glass as half full; bears see it as half empty. It all depends on your attitude.**
>
> —*JUDY ROBINETT, entrepreneur and women's financial coach*

short-term and a long-term goal, you'll want to choose an asset allocation strategy for each goal. (Women in the 28 percent or higher tax bracket may wish to replace taxable bond funds with tax-exempt funds.)

IF YOUR GOAL IS . . .

LESS THAN THREE YEARS AWAY: SHORT-TERM PLAN

For example: You're retired and want to set aside enough cash to cover living expenses for the next two to three years. You may want to consider a portfolio consisting entirely of short-term investments such as money market funds and short-term bond funds.

Stocks	0%
Bonds*	40%
Short-term	60%

*Short-term bonds

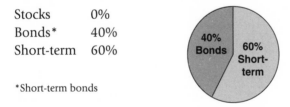

Collins observes, "This type of allocation is appropriate for women who want current income and very little fluctuation in their portfolio. There won't be any growth, but you will be preserving capital and will have liquidity."

THREE TO FIVE YEARS AWAY: CONSERVATIVE PLAN

For example: You want to accumulate the down payment for a house in three years. Consider a portfolio that's heavily weighted toward bond mutual funds and short-term investments.

Stocks*   20%
Bonds   55%
Short-term   25%

*15% Large-Cap,
5% International

"This mix is for investors who may need income now and who want little fluctuation in portfolio value with a slight potential for growth," says Collins.

FIVE TO SEVEN YEARS AWAY: MODERATELY CONSERVATIVE PLAN

For example: Your young teen is five years away from starting college. Consider a portfolio that balances stocks and bonds.

Stocks*   45%
Bonds   40%
Short-term   15%

*25% Large-Cap,
10% Mid-Cap,
10% International

Collins comments, "This plan is for investors who need stability, but would also like the potential for an increase in the value of their investments."

MORE THAN SEVEN YEARS AWAY: MODERATE PLAN

For example: You've just retired in good health and want to dedicate part of your investment portfolio to continued growth. Consider an approach that's heavily weighted toward stocks, with some bonds and short-term investments to balance risk.

Stocks*   70%
Bonds   25%
Short-term   5%

*40% Large-Cap,
10% Mid-Cap,
5% Small-Cap,
15% International

"This is an appropriate mix for longer-term investors who don't need current income, but want reasonable and relatively stable growth," says Collins. "They want less risk than the overall stock market, but are okay with some fluctuation."

AT LEAST TEN YEARS AWAY (NONRETIREMENT): MODERATELY AGGRESSIVE PLAN
For example: You plan to keep working for at least another decade. Since you're in a position to tolerate market fluctuations while seeking the opportunity for growth, consider a portfolio that's more strongly weighted toward stocks.

Stocks*   80%
Bonds   15%
Short-term   5%

*50% Large-Cap,
10% Mid-Cap,
5% Small-Cap,
15% International

Collins notes, "This moderately aggressive mix is good for long-term investors who want growth in their portfolio, but don't need income right now. These women can accept a fair amount of risk, but since they might need to draw on the money at some point, the risk should be lower than if they were invested in 100% stocks."

AT LEAST TEN YEARS AWAY (RETIREMENT): AGGRESSIVE PLAN
For example: You're putting away money earmarked for retirement in an IRA, 401(k), or similar retirement plan, with more than ten years to go before you expect to start taking distributions.

Stocks* 100%

*65% Large Cap,
10% Mid-Cap,
5% Small-Cap,
20% International

"This is an excellent mix for long-term investors to have in their 401(k)s or IRAs," says Collins. "There may be substantial year-to-year fluctuation in value, but there is more potential for higher long-term results than any other portfolio mix."

These models would be considered relatively prudent for most investors. But if you'd like to explore other possibilities, try the interactive asset allocation planners at any of the major financial services companies' Web sites. Just don't get so hung up on searching for the perfect strategy that you put off beginning to invest.

> Worth repeating:
> **Almost any investment is okay to start with.**
> **Success isn't really determined by**
> **investment behavior, but by investor behavior—**
> **whether or not you get started and keep going.**
> —DICK VODRA, a Certified Financial Planner in McLean, Virginia

'Tis a gift to be simple:
the advantages of index funds

Most people are already familiar with at least one market index: the Dow Jones Industrial Average, a group of thirty large-company stocks widely used by the media to symbolize the entire stock market. Because thirty stocks are a fairly skimpy basis of comparison, more stock funds use as their yardstick the Standard & Poor's 500 Stock Index (the S&P 500, for short), which tracks 500 of the biggest companies in the United States. The even broader Wilshire 5000 Equity Index includes the whole universe of publicly traded U.S. stocks, big and small. (If you own only one growth fund, make it a fund that tracks this index.) Small-company funds, international funds, government bond funds, and other market segments have indexes of their own.

An index fund is a mutual fund whose only purpose in life is to mimic the performance of a certain market index. It does this by buying all (or a representative sample) of the securities included in a particular stock or bond index, and holding them in the same proportions in which they're represented in the index. This buy-and-hold approach is considered "passive investing," in contrast to "actively managed" funds whose management team is constantly researching, buying, and selling securities to gain a competitive edge.

Index funds offer several advantages for investors at all levels of experience. They're broadly diversified, they seldom lag far behind the market index (unlike many actively managed funds), and they're cheap. Since the fund manager buys securities when they're added to the index and hangs on to them forever unless they're dropped from the index, trading costs are low and research costs are nil, which helps hold down the fund's annual expenses. If you're investing outside of a tax-deferred account, you'll also like the fact that the low turnover typically means less capital gains tax passed on to you.

So once you've determined the asset allocation strategy you're going to stick with, a simple and potentially effective solution is just to buy the index fund in each category with the lowest expenses. As you get more involved in investing, you may decide later on to select some actively managed funds to fill out your portfolio, or even to switch out of index funds in some categories where actively managed funds have had a slight edge in the past, such as small-company stocks and international stocks.

> **I realized I had to start investing after my divorce.**
> **Now my business and investments are both thriving,**
> **and I'm preparing to sail around the world**
> **while working on board in a virtual office.**
> **Quite a long way from the farm!**
> —*A Kansas graphic designer*

Don't invest in anything you don't understand

You can't really tell if an investment's risk is acceptable if you don't understand it. So don't let yourself be swept into investing in something you know too little about (gold mines, for example). By contrast, if there *is* something you know a lot about—regional banks, say, because you work for one yourself—your expertise and intuition, aided by some research, may allow you to spot a great investment at a bargain price.

Gloria Steinem, the author and founder of *Ms.*, told us that one of her biggest regrets now is that she avoided taking risks on investments she did know something about. Among these missed opportunities was a chance to buy a group of Manhattan brownstones for $95,000 each (the buildings were soon worth millions). "If we had only taken the time to organize what we knew and think about it more carefully," she says ruefully, "we might have chosen differently."

Once you get comfortable with mutual funds, you may want to take advantage of opportunities to "buy what you know" in individual stocks or bonds. (In the next chapter, you'll find more information about ways to add selected individual securities to your portfolio—and have fun while you're doing it.)

In the meantime, keep it simple when you start. You can become a skilled and successful investor without needing to get involved in any of the more complex ways to invest. Here are six things you *don't* need to know about.

1. *Almost anything known by an acronym.* ETFs (Exchange-Traded Funds), CMOs (Collateralized Mortgage Obligations), REITs (Real Estate Investment Trusts), IPOs (Initial Public Offerings), UITs (Unit Investment Trusts), LEAPs (Long-Term Equity Anticipation Securities), SPDRs (Standard & Poor's Depository Receipts) . . . they're all great tools in the hands of sophisticated investors. Beginners can live just fine without them.
2. *Commodities.* Wait to buy pork bellies, wheat, and cocoa until they're turned into bacon, bread, and Milky Ways. Commodities trading takes steely nerves and lots of research—and even then, you're putting your money up against Mother Nature.
3. *Preferred stock or convertible bonds.* Preferred stock guarantees a dividend but is slower to gain value than common stock. Convertible bonds don't pay as much interest as regular bonds and don't appreciate as much as stock. Think of these two investments as stocks and bonds that operate with brakes on and flaps down—the reason that investors with ambitious goals may have a hard time getting into the air with them. However, they can be a way for savvy mutual fund managers to dampen volatility in a fund portfolio.
4. *Options (puts and calls).* These contracts allow you to buy or sell stock within a certain period for a certain price. "Puts" are options to sell; "calls" are options to buy. Given the market's nat-

ural volatility, either one can be an invitation to lose your shirt—even for experts.

5. *Selling short.* This is like borrowing your broker's Jaguar and selling it, hoping that when she asks for it later, you can buy a new one for her at a lower price. Expecting that a stock's value is going to decline, short sellers borrow stock (instead of an XK8) and "sell it short." In other words, they're gambling that the price won't rise during a specified period. If it does, they have to replace the stock at the higher price, plus the interest their broker charged on the loan—a great way to lose big chunks of money. The closest you'll probably want to come to short selling is the wonderful description in James Clavell's *Noble House* of how wily Hong Kong tai-pan Ian Struan bankrupted an archcompetitor who had "shorted" Noble House stock.

6. *Variable annuities.* In our view, the chief merit of an annuity is that when it's time to take payouts, you may elect to receive lifetime income. Retirees can anchor the growth portion of their portfolio with a fixed annuity, which pays a guaranteed interest rate.

With a variable annuity (VA), on the other hand, you're exposed to market risk—and pay a premium for it. These half-investment, half-insurance retirement products allow you to invest in a selected handful of mutual funds, with the assurance that if you die while the market is down, your beneficiaries will get back at least the amount you invested. Unfortunately, VAs are weighed down with so much extra financial baggage that there's no way they can beat straight mutual fund investing.

Adding mortality fees (to cover the death benefit) to expense fees can mean you pay twice what ordinary mutual funds would charge. If the annuity's investment choices sour and you want to get out, you'll often pay surrender charges to exit before five to seven years are up. Perhaps the unkindest cut of all is that while gains from stock or stock mutual funds are taxed at a low capital gains rate, distributions from annuities are taxed at ordinary income tax rates, which can be up to twice as high.

Why pay extra for insurance you're unlikely to need? In retirement, you may want to consider buying a fixed annuity that will start making payments immediately. But in the meantime, invest in the best low-cost mutual funds you can find—and buy life insurance to take care of your heirs.

How to find a good fund

You've probably heard the investment community's mantra: "Past performance does not guarantee future results." But a lot of do-it-yourself investors still grab mutual funds that topped the charts in the last quarter, six months, or twelve months. That's like driving with your eyes glued to the rearview mirror, assuming that the road ahead will be exactly like the one behind you. What happens, all too often, is *BAM! Where'd that tree come from?* It isn't a pretty sight.

Beware, too, of choosing a fund based solely on a third-party rating system, such as those from Morningstar and Lipper. Though relatively sophisticated, they just give you another way to review past performance, with no assurance of similar results in the future. Both systems rate funds against their peers in specific categories:

Morningstar has twenty-eight Star Rating categories for stocks, ten for taxable bonds, and five for tax-free bonds. Within each category, funds are graded on a curve:

- The top 10 percent receive five stars.
- The next 22.5 percent receive four stars.
- The middle 35 percent receive three stars.
- The next 22.5 percent receive two stars.
- The bottom 10 percent receive one star.

Each fund is rated in four different ways: risk-adjusted performance for the last three, five, and ten years; and an overall ranking based on performance over all three time periods (weighted in a 20/30/50 ratio, respectively).

Lipper's risk-adjusted system ranks funds over one, three, and five years. There are twenty-seven peer groups for stocks, two for funds holding both stocks and bonds, ten for taxable bonds, and six for tax-free bonds. Lipper rankings are typically expressed in terms of a fund's position in its peer group—for example, "one out of sixty-eight" funds in a particular category over a particular time period. In mutual fund tables, Lipper rankings often appear as alphabet letters:

- The top 20 percent receive an A.
- The next 20 percent receive a B.
- The middle 20 percent receive a C.

- The next 20 percent receive a D.
- The bottom 20 percent receive an E.

As helpful as they may be, stars and grades can't take the place of portfolio planning tailored to your own needs. When you evaluate funds you already own or are thinking of buying, look at these key factors:

- *A clear objective.* Call the fund company or look on its Web site for a prospectus, which tells you what the fund is allowed to do, and the most recent annual report, which tells you what it has actually done.

  What does the fund focus on? Growth or income? Does it have a high-risk objective such as aggressive growth or high yield, or does it aim for protection of principal? Does it invest in large-cap, mid-cap, or small-cap stocks? Long-term, intermediate-term, or short-term bonds? What sectors are favored?

- *A good fit with your asset allocation strategy.* Does the fund's investment objective qualify it to belong in your portfolio?

- *Low annual costs.* To compare sales charges, fees, and other expenses, see the example in the fund prospectus. In particular, you want to find a low annual expense ratio. The American Association of Individual Investors suggests that you focus on funds with expense ratios of no more than 1.2 percent for a domestic growth fund and 0.75 percent for an income fund. Index funds should have expense ratios well under 1 percent, since all they do is buy and hold the securities included in a given index.

  While high research costs may justify higher ratios on some kinds of funds, such as international or small-company stocks, be aware that you'll need to earn correspondingly more to net the same rate of return. For instance, a fund with an expense ratio of 0.5 percent would only have to earn 10.5 percent for you to net 10 percent, while a fund with a 1.75 percent expense ratio would have to earn 11.75 percent to give you the same 10 percent rate of return.

  Armed with prospectuses for funds you're interested in, you can compare the annual cost per $1,000 or $10,000 invested by referring to the hypothetical example following the Fee Table, which includes any sales charges as well as the fund's operating expenses. For every $1,000 invested in the Vanguard 500 Index Fund, for example, your annual cost would be $2.

- *Strong long-term performance against its benchmark.* In the annual, semiannual, or quarterly report, look at the fund's performance over the past five and ten years versus its benchmark. Over these longer periods, the fund should have pulled ahead of its benchmark, allowing investors to accumulate more wealth or receive more income.

- A *level of volatility you can live with.* The newer profile prospectuses now graphically display the fund's annual return over the past ten years, letting you see how high the "ups" have been and how low the "downs." This can prepare you for the fluctuations you may face if you invest in the fund.

- *Expense subsidies.* If a footnote in the prospectus tells you that the fund sponsor is absorbing some of its expenses (often true of newly launched funds with a small asset base), that's good news now. But be aware that the full cost can be restored at will, perhaps without your noticing.

- *Low portfolio turnover.* While trading costs don't appear in the expense ratio, they're still deducted from your account—so it helps if the fund manager doesn't do a lot of buying and selling. On a typical domestic equity fund, this hidden cost reduces gross profits by up to 0.25 percent, according to Lipper. High turnover may also expose you to a steep capital gains tax if your account isn't tax sheltered.

  How high a turnover rate is too high? A 50 to 75 percent rate is pretty steep, meaning that the manager replaced one-half to three-fourths of the fund's holdings during the year. If the turnover rate is over 100 percent, it means the manager isn't a buy-and-hold investor—so this fund may not be a good choice for an investor who is. (If the prospectus's Annual Highlights section doesn't include the turnover rate, find it out from the fund company.)

- *Experienced, committed fund management.* Who is the fund manager or management team? How much experience do they have? Look for indications that subpar performance will be addressed promptly. For example, it's a good sign if they have any of their own money in the fund, their name on the fund, or they have an ownership stake in the fund company.

EARN MORE WITHOUT RISK BY CUTTING YOUR COSTS

The only surefire way to improve your investment returns is to keep more of what you earn. The more you can cut your costs, the more profit you can put in your own pocket.

Every mutual fund investor pays a share of the annual operating costs charged by the fund company. You'll also pay a sales charge (or "load") if you buy your fund shares through a broker.

"A" shares have a front-end load—a commission you pay upfront. This typically eats up 3 to 5.75 percent of your initial investment, shrinking your returns for years. For example, say you invest $10,000 in a fund with a 5 percent front-end load. Immediately, $500 is taken off the top for sales charges, leaving only $9,500 that's actually invested. If the fund earns 10 percent a year, in thirty years your diminished investment would grow to $165,769. By contrast, $10,000 in a no-load fund with the same rate of return would have turned into $174,494 . . . $8,725 more.

Financial advisor Peg Downey points out that in the real world, you may lose even more potential profit to front-end sales charges. That's because the average investor holds on to a fund for only about three years. Thus, in buying and selling funds over thirty years, you'd typically pay a load not once but nine times—which would shrink your nest egg to just $82,627. That's only 47 percent of what you'd have made with comparable no-load funds!

"B" shares levy a back-end load when you sell your shares. This load is usually a Contingent Deferred Sales Charge, or CDSC, which shrinks to zero over six or seven years. Since buy-and-hold investors never pay the CDSC, fund companies usually compensate brokers by jacking up a component of the fund's annual operating expenses that's called the 12b-1 fee. Because this higher fee nibbles away at your balance year after year, B shares can actually cost more in the long run than A shares. (To complicate matters further, some fund firms convert B shares to A shares after the CDSC disappears.) Generally speaking, the lower your returns, the bigger a bite loads will take.

Before you begin working with a financial advisor, find out if his or her compensation comes from sales charges. If it does, you may feel that the knowledge and expertise you'd be getting is well worth the extra cost. But if you'd rather have the opportunity to boost your returns by avoiding these sales charges, look for a fee-only advisor who focuses on no-load funds. Of course, you can also buy no-loads directly from the fund company or through a fund supermarket like Schwab OneSource or Fidelity FundsNetwork.

HOW MANY FUNDS ARE ENOUGH?

Many funds have minimums of $1,000 or more, or $500 for retirement accounts. If you can afford only one to start with, a good choice would be a total stock market index fund that tracks the Wilshire 5000.

When you've accumulated $5,000 to $10,000, you may want to begin diversifying. To target big, relatively stable blue-chip companies, for example, you might move into an S&P 500 Stock Index fund. As your balance builds, you can start filling the other slots in your asset allocation strategy.

Typically, you should be well diversified with five to eight funds, assuming there isn't a lot of overlap in the areas they invest in. But that doesn't mean every fund needs to be from a different fund company. For one thing, you'll go batty trying to cope with all the prospectuses, quarterly reports, and account statements. What's more, segregating investments in this way can lead you to focus on the performance of individual funds instead of your total portfolio.

Our suggestion: Choose all your funds from the same big fund family, or buy funds from different families through a fund supermarket that will give you consolidated reports on your entire portfolio. You can still get the quality you want, without the quantity of record keeping. And it's a lot easier to move your money to a different fund if you ever want to.

Common mistakes new investors make, and how to avoid them

- *Putting their money in investments that feel most like savings accounts.* While money market funds and bonds may have a comforting stability, the fact is that over the past seventy-four years, stocks' average annual return of 11.3 percent has far outpaced other kinds of investments. Of course, this long-term growth rate has been accompanied by volatility—the short-term price variations that so unnerve inexperienced investors when they follow the daily stock or mutual fund listings. To build your own wealth, you'll almost certainly need a healthy dose of stocks or stock mutual funds in your portfolio, but skillful asset allocation can help hold down the overall volatility by mixing in investments that tend to cushion stocks' fluctuations.

- *Compulsively checking whether their investments are up or down from one day to the next.* Once you have a customized strategy in place, remember that what's important is the performance of your overall portfolio, not individual pieces of it. So if you're prone to jitters, pass up the daily listings. Wait until you get your quarterly and annual statements to see how your portfolio's doing.

  Some advisors would say that when it comes to reviewing stock or stock fund performance, once a year is too often. In an experiment conducted by two economists a few years ago, one group of university employees who were shown a chart displaying the short-term fluctuating returns of stocks and bonds put most of their money into bonds. But another group of employees who were shown a chart displaying total stock and bond returns over a thirty-year period put 90 percent of their money into stocks.

- *Jumping in and out of investments in reaction to short-term fluctuations.* This goes hand in hand with the previous mistake, since your anxiety level tends to rise in direct proportion to the frequency with which you check the value of your holdings.

  Don't let yourself be panicked into making portfolio changes because of today's headlines. If you try to move your money in and out of investments based on what you think the market's going to do, you're likely to miss out, because big gains happen fast. For instance, if you'd stayed fully invested in the S&P 500's stocks between January 1992 and January 1997, you'd have earned an average of 15.2 percent a year. But according to *Money* magazine, if you were out of the market during the forty best days in that five-year period, you'd have earned only 2 percent. If you missed the best sixty days, you'd have actually lost money! The moral is If you're going to invest, stay invested.

When to hold 'em and when to fold 'em

Many successful investors believe in making the best investment choices they can, then monitoring their portfolio's progress just once a quarter, once every six months, or even once a year. Remember that your strategy is a long-term one and that short-term market fluctuations are normal. Be prepared to buy and hold.

How do you know when to get out of an investment? The pros—mutual fund managers who make these decisions every day—usually make "sell" decisions based on how an investment performs against their expectations. As an investor in a mutual fund, you have a more objective way to measure performance: by comparing it to an industry benchmark, such as the S&P 500 Stock Index.

When your fund publishes its quarterly or semiannual report, it must tell you how it did compared to its benchmark. If it underperformed the benchmark for a year or more, try to figure out why. Is there a new manager who's making a lot of changes? Is the fund really invested where it's supposed to be? By checking the actual holdings listed in the report, you may find, for example, that a so-called small-company growth fund is really investing in big blue-chip stocks—thus producing odd results when measured against a small-company benchmark. Or are the anemic results simply due to a lot of bad judgment calls, like being heavily invested in a certain sector just before the roof falls in?

Anyone can slip up once. But if a fund keeps performing poorly in comparison with its peers in the same category, this sign of weak management should prompt you to start looking for a replacement. Remember, selling can trigger taxes on nonretirement accounts, so don't switch funds on a whim.

> **We're often afraid to make a decision, when the real issue is that we don't have enough information. But people are more than happy to help you.**
>
> —JUDY ROBINETT,
> *entrepreneur and women's financial coach*

Where to find out more

Although this chapter has only covered the fundamentals, we hope you've already begun to be a lot more comfortable with the idea of investing. If you decide that you like the lower risk of diversified mutual funds so much that you never want to own an individual stock or a bond, that's perfectly fine. Used as fuel for your asset allocation strategy, mutual funds can take you just about anywhere you want to go.

To find out more about prudent investing, read Andrew Tobias's friendly and informative book, *The Only Investment Guide You'll Ever Need*. An excellent free resource is the Vanguard Group's "Women and Investing" brochure, available on-line at www.vanguard.com or by calling 1-800-662-7447.

Investment seminars for women are usually free and well worth the time. Go with a pal, so the two of you can discuss later what you learned, and ask lots of questions. Just don't make any snap decisions about proprietary products the seminar's sponsor may try to steer you toward. If they sound interesting, ask what the drawbacks are.

Personal-finance magazines are great for general financial information. But when it comes to investments, they have an annoying tendency to lunge out and grab you by the lapels to tell you what's hot right this minute, whether you care or not. As for investment newsletters . . . well, let's just say read and learn as much as you can but don't necessarily swallow the advice.

For our money, the best investment publication, bar none, is the *Wall Street Journal*. The writing is great, the headlines are witty, it's full of personal stories about the people behind financial trends and events, and the reporters never assume that you know what *bond duration* means or how the New York Stock Exchange works. A daily subscription is expensive—over $100 for a year—but you may be able to get a pass-along copy at the office (or from your partner's office), split the cost with friends, or at least catch up on recent issues at the library.

There are zillions of good places to find investment advice on-line, but we know most women don't have time to browse around on the Web for information. (Hmm . . . not enough time? Sounds like a good topic for the next chapter.) Also, these sites open, close, change, and move around with a frequency that might quickly outdate any specifics mentioned here.

However, this might be a good moment to warn against investing based on a tip in an on-line chat room. While there's a slim chance that some brilliant self-taught stock analyst has discovered a diamond in the rough (and is enough of a philanthropist to tell the world about it), it's equally possible that the tipster has an ulterior motive for touting that stock—like unloading it to gullible investors at an inflated price.

Exercise for newcomers: becoming a virtual investor

Many investors rely on a knowledgeable investment representative or financial planner to help determine an asset allocation strategy that suits their goals and sensitivity to market risk. In the next chapter, we'll discuss ways you can get expert help, support, and information if you still feel unready to begin investing. But if you've been trusting others to make money decisions for you up to now, it's important to begin learning to have more confidence in your own financial judgment—and this exercise can help.

We're inviting you to buy and monitor a virtual portfolio made up of two mutual funds: Vanguard 500 Index Fund, a stock index fund that tracks the S&P 500, and Vanguard Total Bond Market Index, an index fund that tracks the broad bond market.

Why these funds? They give you a sense of how the stock and bond markets move, independently and relative to each other. Why Vanguard? Because this large, well-respected mutual fund company deals directly with investors at all levels of experience and charges very low fees. (Another strong contender for the low-cost title is New York–based money manager TIAA-CREF at 1-800-223-1200.)

Here's what to do:

- Call Vanguard at 1-800-871-3879 and ask to receive copies of the prospectuses and annual reports for both funds. Or if you have Internet access, go on-line to www.vanguard.com, review the highlights provided for these two funds, and download the prospectus and reports for each.
- Read the literature for both funds, with our tips from pages 97–98 in mind. Do they meet the criteria for funds worth considering? How did they perform over the past five and ten years? How well did they do versus their respective benchmarks?

- Fill out the applications for both funds (use the non-IRA forms). But don't send them in . . . not yet, anyway.
- "Invest" $1,000 in each fund. On a plain piece of paper, write two phony checks, one made out to "Vanguard 500 Index" and the other to "Vanguard Total Bond Market Index." Staple the checks to your applications.
- Pretend you did open your account with Vanguard. To find out how many shares of each fund you'd have "bought" at the most recent closing price, look under "Vanguard" or "Vanguard Index" in your daily paper's mutual fund listings, then find the two fund names (usually abbreviated to "500" and "TotBd"). Once you locate the NAV (Net Asset Value), divide this per-share price into 1,000 to find out how many shares of each fund you now "own" in your virtual portfolio. For example, if the share price was $50, you'd have bought 1,000 ÷ 50, or 20 shares.
- Check the newspaper every day and write down the two funds' current NAVs. Multiply this by the number of shares you own to see how your portfolio value changes from day to day. (This exercise is an exception to the rule about not checking your investment balance frequently. Our goal is to help desensitize you to the markets' normal fluctuations, by encouraging you to see how temporary dips and rallies affect your portfolio.)
- Keep doing this exercise every day for at least two weeks, or for as long as you wish. At the same time, make yourself more aware of national and international political and economic developments that have a direct effect on daily market prices. For example, what happens when there are rumors that the Federal Reserve Board will raise interest rates, or when a big technology company announces an earnings setback?
- Once you decide to end the exercise, tally up your portfolio's current value. (Bear in mind that you held your investments for an extremely short period of time—much shorter than that recommended to reduce market risk.) How did you do? Did you gain or lose a lot or a little? Or did the value of your virtual portfolio stay about the same?

After doing this exercise, chances are you'll feel more comfortable about investing and about market risk.

> **I think we're into a second wave of empowerment.**
> **In the seventies and eighties, women made strides**
> **in the workplace. And now it's time for them**
> **to get excited about protecting and investing**
> **the assets they're earning.**
>
> —*ELLIE WOTHERSPOON, a financial advisor in Washington, D.C.*

Where are you now?

By taking the seventeen steps suggested in this chapter, you'll find you no longer feel that "if I take risks with my money, I'll lose everything."

1. Find out how risk-tolerant you are. If you're a Risk Avoider or a High Risk Taker, work on becoming more of a Risk Manager by learning to assess risks realistically to make calm, confident decisions.

2. Take time to explore "bag lady" fears that may have been undermining your willingness to take risks. Bring these fears out into the light of day and see how realistic they really are.

3. Learn the differences between savings vehicles and investments.

4. Examine whether what's been scaring you is short-term market risk (which doesn't make a significant difference in the long run), when you should be more concerned about the more serious risk of not having the money you'll need in the future.

5. See how other women overcame their fear of investment risk. Do any of their motives inspire you? If so, focus on them and let them help you reduce your own anxiety.

6. If you're just beginning to invest, learn the three building

blocks of an investment plan: stocks, bonds, and short-term investments.

7. Explore the fear of "losing it all" in the market, and review how stock investors have actually done in the past. Does it seem to you now that the real risk may be much lower than you'd feared?

8. Be aware of the risks involved in leaving financial decisions to someone else. Vow to protect your financial security by educating yourself, ideally with the help of an impartial money mentor.

9. Take advantage of the three secrets of successful investors:
    • Start as soon as possible.
    • Invest steadily through market ups and downs.
    • Diversify your investments.

10. Learn how mutual funds work, and what they can do for investors. Remind yourself to take risk-return charts with a grain of salt when building a portfolio.

11. Assess your current asset allocation, and compare it to the sample on page 85 to see how it would have performed in the past. Is it likely to help you reach your goals within your time frame?

12. Develop an asset allocation strategy focused on your personal goals, guided by the asset allocation models on pages 89–91.

13. Consider index funds as a low-cost way to begin your investment program.

14. Review the guidelines on pages 96–100 to learn what to look for in an investment—and what to avoid.

15. Watch out for the three common mistakes many new investors make:
    • Putting their money in investments that feel most like savings accounts.
    • Compulsively checking every day whether their investments are up or down.
    • Jumping in and out of investments in reaction to short-term fluctuations.

16. Be familiar with the signs that it may be time to get out of a fund.

17. Deepen your understanding of mutual-fund investing from other knowledgeable sources. Make a commitment to send for more information, attend a seminar, read a book, and/or regularly read the *Wall Street Journal* or another financial publication you like. Practice being a virtual investor.

Congratulations! You've moved past a major myth that stood in the way of your financial security.

Myth 4:
"I Don't Have Enough Time to Manage My Money"

It's a question of priorities. We don't make money a high priority, in part because we're not comfortable with it.
—KAREN GROSS, *professor of law at New York Law School*

* * *

Both men and women feel starved for free time these days. Three-fourths of adults in a 1998 study by time management firm Franklin Covey said they wish they had more time to "stop and smell the roses."

In that survey and others, women tended to feel more strongly than men about having too little time to accomplish everything they need or want to do. When an informal poll at *Redbook* magazine's Web site recently asked women if they would prefer a 20 percent pay raise or a four-day workweek, nearly two-thirds said they would pass up more money in favor of having more free time.

Women struggle with multiple roles and tasks as wives, mothers, daughters, housekeepers, employees, and entrepreneurs. While men usually devote most of their energy to being the family breadwinner (even if their wives work), women often carry the double burden of working hard for money, then coming home to a "second shift" of keeping the family running smoothly.

If a busy woman isn't totally confident of her ability to make the right decisions about money, it's natural to put financial matters toward the bottom of her long, long "to do" list—or keep it off the list altogether. Even with the best of intentions, there never seems to be time to read a magazine about personal finance, research the best mutual funds, or set up an IRA for herself.

When we asked CNN newscaster Judy Woodruff about the common perception that "I don't have enough time to manage my money," she not only admitted "buying into that one" but added, "It doesn't seem like a myth to me—I think it's a reality!"

A typical time-impoverished role juggler, Judy combines a challenging and stressful job with a second shift as mother of three children and wife of Al Hunt, the *Wall Street Journal's* executive Washington editor. When it comes to learning more about money and keeping track of investments, she said, "I don't know what the answer is. Frankly, if you have a career and a family and you're busy, when are you going to have time to do the research? Especially since Al is knowledgeable, I leave a lot of it up to him."

It *is* hard to find time to deal with your money when every available minute seems to be taken up with family and work. But many of us aren't fortunate enough to have a financially savvy family member whom we can trust with our future security.

So if we're too busy to do it ourselves, nobody does it.

"I regret not making the time": a cautionary tale

"I told myself it was enough that I was making good money for a girl" in an era when most women didn't, says Betty Carter, explaining why she never took time to learn about managing her finances. Now semi-retired, Betty is a renowned family therapist, cofounder of the Women's Project in Family Therapy, and author of *Love, Honor, and Negotiate* and other books about intergenerational family relationships. She recalls:

> My grandmother set the tone for our family's view of money when I was growing up. Anytime the subject arose, she would end the discussion by saying, "It's only money," meaning that it was tacky or uncultured to be concerned with money, and that one should focus on higher things in life.
>
> So my sister and I were brought up believing that it was crass and materialistic to devote our time and energy to dealing with money. And when I got married, my husband, who was an opera singer,

also had the attitude that money was not something an artist should focus on.

Somehow my younger brother got past these messages. Starting with his pilot's pay, he spent a lot of time learning about investing. He's become the world's best money manager. He kept advising my sister and me to do more with our money, suggesting ways to make it grow. But I was always too busy. I thought it would take too much time and effort to read about it, or even to contact a broker and commit to that.

Now we're both retired. He's wealthy, and I'm not. And I have real regrets about not making the time to follow at least some of his advice.

As this story points out, if you don't make time to safeguard your financial independence now, you may end up with a pocketful of regrets.

However, many of us women were taught to take care of our families' needs first and put our own last. Thus it can seem natural to place a low priority on making ourselves financially comfortable and secure, and on achieving our fondest dreams—benefits we would stand to gain by taking the time to manage our money more effectively.

And certainly "I don't have time" sounds more acceptable to our own ears than "as long as I do all the things today that tell me I'm a good daughter, good worker, good wife, or good mom, the future will hopefully take care of itself."

According to Ellie Wotherspoon, a financial advisor in Washington, D.C., "Women are starting to make time, because they're realizing they *have* to make time." But she thinks there are still many women who lack financial knowledge—or a sense of urgency about acquiring it. "I have an ad, a three-paragraph statement to help and educate women, that I run in a women's newspaper," she explains. "And almost consistently, women who call me and make an appointment never show up. Why aren't women consulting financial professionals more? Why don't they come see me after reading the ad?" She answers her own question: "Too many of them are still stuck, not ready to take any action."

If you've been putting off taking an active role in money management, you may be rationalizing your failure to act by telling yourself you just don't have time—not enough time to consult a financial advisor, to attend a seminar on investing, to call a mutual fund company for information (or read the information when it comes). Worse yet, you may believe that the longer you put off taking charge of your money, the more time it will take to catch up—a quantity of time you would absolutely never be able to find.

Fortunately, that isn't true. Getting started takes the same amount of time whether you begin at twenty or at sixty. So don't let yourself be paralyzed by regret for the time you've let go by. You might just as well regret not having flossed more often or not having taken more pictures on your last vacation. You've still got years ahead of you—and it's never too late to get going.

> **I don't understand how women can think**
> **they have control over their own destiny**
> **if they're not comfortable with money.**
> —SACHA MILLSTONE, *a financial planner in Washington, D.C.*

Some women simply believe that money matters are too tedious to make time for. And when you're just starting out, it's understandable to feel you'll never be able to wade through a personal-finance magazine. The five best mutual funds to buy now? Yawn. Tax advantages of deferred annuities? Snore.

But taking charge of your money is much more exciting than you might think. It's a basic part of the plot in the drama of your life—one of the few parts, in fact, that you can use to direct yourself toward a happier ending.

- You might come up with a great idea, bankroll it yourself, and start a wildly successful company.
- You might meet the partner of your dreams and cruise off into the sunset together, funded by your combined investment portfolios.
- Using the savings you accumulated, you might send your flaky son to college, where he discovers a flair for biochemistry that eventually leads to a Nobel Prize.

- Or someone you love might need help, and you'd have the financial resources to provide it.

Pat, a workshop participant, had always thought that dealing with her money would be tedious and boring. "But once I decided to make my own decisions," she enthused, "the more I had to know—and the less boring it was."

Laura, another of our interviewees, discovered an interest in discussing money with friends and colleagues: "I realized how important it is, and that others think about it too! It's actually a good topic of conversation."

"I always say I don't have time enough to learn about money," admitted another of our interviewees, a forty-nine-year-old performing artist. "But I could make the time if I wanted to."

If you're creative, you'll find that making time to take care of your financial well-being can be very enjoyable. For example, maybe you have a money-savvy friend who'd be glad to trade her specialized know-how for yours. As Susan Freed, a financial advisor in Washington, D.C., told us, "I'm short of time, too! I'd love to be a money mentor for a woman who'd be willing to be a walking partner for me, or coach me about gardening."

So give it a try! You're apt to find (as Judy Robinett suggests) that money, like sex, is a lot more interesting than you thought it would be when you were younger.

As for those eye-glazing articles, save them for later. Eat your dessert first by reading the ones that tell you "You *can* retire early!" or "How one couple financed their dream." Once you get more involved in directing the story of your life, there'll be plenty of time to discover how technical tips can help produce the special effects you want.

To make managing your money an important priority, you may need to challenge three underlying assumptions.

1. *Your family and work relationships are more important than taking care of yourself financially.* This is really a separate myth ("It's selfish to put myself first. I'm supposed to take care of everyone else"), which we'll discuss in the next chapter. The truth is that time spent planning your future is not time stolen from your

family. On the contrary, it's one of the best things you can do for them—and for yourself.

2. *Managing your money is no fun, and you won't be any good at it.* But if you've been working through the preceding chapters, you know you *can* get good at it. And you've heard such former Money Avoiders as Daria Dolan and Gerri Detweiler say that once they started taking charge of their money, they began to enjoy themselves tremendously. (Later in this chapter, you'll learn more about a strategy that has helped thousands of women have fun while they improve their money skills: joining an investment club.)

3. *The day is too short to accomplish everything you need to do.* Because this assumption is probably true, the rest of this chapter will focus on ways you can address the important priority of money management more efficiently. You'll learn shortcuts that can help you get information faster, make everyday financial choices more easily, and manage an investment portfolio in just a few hours a year—whether or not you consult a financial advisor! You'll see that it doesn't require vast amounts of time to manage your money much more effectively. And by establishing new habits and new attitudes, you'll reap the additional reward of feeling less stressed, knowing you're taking charge of your future.

The one-hour-a-week money-management plan

Unless you're a very disciplined individual, ad-lib financial management usually doesn't work any better than ad-lib saving. At the end of the day (or month), there's never any time left to fill out that IRA enrollment form or to check on refinancing the mortgage.

The solution: Set aside an hour every week for money matters. Designate this time to yourself (and to everybody else) as My Money Time. Ideally, it should be the same hour from week to week—for example, a specific weekday evening, Saturday morning after breakfast, or Sunday afternoon when your partner is watching sports on TV. Try to pick a time when you'll be relatively relaxed and a location that's private and peaceful. During this hour, you'll focus on activities affecting your moneylife. These might include:

- Reminding yourself of your near-term (next five years) and long-term financial goals.
- Reading a magazine article or a book chapter about making your money work for you.
- Catching up on annual reports for mutual funds or stocks you own.
- Balancing your checkbook.
- Paying bills.
- Filling out an IRA application or transfer form.
- Calling for information about on-line banking or current interest rates on a loan.
- Researching college costs and financial aid possibilities for your teenagers.
- Deciding on one new step you'll take to improve your financial skills (perhaps attending an investment seminar or course, or discussing a financial issue with your partner, financial advisor, or other money mentor).

Before the end of the session, decide what action steps you'll take during the next week and what will be on your agenda for the next money hour. Put the date on your calendar right away so you can begin making this a habit. (If your schedule requires, your money hour can float from week to week, as long as you decide at the beginning of each week when it will be or reschedule promptly if you need to make a last-minute change.) Last, be sure to reward yourself for having taken time to make order in your moneylife.

If you find it difficult to make time for yourself in this way, consider asking a friend to join you—someone you can trust not to disrupt this important new routine. Week by week, you'll learn to take care of yourself in a deeper way as you make time to manage your money wisely.

If you're in a relationship where your partner has been taking care of money management, it's all the more important to have this time to yourself to address your own needs and plans. Once or twice a month, the two of you should get together at a different time to discuss household finances and goals. (You might choose the first weekend after every payday, if that's easy to remember.) Make a habit of rewarding yourselves afterward, perhaps by going out for a romantic walk or lunch together.

Here's how some busy women manage to set aside "money time" for themselves.

- Sondra: "Every Saturday morning while the kids are watching cartoons, I take about an hour to catch up on the financial magazine I subscribe to, look at any account statements that have come in, pay bills, and so on. At first it was hard to do, but now I look forward to this quiet time for myself."
- Lillian: "I like to set aside one evening a week for about forty-five minutes to an hour to bring my account information in Quicken up to date, pay bills on-line, and maybe play around with viewing the data in different ways to see if I'm making progress or spending too much in certain areas. If there's time, I might take a look at some of the personal-finance sites on the Internet to see if there's any interesting information I can use. Because of my complicated schedule, it's not always the same evening every week. But I decide at the beginning of the week when I'll do it, and put it in my schedule book. It's like a date with myself."
- Myrna: "I'm still nursing a very active baby. So once a week, I use his nap time for 'money stuff' like paying bills and reading a chapter in a great personal-finance book I found. Last week I looked at information I'd sent for about our state's guaranteed college tuition plan. Taking this time makes me feel more in control of my life."
- Keisha: "My husband and I decided to take an hour or so every Sunday after we get home from church to look at our money, see whether we're sticking to our spending plan, and check on how our savings are doing. At first we used to get tense about these meetings, but now we really look forward to them. My husband feels like we're sharing the burden of 'worrying about our money'—and when we do it together, it makes me worry less and less about it."
- Rita: "My boyfriend goes to work a lot earlier than I do, so once a week I use that time to read articles about money that I've torn out of newspapers and magazines. Every three months it's my turn to pay the bills out of our joint checking account, so I do that too. And I have a little folder that I put notes and articles in, stuff I want to discuss with him later on."

How to Get in Touch with Your Feelings About Money

If you're feeling some resistance to getting more involved with your money, take the first thirty minutes of your "money hour" to create a new money dialogue for a few weeks.

This assignment consists of imagining a conversation between you and Money about how the relationship between the two of you is going. Most people write down their conversation, but you can record it on a tape recorder if you prefer. The idea is to assume that Money is someone with whom you have an ongoing relationship, and to imagine both sides of a dialogue about the nature of that relationship right now.

For example, are you happy with Money? Are you trying to do what's best for it? Is it forcing you to do something you don't like? Is Money pleased with the way you're using it? Does it have comments or complaints about what you should be doing differently?

Let the conversation continue for about fifteen minutes or until it winds down by itself. Then imagine how the dialogue you've just created would be viewed by major influences in your life—for example, your mother, your father, and the voice of your inner wisdom (or God or your Higher Power). Jot down in a sentence or two what you think their comment(s) would be. If you're especially pressed for time, go straight to the voice of your Higher Power.

This assignment usually yields powerful results. It helps show you how you've progressed in paying attention to Money in your life and indicates which way to move (emotionally or practically) to experience "money harmony." As you become more and more comfortable with your relationship with Money, and vice versa, you may need to do a money dialogue only once a month or even less frequently.

Alana, a workshop participant, chose to start her empowerment process by doing a money dialogue every week or two. She explained why she made time for this assignment: "Writing a money dialogue on Monday nights helped me feel better and better about the attention I was paying to my money. The 'inner wisdom' voice would help me be loving toward myself, and Money itself started giving me advice about the next step to take in making better use of him/her (it changes sexes, believe it or not!). Thanks for this great idea!"

Thirteen creative money shortcuts
that can save you time and hassle

1. *Make balancing your checkbook "centslessly" simpler.* When you're adding a deposit or subtracting a withdrawal, forget about the cents column—just keep track of the dollars. This makes it easier to keep a running total, since you'll probably be able to do the arithmetic on the spot. (Try it. It's easier than you may think.) At the end of the month, when you get your account statement and see what your actual balance is, enter an adjustment (either a credit or a debit) in your check register to compensate for the pennies you omitted earlier.

   As noted in chapter 2, a variation on this scheme is to round up every debit to the nearest dollar and round down every credit. Every month, transfer the accumulated spare change into a savings account.

   Whatever method you use, it's important to balance your checkbook regularly. Otherwise, you'll be forced to keep a lot of extra money in your account to avoid unpleasant surprises—a practice we frown on, since you won't earn much (if any) interest on it.

2. *Sign up for automatic monthly payments to meet long-term commitments.* Check to see if you can have payments automatically deducted from your checking or savings account for your mortgage, life insurance, and auto and home insurance. It's often possible to pay car loans and utility bills automatically, too. But beware of agreeing to make automatic payments to any company you don't know to be reputable—if you have any difficulty getting the process to stop when it's supposed to, you want to be dealing with someone who'll make amends promptly.

   Some women are reluctant to give up control of when their bills are paid, especially if it's a juggling act every month to make sure the money's in their account at the right time. Only you can judge whether automatic payments would work for you. But knowing when the debit will be made to your account (it's usually the same date every month), you can simply subtract that amount in advance from your account balance during your weekly money hour.

By the way, places of worship and charitable organizations are increasingly offering patrons the convenience of automatic payments, too. So if you've made a pledge to your college or want to support your church building fund or public TV station, automatic debits can allow you to make smaller monthly contributions without having to write and mail a lot of checks.

3. *Automate your income by signing up for direct deposit.* When your payroll check is directly deposited by your employer, you still get a stub itemizing your deductions. But you avoid the hassle of having to rush to the bank with your check, or letting it sit around undeposited while you're out of town or on vacation.

Direct deposit of Social Security and pension benefits has also been a godsend for folks who hate having to worry about a check being lost or stolen. And if you're having investment income paid to you regularly, it's much easier to have it automatically deposited into your checking account or asset management account.

A tip from financial advisor Peg Downey: To help slow down your spending, have all deposits made directly to your *savings* account. Then withdraw or transfer to checking only as much as you need, when you need it. (Before putting this plan into action, be sure to find out if your savings account restricts withdrawals in any way.)

4. *Set up an automatic investment plan.* By having your IRA or non-retirement investment contributions pulled automatically out of your bank account, you save writing still more checks. (But again, remember to enter those automatic debits in your account register *ahead of time,* during the previous week's money hour.) Contributions to 401(k) plans are ultraconvenient: You never get a chance to spend the money, because it goes straight into the investments you've designated.

5. *Get a debit card.* Also known as a check card, this piece of plastic looks like a credit card but pulls money out of your checking account. You can use it with merchants or at ATMs just about anywhere major credit cards are accepted. If it's lost or stolen, you're protected just as you are with a credit card.

If you're used to writing checks, you'll find it's a lot faster to run your card through a payment terminal at checkout. What's more, you'll be able to use your checking account worldwide, instead of having to charge everything to a credit card or lug around traveler's checks. To obtain a debit card linked to your checking account, just ask your bank. There may be a modest monthly fee of $1 or so, but merchant purchases and transactions at your own bank's ATMs are usually free.

6. *Avoid trips to the bank by going on-line.* All large banks, and many small ones, now offer Internet banking. It's highly secure and allows you to check your balances, review account activity, and transfer money between accounts.

   The two tasks you can't yet do on-line are to make deposits and get cash. The first may be solved, at least partially, when more checks are direct-deposited. As for the second, you may soon be able to plug a smart card into an appliance hooked to your PC, download money onto it from your checking account, and then use the card to make purchases from vending machines and other places where you'd normally reach for cash. But except for nickel-and-dime transactions, you can already do this with a debit card (which offers the added advantage of leaving money in your account until you actually spend it).

7. *Cut your tax-preparation time in half for less than $10 a year.* Many women swear by TurboTax or Tax Cut software—both of which have made it possible for millions of people to continue doing their own taxes instead of having to consult a tax professional. But no matter how your tax return is prepared, you can save time and simplify the process tremendously in just three steps.

   First, buy a big accordion file—the kind with lots of individual pockets—at your local office supply store. Next, label each section with key categories found on your Form 1040 and other tax schedules, such as Wages, Interest & Dividends, Deductible IRA Contributions, Mortgage/Home Equity Interest, and so on. If you run a small business or have rental property, you may want to set up a separate accordion file labeled with the key categories for Schedule C or E. Then, whenever you pay a bill or receive a financial statement with tax implications, just toss it into the right file pocket.

8. *Consolidate your accounts.* As you go through life, you may develop ties with a variety of financial institutions. Do you have a no-fee checking account here, a mortgage there, a car loan or home equity line somewhere else, and an assortment of invest-

ments from Company X, Fund Supermarket Y, and Bank Z? If so, you may find that you're drowning in account statements and don't have a good handle on how your money is allocated or whether it's working hard for you.

Our advice is simplify, simplify. Work on consolidating all your loans and deposit accounts at one bank or credit union. (Find one that will reward you for giving it so much business.) For example, if the time is right to refinance your mortgage, go to your chosen financial institution, say that you're interested in doing business together, and be specific about what you're looking for. For example, you might say, "I'm looking for a thirty-year mortgage with a fixed rate of X percent and no points." There's a good chance the institution will meet your specifications—or at least come back with an attractive counteroffer.

If you own mutual funds in several far-flung fund companies, consolidate your holdings at one of the larger fund companies or fund supermarkets, where you'll still have plenty of choice. (Caution: IRA investments should be transferred directly from one custodian to another. If the check is sent to you, the fund company is required to treat it as a distribution and withhold taxes.)

Send all your stock certificates to one brokerage and have it hold the shares "in street name" for you. This means that the stock is registered in the brokerage's name, although you remain the "beneficial owner," fully entitled to the privileges of ownership that you had before. Street-name ownership simplifies trading and relieves you of trying to remember later where you put the darn certificates.

9. *Consolidate your credit cards, too.* Most people can get by with just one card, as long as it has an adequate credit limit. If you buy on plastic a lot, you may want two—perhaps a low-rate card for special purchases you'll need to pay off over time, and a second card that rewards you with rebates or frequent-flyer miles for purchases you'll pay off every month. By owning only one "everyday" card, you may end up charging less, since your choice will be "Should I buy on credit or pay cash?" instead of "Which credit card should I use?" If possible, carry a card with your photo on it, so it will be less likely to be used by someone else if it's lost or stolen.

10. *Consider converting your traditional IRA to a Roth IRA.* Some advi-

sors qualify this with speculation about whether your tax rate will be higher or lower in retirement. Who knows? But in our view, in return for a little pain now, you could enjoy a big gain later. The big gain is that after you convert, all your earnings will be tax-free. In fact, you'll owe no tax at all on qualifying Roth IRA withdrawals—compared to the mind-numbing calculations to determine your tax liability when you begin taking money out of a traditional IRA.

But conversion does mean paying all the income tax you've deferred to date, which not everyone can afford to do. Don't convert if the only way you can swing it is to pay the IRS with money from your IRA. Depending on your tax bracket, you could lose as much as 50 percent of your withdrawal to federal income tax and IRS early-withdrawal penalties. Worse yet, the savings you withdraw will no longer be there to keep compounding for you.

11. *Prepay several months' worth of small recurring bills.* For example, instead of paying the cable company $30 a month, send it a check for $90 and don't worry about another bill for the next three months. The next month, pay your newspaper carrier three months ahead. The third month, you might prepay your parking-lot fee or something similar. You'll cut your bill-paying time by two-thirds, without spending any more than you are now.

12. *Consolidate your advisors.* Do you use one insurance agent for your life and disability coverage, another for the house, and a third for the cars? Do you and your partner each have a different financial advisor? Try to come as close as you can to the busy woman's ideal: a single experienced professional who can either execute or direct all your financial planning, from investments to insurance to estate planning. (Tips later in this chapter will help you locate such a paragon.)

13. *Sign up for telephone or Internet bill payment.* You can typically register any number of payees with your bank's bill payment service. From then on, paying a bill is as easy as punching in the payee code and the payment amount on your TouchTone phone, or point-and-clicking the same information on-line. In a matter of moments, you can whisk through a stack of bills that

might take half an hour to pay manually. You can also arrange to have recurring payments for the same amount (e.g., mortgage, cable TV, car loan) made automatically on the same date every month, without having to lift a finger.

Traditional banks usually charge $6 to $10 a month for this service, while Internet banks often offer free on-line bill payment. Even the U.S. Postal Service has begun to offer electronic bill payment. You may be courted by other service providers hoping to profit from your bills, but be careful of entrusting less familiar firms with access to your checking account.

Should you use personal-finance software?

Will personal-finance software save you time? Perhaps not—but there are other benefits. It's definitely worth considering Quicken or Microsoft Money if you can get on-line access to your bank and investment accounts and do most of your bill paying on-line. By allowing you to download details of your account activity into your own computer whenever you wish, this will help you keep better track of your money.

However, software can't substitute for manually maintaining a running total of your checking account balance in your register. After all, the bank doesn't know what other checks you've written that might not have been presented for payment yet.

The big advantage of personal-finance software is being able to see in one place where you stand in regard to your financial goals—where you're spending your money, how your savings and investments are doing, and whether they're divided up among investment categories in a way that matches your asset allocation strategy. These programs also come with built-in calculators that can help you figure out such otherwise-impenetrable mysteries as monthly payments on different loan amounts at different interest rates, or see how much you could accumulate by investing different amounts at different rates of return.

So if your computer came with a preinstalled version of Quicken or Microsoft Money, try it. The time you spend could pay off in confidence that you're really on top of your finances.

The Importance of Being Wired

According to a recent Money magazine survey, 44 percent of women use computers to help them manage their money or invest. And the busier you are, the harder it is to beat the advantages of the Internet.

If you don't own a computer and aren't sure you want to buy one of the simpler-to-use "Web appliances," why not try going on-line with a friend's PC? Alternatively, more and more libraries now have public-use computers that are set up for Internet access, with plain-English instructions that help make it easy for a neophyte.

The Web sites you'll see on-line are hosted by various individuals, companies, institutions, organizations, and government entities around the world. When you visit a site, your computer is actually connecting with a host computer where the site is stored. Every time you click on a hyperlink—underlined text on a Web page—its embedded code will automatically zip you to a related section of the same Web site or perhaps to somebody else's site half a world away. A "Back" button at the top of your screen allows you to retrace your footsteps, and another button labeled "Home" will always return you to the place you started from. That's really all you need to know to get going.

Whether you're a novice or an old pro, there are dozens of ways to save time by going on-line. Among them:

- To look up a tax law or download a tax form from www.irs.gov.
- To review your investment accounts, transfer money between mutual funds, or redeem some of your holdings through the Web site of your bank or brokerage.
- To look up information about a potential new investment at its sponsor's Web site or at the site of a third-party rating service such as www.morningstar.com
- To check the latest financial news from cnnfn.com or your favorite site.
- To compare mortgage types and current rates (try www.eloan.com or www.quickenmortgage.com).
- To check on the lowest credit card rates (www.bankrate.com or www.cardtrak.com).
- To buy or sell stocks, bonds, or mutual funds through an on-line discount brokerage.
- To use interactive calculators that can help you determine whether your retirement plan is on track, how much you might need to put aside for your child's college education, or how long it would take to pay off your credit card balance with different monthly payment

amounts (at personal-finance sites such as www.smartmoney.com, www.kiplinger.com, or www.money.com).

- To get financial tips and advice from online versions of financial publications, as well as from organizations such as the Mutual Fund Investor's Center (www.mfea.com), the Investment Company Institute (www.ici.org), the American Association of Individual Investors (www.aaii.com), and the National Association of Investors Corporation (www.better-investing.com).

I didn't think it was worth the time, but now I see that the simple act of tracking my expenses carefully gives me the power of truth—about what's real in my life versus what I'm imagining.

—ANNE SLEPIAN, *cofounder of* More Than Money, *a journal that explores issues of wealth and values*

The pros and cons of working with a financial advisor

The busier you are, the more tempting it may be to turn over the lion's share of your longer-term money management to a professional financial advisor. In a 1999 poll of professional women by Stern Marketing Group, 47 percent said they use financial planners (including tax consultants or stockbrokers) to help them plan and manage their long-term household finances.

Should you link up with a money pro? "That's why you hire expert help—because you don't have enough time to do everything yourself," urges Peg Downey, who was rated one of the top financial advisors in the United States by *Worth* magazine.

You'll find that financial advisors are increasingly interested in working with you. Women represent a large pool of potential clients who were overlooked "for decades" by the financial services industry, said the *Wall Street Journal* in 1997. In particular, many female financial advisors feel an almost evangelical calling to help other women.

"Part of my job is to put the word out to women that I can take the load off them," says financial planner Ellie Wotherspoon. Unlike some other advisors, Ellie doesn't expect her clients to be wealthy when they walk in the door. She explains: "Before I became a planner, I worked as a tax lawyer and a foundation executive, and I noticed that many advisors seemed to have a bias against the average person. I think there's a huge group of people who are being completely ignored, and they're open to working with somebody who respects them."

You may want to consider working with an advisor if you're having a hard time keeping tabs on your assets or feel uncomfortable making money decisions by yourself. Also, if you're venturing into deep waters—tax planning, say, or estate planning—an expert's advice can often save you a great deal of time and expense.

Sally Nash, for one, was grateful to find the right person to help her. "When I inherited money, I was terrified that I would somehow mismanage and lose it," says the dancer and director of Workspace for Choreographers in Sperryville, Virginia. "I just wanted to put it under my mattress! But I followed my better instincts and hooked up with a stockbroker who has slowly educated me, respects me, and never takes advantage of me. I'm proud that I faced up to the responsibility and did what I felt was best—even if I lost stature in the family by sharing the job with someone else."

> **Ultimately, no one can take the responsibility away from you. . . . But that doesn't mean you have to do everything.**
>
> —BOB VERES, *financial journalist and industry commentator*

Depending on what kind of help you need, you can choose from several types of financial advisors. The industry is in the throes of rapid evolution, so be prepared to ask a potential advisor, no matter what his or her title, about actual responsibilities and compensation structure. In the following summary of the most common categories, we'll assume for the sake of simplification that your advisor is a woman.

- *An investment consultant* usually works for the brokerage arm of a bank or other financial institution. She's licensed to sell mutual funds and often stocks, bonds, and annuities as well. Many are still paid on commission (which means they take a percentage of every purchase), while others are compensated by "wrap fees" based on a percentage of the total assets in your portfolio. Though she'll help you put together a portfolio designed to meet a specific goal, she normally focuses on investments, not on your total financial picture.

- A *stockbroker,* like an investment consultant, is a registered investment representative licensed to sell securities. Because she typically works for herself or for an independent brokerage firm, she may be more sales-oriented and actively strive to extend your relationship. She usually works on commission.

- *An accountant* specializes in helping you keep track of your money. Depending on her training, she may also be able to offer tax guidance and prepare your tax returns. If she's a Personal Financial Planning practitioner, she'll also be able to help you with longer-term money-management strategies. Her compensation is usually based on an hourly rate or on a fee that's a percentage of your assets.

- *An insurance agent* specializes in various types of insurance but may also offer annuities and mutual funds. Unless she has had considerable experience or special training as an investment advisor, she may not be prepared to provide overall financial leadership. She is compensated with a share of the insurance premium or sales charge you pay.

- A *financial planner* often has a broader area of expertise than any of these others. She may have passed rigorous tests to measure her understanding of investments, tax law, estate planning, and other specialized financial disciplines. Some planners offer cradle-to-grave services that include college planning, insurance, and eldercare. Compensation may be based on a percentage of the assets she manages for you, on a fixed fee, on a commission for investment transactions, or some combination of these.

While you can expect an advisor to research your choices for you (saving you a lot of wading through prospectuses or long-term-care policies), she won't want you to give up all responsibility for making decisions. She even may present you with a variety of choices that are more complex and sophisticated than you would have come up with by yourself. A good advisor will indicate which option(s) she thinks make the most sense for you, but you need to be able to understand how they differ, and determine which to choose.

So even if you find the perfect professional, don't count on simply handing over all your financial affairs and walking away. You need to understand at all times where your money is, why it's there, and how it's doing.

> **Ultimately, it's your responsibility.**
> **You fulfill part of your responsibility by finding**
> **a person you trust, and then the rest of your**
> **responsibility is to continue understanding**
> **what's going on with your finances.**
> —PEG DOWNEY, CFP, a fee-only financial advisor
> in Silver Spring, Maryland

If you decide to seek out an advisor, gather the names of two or three candidates by asking friends for referrals, checking with your attorney or accountant, or calling your bank's investment affiliate. Then make an appointment with each one to see whom you're most comfortable with. Ask if there's a fee for this initial getting-acquainted session. Some advisors charge; others don't.

It's crucial for the chemistry to be right between you and your advisor. Is she (or he) attuned to your needs, goals, and personality? Are your questions answered patiently and respectfully? If you're not happy with an advisor's philosophy, communication skills, or attitude, keep looking until you find someone you can trust.

Some important questions to ask as you interview the candidates:

- *What is your area of expertise?* Try to find someone with several years of experience in dealing with your kinds of needs. For example, if you're a retiree looking for strategies to conserve money, don't choose an advisor who specializes in helping young professionals build wealth. Ask if you may contact some of the advisor's other clients.

- *What is your investment philosophy?* If you can't clearly understand the answer or the advisor's approach doesn't jibe with your own, it should raise a red flag.
- *How are you paid?* You'll see in a moment why this is important.
- *What are the average and minimum account sizes you handle?* You don't want to be too big a fish in a small pond or too small a fish in a big one.
- *May I see a sample of the kind of plan you'll provide me?* Check to make sure it's clear, well put together, and comprehensive.
- *Do you have access to other financial specialists?* If you need an expert in personal or business financial services, taxes, or estate planning, can the advisor put you in touch with one?
- *How would we continue working together?* Make sure you know what's expected of you as well as what the advisor will do.
- *How will I know whether you're doing a good job?* You should agree upfront on how success will be measured—on progress toward your goals, for example, or performance versus a benchmark.
- *What do you want to know about me?* The advisor should ask about your income, financial situation, investment and other relevant goals, and attitude toward risk.

This last point is crucial. "If you're just going for investment advice, that's all you'll get," points out financial planner Peg Downey. "But if what you need is financial planning, your advisor should have a comprehensive view of your life situation as well as your plans and goals."

Once you establish a relationship, there are several things you should expect from your financial advisor, says planner Susan Freed. "One is education. They should be able to tell you why they've recommended what they've recommended. If you think that other alternatives might be appropriate, your advisor should be willing and able to point out the relative advantages and disadvantages of different options." She adds, "There is no single right answer, but often there are wrong answers—and it's important to avoid a decision that could jeopardize your financial security."

What else should you expect? "For your advisor to provide you with progress reports and performance measures," Susan says. "You want to know that their recommendations are appropriate to the extent that they meet your needs and goals."

> **Bill—my broker—has become a friend.**
> **He works hard to earn my trust and is willing**
> **to listen, willing to agree and to disagree with me**
> **—the "disagree" part is very important.**
> —LORI SMITH, *higher education operations director of Dell Computer*

How to Find a Reputable Financial Planner

You probably have an idea of how to find an investment consultant, broker, accountant, or insurance agent. But how do you find a financial planner? If you don't have any luck getting referrals from friends, try the following industry associations.

- *The Financial Planning Association can connect you with individuals who have earned the rigorous CFP (Certified Financial Planner) designation or are working toward it. For information on planners in your area, including services offered, backgrounds, and fees, go on-line to www.fpanet.org, or call 1-800-322-4237.*
- *The National Association of Personal Financial Advisors provides names, addresses, and phone numbers of fee-only planners. See its Web site, www.napfa.org, or call 1-800-333-6659.*

If you decide that consulting a financial advisor is the best way to get your moneylife sorted out, keep in mind that you still must become knowledgeable about your money in order to judge whether your advisor is doing a good job.

Whenever someone else makes investment recommendations for you, you risk buying that person's biases. Your insurance agent may steer you toward annuities or life insurance policies with an investment component. Investment consultants and brokers may aim you toward "house brand" mutual funds or other products on which they receive higher commissions (and which may cost more, or not perform as well, as those a less-biased advisor might choose). And since commission-based advisors earn money whenever they persuade you to sell an investment and buy another one, their interest may not be aligned with a buy-and-hold investor's. Many people believe that fee-only financial planners are more objective.

Even so, some women told us that disappointment with a particular financial advisor had prompted them to take over investment responsibility themselves. Kay said: "Before I got married, I had a boyfriend who was an investment advisor. He stole some of my money—so now I manage my own investments, as well as my husband's."

"Past losses made me realize no one else can know what I want as well as I can," reported Daryn.

Enid agreed: "I found their recommendations were no better than my choices!"

"They can't know it all," concluded Bernadette.

In fairness, *nobody* can know it all—not even experienced professionals. There are many excellent, ethical advisors out there. But the better *you* understand what's going on with your money, the more confidence you'll have about making the right decisions with it.

> **Even if I don't have enough time to invest it myself,**
> **I wouldn't hand my money over to someone**
> **if I don't understand what they're doing.**
>
> —GEORGETTE MOSBACHER, businesswoman
> and political fund-raiser

The busy woman's guide to do-it-herself investing

If you've decided to manage your investments on your own, how can you invest as *efficiently* and *effectively* as possible? (According to renowned business consultant Peter Drucker, "*Efficiency* means doing things right. *Effectiveness* means doing the right things.")

MUTUAL FUNDS

You learned in chapter 3 how to quickly build a plain-vanilla portfolio of index funds in three easy steps.

1. *Narrow your search.* Having chosen an asset allocation strategy that suits your goals (see pages 90–91), find two or three funds that might be appropriate in each asset category. For simplicity's sake, you may want to draw all your choices from a single fund supermarket such as Fidelity FundsNetwork or Schwab One-Source; or from the Vanguard Group, which specializes in a wide variety of low-cost index funds.
   - Fidelity FundsNetwork: 1-800-544-8666 (www.fidelity.com)
   - Schwab OneSource: 1-800-435-4000 (www.schwab.com)
   - The Vanguard Group: 1-800-871-3879 (www.vanguard.com)
2. *Choose the funds you want.* Using the criteria we've provided (pages 97–98), pick the low-cost fund in each category that looks most promising. If you have Internet access, you can view many fund prospectuses and annual reports on-line and then download an account application. Otherwise, phone the fund company to get information for funds you're interested in, along with an application.
3. *Send in the completed application with your check.*

BONDS

With an investment of just $1,000, you can buy Treasury bills, bonds, or notes directly from the Bureau of the Public Debt. To encourage smaller investors, there's no transaction fee for accounts under $100,000. To set up a Treasury Direct account, contact your nearest Federal Reserve Bank; call 1-800-943-6864, or go on-line to www.publicdebt.treas.gov/sec/sectrdir.htm. Once your account is open, you can buy by phone or on-line. Purchases are deducted from your bank account.

The Internet, thankfully, is democratizing what once was a closed system of buying and selling individual corporate and municipal bonds. To find out whether you were being offered a good deal on a particular bond, you used to have to call a number of bond traders, each of whom might have a different opinion on the bond's value based on interest rates, supply and demand, credit quality, maturity and call features, tax status, state of issuance, market events, and the size of the transaction. As a result, it was easy to pay way too much.

Today, bond information is available on Web sites like that of the Bond Market Association (www.investinginbonds.com), and a true Internet bond exchange may exist by the time you read this book. When that happens, you'll be able to buy bonds much more efficiently.

STOCKS

Folios—also called personal funds—are a nifty innovation for online investors. Like its mutual-fund cousins, a folio is a basket of selected stocks. The big difference is that you're the manager of your folio, buying and selling stocks as you wish (and taking capital gains only when you're ready). You may start with a preselected folio and customize it as you wish, or build your own folio from scratch. Typically, you can trade the most popular stocks as often as you wish for a monthly service fee of $20 to $30.

What's particularly good about folios is that you don't have to buy whole shares, the way you do when you buy stock on the open market. If, for example, a stock is trading at $66, you can simply instruct the folio firm to buy you $50 worth of it. For more information, go on-line to Folio*fn* (www.foliofn.com), Netfolio (www.netfolio.com), eInvesting (www.einvesting.com), or UNX.com (www.unx.com).

If you'd rather build an investment portfolio the traditional way—one stock at a time—rock-bottom commissions make on-line deep-discount brokerages such as E*Trade and Ameritrade a bargain for computer-literate investors who know what they want. Ameritrade, for example, currently charges a flat fee of $8 per trade. "Now that you can do investment research on-line, the broker doesn't have to be there for you," says Andre Scheluchin, managing editor of the New York research firm Mercer, which has studied the discount brokerage market.

Cheaper isn't always better, though; high on-line volume occasionally causes delays in execution of trades, prompting some investors to choose brokerages with better service reliability and slightly higher fees. Detailed information about discount brokers' fees and services is available annually to members of the American Association of Individual Investors (cost to join: $49 a year; call 1-800-428-2244).

If you value savings more than speedy trades, you can purchase one share of some companies' stock through the National Association of Investors Corporation's Low Cost Plan, then buy more stock directly from the company. (For more details, call the National Association of Investors Corporation (NAIC) toll-free at 1-877-275-6242, or go on-line to www.better-investing.com.) Some companies will even sell you the first share of their stock themselves—and most permit no-load dividend reinvestment. (You can check out a list of companies with direct-purchase plans at www.net stock.com.) However, the timing of your trade is usually dictated by the company's stock transfer agent.

With smaller stocks, be aware of the hidden cost of dealer markups. When a share of stock is sold through a broker to a dealer on the New York Stock Exchange or the Nasdaq Stock Market, the dealer marks up the resale price. The markup (the spread between the "ask" and the "bid" prices) tends to be higher for smaller stocks to compensate for their higher risk. According to Wharton finance professor Jeremy Siegel, the average markup on smaller stocks is 2.65 percent, compared to 0.40 percent for larger stocks. If you're comparing a large and a small company whose stock seems to be equally suited for your portfolio, compare the spreads too. You're likely to pay a bigger markup for the smaller company.

REBALANCE YOUR PORTFOLIO ONCE A YEAR

Once you've put together your portfolio, practice benign neglect. School yourself not to react to bad financial news, and don't worry about short-term setbacks. University of Chicago economist Richard Thaler once confided, "When other professors ask me what to do with their retirement money, I tell them to put it all in stocks and then don't open the mail."

However, you do need to take time periodically to see how your current portfolio allocation compares to your target asset allocation strategy, and make adjustments if necessary. For example, suppose you start the year with $15,000 in large-company stocks and $10,000 in government bonds. It happens to be a great year for the stock market, and you end up with $25,000 in stock holdings and $11,000 in bonds. In other words, your original allocation of 60 percent stocks and 40 percent bonds is now 70 percent stocks and 30 percent bonds.

To get back to your original asset allocation, you'll need to sell what you have too much of and buy what you have too little of. We suggest doing this only once a year. Any more often, and you may overreact to short-term market wrinkles, which might iron themselves out in a few months. Also, it can be expensive to trade frequently—even with no-load funds, which sometimes levy a fee on investors who sell shares within a few months of buying in. (Anyway, you don't have a lot of extra time for this stuff, do you?)

Portfolio rebalancing may not sound terribly important, but it can have a substantial impact on your final results. Not long ago, the mutual fund company T. Rowe Price studied two hypothetical $10,000 portfolios made up of 60 percent stocks, 30 percent bonds, and 10 percent Treasury bills. One portfolio was allowed to grow unchecked, while the other was rebalanced back to its starting allocation every quarter from the end of 1969 through September 1995. (Money managers have more time for this.) The results were that the unchecked portfolio was worth $141,000; the rebalanced portfolio, $145,000. Why the difference? One big reason: At the bottom of the 1973–74 market crash, the unchecked portfolio's stock allocation had shrunk to only 49 percent of its total holdings. The rebalanced portfolio, with 60 percent of its assets in the stock market, was in a far better position to profit from the subsequent market rally.

When You Yearn to Walk on the Wild Side

So far, our focus has been on the basics of building a long-term investment portfolio, diversified across several different asset categories and sectors to reduce risk. This prudent portfolio may tick along quietly without needing much attention, other than rebalancing once a year. That may be just fine with you—or maybe it isn't. Maybe you'd like to dabble in a fast-growing market sector now and then, or buy a long-shot stock that you think is going to zoom.

If you get these hankerings, open a separate money market fund account and put 5 to 10 percent of your money in it. Use this money for higher-risk investment choices—knowing that even if you make some wrong calls, 90 to 95 percent of your portfolio is still invested more conservatively. One caution: If success makes this account balloon, rebalance so you have no more than 5 to 10 percent of your money exposed to higher risk at any time.

The ins and outs of investment clubs

If you'd like to have a lot more fun while you learn about investing, consider a women's investment club. Over 30,000 clubs around the country are registered with the National Association of Investors Corporation, and many more operate on an informal basis. Women make up almost 70 percent of NAIC membership, often in women-only groups.

> **I've helped start four women's investment clubs.
> It's a wonderful way for anybody, but particularly
> women, to educate themselves about investing.
> Women like to do things in groups. We learn best
> that way, and we encourage each other.**
>
> —ELLIE WOTHERSPOON,
> *a financial advisor in Washington, D.C.*

Women who are too busy to do anything else somehow find the time to engage in this pleasurable meeting with other women—friends they don't get to see enough in their busy lives, cohorts from work, acquaintances from church or temple or from their kids' school. Getting together once a month, they coach each other on investment basics, then try out their expertise by pooling their money (sometimes as little as $10 to $25 a month) to build up a carefully selected club portfolio.

"What's so fascinating to me about these clubs," says financial advisor Ellie Wotherspoon, "is that it's the old sewing circle reinvented." Indeed, women seem to be quite effective when they get together: As of 1999, women-only clubs had earned a lifetime annual average of $1.39 for every $1 earned by men-only clubs, according to the NAIC.

In an NAIC-affiliated club, you'll have specific guidelines to follow. Typically, all members learn how to research potential stock purchases. (Some clubs also buy mutual funds.) You'll discover how to use such information tools as ValueLine reports, corporate annual reports and other financial publications, and the Internet. If the club decides to make a buy, someone is assigned to follow the new acquisition and report periodically on how it's doing. Profits are generally reinvested. The idea isn't to become wealthy by joining the club, but to apply what you learn in order to create your own successful portfolio.

Like Christine Moore's Gourmet Investment Club (mentioned in chapter 1), some clubs combine an epicurean meal with investment activities. Others regularly invite knowledgeable financial professionals to speak on various aspects of investing. In Washington, D.C., alone, there are the Helen Keller Investment Club (tongue-in-cheek motto: "The blind leading the blind"), Bucks Are Us, the M Street Moguls, and the Great Potential Investment Club, to name just a few.

Women report that they get a tremendous amount from these sessions. "I never feel stupid asking questions, knowing that I'm not the only one who doesn't know everything," one club member said candidly. "And there's always someone there who can help me understand anything I don't know." Another commented, "Something about being in a group that's all women makes me feel comfortable and relaxed—even when I'm learning about price-earnings ratios!"

Investment clubs can give women a safe, nurturing environment to venture small amounts of money—a big advantage if you have conflicting feelings about how much risk you're ready to take. That was a major benefit to Teresa, a young California entrepreneur with her own consulting business. Brought up in a family with a lot of chronic money tension, she told us:

> My dad was superconservative, always putting his money in very low-risk places, never in the stock market. In fact, our granddad had lost almost everything during the stock market crash of 1929 and the Great Depression. My mom, on the other hand, was a superspender who loved taking all kinds of risks. Some paid off—starting her own talent agency, for example—but many didn't.
>
> When I was thirteen, they divorced. My mom spent an enormous amount on her high-living lifestyle, lost a great deal of money in stock market options and futures, and eventually had a stroke. I vowed I would never be as irresponsible as she was about money. So, following my dad's lead, I've been too scared to invest in the market at all.

Teresa's turning point came when, realizing how much she was missing by not knowing how to invest intelligently, she joined a women's investment club. The other members have helped her learn how to manage investment risk wisely. As one of its most active members, Teresa now believes that joining a women's money group was absolutely the right move. "When I don't understand something," she says, "I don't feel dumb asking as many questions as I need to." It's been a real journey of self-discovery for this woman, whose attitude toward financial risk was shaped by an impulsive, risk-taking mother as well as a risk-averse, security-minded dad.

If the idea of working with a group of fellow investors intrigues you, by all means ask around for groups in your area, or call NAIC toll-free at 1-877-275-6242. Women starting out fairly low on the learning curve, as Teresa was, might consider seeking out a women-only investment club. While the camaraderie and supportiveness of a women's group attracts investors at all stages of the journey toward financial enlightenment, it's particularly valuable for those with a lot to learn. Though some mixed gender clubs work well, men in groups are sometimes inclined to be less patient with learners and may tend to focus on competitiveness instead of collegiality. (One prolific founder of women's investment clubs confided that only one of her groups had folded: a club that had accepted a few men, who proceeded to dominate the proceedings and discourage the other members.)

No matter how busy you are, setting aside a few hours a month to bond with other women as you learn about investing can be an investment in itself . . . one that may be well worth your while.

**Don't let your fears stop you.
Just do it!**

—BETTY FRIEDAN, *author of*
The Feminine Mystique

Where are you now?

Have you taken the following steps to debunk the myth that "I don't have enough time to manage my money"?

1. Think about the potential cost of this belief. Do you know other women who didn't make time to take charge of their money? What has happened to them?

2. If you're reluctant to take time for your finances because you think they're boring, review your goals. Do you need to make them more specific and enticing? For example, "a comfortable retirement" is pretty ho-hum. How about "living in New Mexico [or somewhere else you've always loved] and traveling to Fiji [or another exotic place] for a month every year"?

3. Don't like to make time to read financial magazines? Glance through them anyway, and look for stories that get you fired up, like "How to Buy the Home of Your Dreams on a Shoestring" or "We Quit the Rat Race—and Now We Love What We're Doing."

4. Determine when you could set aside an hour a week for money education and management. If you haven't been taking time to focus on your finances lately, try writing a short money dialogue every week to explore the relationship between you and Money.

5. If you have a partner who has been managing the money, establish a separate time once or twice a month to discuss joint financial matters with him or her.

6. Try some of the thirteen creative shortcuts we've suggested to streamline your money management, saving you time while helping you organize your moneylife better.

> **Don't expect to do everything at once.**
> **Successful investing is a process.**
> **One of my mentors told me, "Judy, the**
> **first ten thousand dollars is hard. Then the first**
> **hundred thousand. Then the first million."**
> **Can you imagine having a million dollars?**
> **Why not? The opportunities are out there."**
>
> —JUDY ROBINETT,
> *entrepreneur and women's financial coach*

7. Explore the Internet, if you haven't already done so. Find a friend who can help you get launched, or ask your librarian if there's a public computer you can use.

8. If you have access to a program like Quicken, consider using it to help you stay on top of your finances—especially if you can download current account information from your bank's or investment company's Web site.

9. Review the pros and cons of working with a financial advisor. If you're willing to take on the challenge yourself, consider the gains in knowledge and self-confidence that might result from handling your own money management. If not, it's fine to seek professional assistance; but keep learning from (and with) your advisor, so you can stay in charge of your financial well-being.

10. Review our time-saving suggestions on pages 131–35 for building and managing your own investment portfolio of mutual funds, stocks, and bonds.

11. Find out about women's investment clubs in your area and attend a meeting as an observer. Was the time well spent? If the personalities of that club weren't your cup of tea, think about checking one or two others. Don't give up on the possibility of learning in a group—it's often quite wonderful!

CHAPTER FIVE

Myth 5:
"It's Selfish to Put Myself First. I'm Supposed to Take Care of Everybody Else"

In a plane, adults are instructed to put on their own oxygen mask first, and only then to put one on their children. It should be the same way with our financial security.
—SHARON RICH, *president of Womoney, a financial planning firm for women in Belmont, Massachusetts*

* * *

Over the ages, many of us have been taught that a woman's purpose in life is to give to her loved ones—her partner, children, parents, friends—and those less fortunate. Taking care of ourselves isn't just low on the priority list; it's a focus that many of us learn is bad.

The two of us are prime examples of this conditioning. Olivia notes that "the worst thing my mother ever called me, when I was not being overgiving enough to her, was selfish—said in a voice laced with contempt and anger. After that, I spent years trying to give to everyone else to avoid ever hearing that awful word again." And Sherry recalls her mother chiding her for "selfishness" with the biblical reproach that "though I speak with the tongues of men and of angels, and have not charity, I am become as sounding brass."

Many of us are so afraid of seeming selfish that we go overboard spending our time, energy, and money on others. Our desire to meet other people's needs makes our days an exhausting cycle of working overtime to please clients, bosses, and coworkers; rushing home to prepare the three-course meal we think our family should have;

spending evenings and weekends taking the kids to Scout meetings, ball practice, and birthday parties; then meeting our partner's need for companionship. If we have elderly parents to care for, time for them has to be squeezed in, too.

As author and therapist Harriet Lerner puts it: "Women are raised to care for others at the expense of caring for the self. Some women feel guilty if they are anything less than an emotional service station to others."

So if our loved ones need or want something, we often find it hard to keep money for ourselves. Sometimes it's an affectionate impulse—buying gifts on a whim, taking friends out to dinner whether or not we can afford it—or just a desire to give our family the best: a private school to ensure that the kids can get into a good college, elaborate sound systems and computers, designer sneakers, GameBoys . . . and on and on. After so much giving to others, no wonder we feel we have too little time and money to plan for our own future!

Even single women without children often fail to make their own requirements a high enough priority. Although you may care for yourself physically with nice clothes, cosmetics, and a health club membership, as well as vacations and other rewards, is providing for your future financial security even on your radar screen?

> **I'm much more comfortable spending money on my husband, child, relatives, and friends than on myself. I think it would be better if I could spend or save for myself as easily and with as much pleasure as I can for others.**
>
> —KAREN GROSS, *professor of law at New York Law School*

But the consequences of ignoring our own needs can be devastating. Chances are, you know someone who was once a loyal wife, deferring her own career in order to help her husband up the corporate ladder—only to be dumped later for a younger woman. After a divorce, these ex-wives are typically much poorer than before, without the job skills to make up the difference in their financial security.

Those who end up in therapy often can't stop kicking themselves for their shortsightedness in taking absolutely no steps to protect their own future.

Even a woman in a happy relationship may find that her partner's death or incapacitation leaves her in a desperate financial situation. One widow told us: "I can't believe my husband provided for me so poorly. He actually sold insurance, and he had almost no insurance for me!" Another said that she "always assumed [her husband] was good at managing money. He never let on that he was so lousy at it."

It's never too late to begin learning self-defense. The first step is acknowledging that taking care of yourself, and even putting yourself first when it comes to financial security, is healthy and necessary.

Olga Silverstein, a codirector of the Women's Project in Family Therapy, often asks women, "What's the opposite of *selfish?*" She reports, "They usually say, '*Unselfish.*' And I say, 'No, I think it's *self-less.* Having no self.'"

"Having no self" is definitely not a positive life-goal. But there's a middle road between being self-less and being selfish. It combines healthy self-nurturing with helping others—a natural balance that most women feel comfortable and satisfied with. "Assertiveness training—becoming more self-centered—just doesn't work for most women," says Judith Jordan, Ph.D., assistant professor of psychiatry at Wellesley College and coauthor of *Women's Growth in Connection.* "What you're looking for is to find a balance: to take care of your needs and interests while still taking care of those you love."

We call it self-care.

**Women's primary responsibility is to ensure
our own economic and emotional viability.
This doesn't mean to neglect others.
On the contrary, all other relationships will suffer
if we don't put our primary energy into
our own life plan.**
—HARRIET LERNER, *Ph.D., author of* The Dance of Anger

To find the right balance of self-care, you need to be aware of your deepest goals and longings, so you can do what's best for you ultimately, not just for today. Because so many of us are still gripped by the myth that taking care of ourselves (financially and otherwise) is selfish and should come last on the list—if it makes the list at all—finding the path to self-care is a painstaking process that may require some new learning.

You may find it especially difficult to focus on your own financial needs if you're what Olivia calls a "Money Monk." Money Monks tend to think money and power will corrupt them. The way they see it, there's more virtue in being a poor but idealistic "have-not" than in being a "have" who is greedy and selfish with money.

If this rings a bell for you, your beliefs may have been reinforced by a hippie or activist youth, or by strong religious training that espoused service to others and warned that money is the root of all evil. (Actually, it's the *love of money* that earned this biblical rebuke.) In any case, the idea of setting goals to accumulate money may seem a grievous sin or, at best, like selling out.

> **Women don't want to be greedy.**
> **"Money is bad." ... "People focused on money**
> **are focused on the wrong things." ... "Caring about**
> **money is not an ethical thing to do"**
> **—these beliefs are rampant among women.**
> —SACHA MILLSTONE, *a financial planner in Washington, D.C.*

To overcome this inner resistance to taking care of yourself, start by separating money from greed and avarice. Think of women you know who seem power-hungry and corrupt in a way that has nothing to do with how wealthy they are. Then look for female role models who accomplish admirable things with their money while still taking good care of themselves. Here are a few examples.

Rebecca Adamson, who is part Cherokee and part Swedish, comes from a family of strong women who made their dreams materialize from virtually nothing. Left with a young daughter when her first marriage ended, Rebecca married again; but within a few months, tragedy struck. Her young husband was killed in a hunting accident, her brother died, and she herself was diagnosed with cancer.

Harshly reminded of the fragility of existence, Rebecca decided to take a gamble on her longtime dream of a better life for poor and indigenous peoples. Cashing her last unemployment check, she traveled to New York City and persuaded the Ford Foundation to give her $25,000 in seed money to found First Nations, a development institute that sponsored the first microenterprise fund in the United States. As she worked hard to learn all she could about raising and lending money, her fund for grants and loans grew to $4.5 million—capital that was parceled out in small start-up loans for people and communities that needed it most.

Rebecca told us, "As long as I had a cause, I could do and learn anything immediately." Her devotion to First Nations prompted her to set up a retirement program for the organization. Committed to socially responsible investing, she joined the board of the Calvert Social Investment Fund. Next, she began buying stock as a birthday present for her daughter, by then a teenager.

But although she was helping hundreds of others, she wasn't doing anything about her own financial well-being. She recalled: "I'd learned how to do asset allocation, how to compare investments. Although I didn't pick my own stocks, I'd learned how the financial markets work, and how you work the financial markets. But pay attention: I'm still not saving for myself yet! I put off beginning my own personal investment program for another four years."

What finally motivated Rebecca to begin taking care of herself was the realization that every part of her life was working better financially—except her own retirement planning. She said to herself: "This is stupid. I know what I'm supposed to be doing, and it isn't that hard. I can be more effective if I'm providing for myself."

Over the next few years, she made up for lost time, putting aside six months' worth of expenses for emergencies, consolidating her bills, prepaying her mortgage, maxing out her 401(k), establishing a savings program with a budget, setting up a custodial account to pay her bills promptly when she's traveling, and shunting excess cash into a money market fund. Finally, she shopped around for a financial planner to help her invest and grow her money over the long haul.

It's fascinating to discover that this remarkable woman, who was savvy enough to found and develop an organization that has changed the quality of life for people around the world, took many years to transfer everything she was learning about money and power into her own life. Even then, she began the shift by focusing on her daughter's welfare, and only later extended that concern to herself. Her journey down this long road, through altruistic community service work and her love for her child, finally brought her to the understanding that she could (and should) take better care of herself.

Like Rebecca, you may find it easier to segue into taking care of yourself by using what you've learned in taking care of others. Becky Berube, who is married to professional hockey player Craig Berube, told us that running charity events for the Capitals hockey team wives made a difference in her own ability to care for herself: "I did all the budgeting, managed the whole event, handled the money, et cetera. This gave me a lot more confidence about my financial and management abilities." Maybe you've taught your children how to manage their allowances more wisely, or contributed to help your church, temple, or college prepare better for the future. If so, isn't it time to extend this commitment to yourself?

Other women have found balance in helping others as they help themselves. For example, dancer and choreographer Sally Nash, whom we met in chapter 4, grew up haunted by a fear of seeming selfish if she focused solely on her own interests. As founder of Workspace for Choreographers in Sperryville, Virginia, a woodlands retreat where dancers dig deeply into their own creative process, she can now exercise her own talents while making it possible for other individuals to do the same. "In planning how the Workspace would work," Sally said, "I was exhilarated to find that I didn't need to choose between serving myself and serving others." Her resourcefulness led to an innovative and satisfying way to nourish herself while giving to others.

Susan Berkley also combines caring for others with caring for herself. A voice-over artist, international communications expert, and author, she started her own company after a fifteen-year career as a radio personality. Initially, the business took off like gangbusters, but with no management experience she soon found that her growing staff and other overhead expenses were swallowing up her profits. Closing down her New York City offices, she began to work solo out of her house. But an odd thing happened, Susan told us:

I became physically ill—double vision, nausea—and I said to myself, "This is a message from my unconscious, because I'm not giving to others." So I opened another office, this one in Englewood Cliffs, New Jersey. The second time we did it right by keeping the overhead low.

I have three full-time employees now, and last year our business grew 25 percent. We have a training division that trains sales and customer service groups and a division that does voice recording for phone systems all over the world, in any language, for clients including AT&T, Citibank, and Prudential. I'm a firm believer now that giving to others and taking care of yourself are related—but it took a struggle with my own attempt at self-sabotage for me to get there.

Susan's story raises an interesting point. When you haven't yet found the right balance between self-care and caring for others, you may sabotage your own efforts—overworking or overspending, neglecting your loved ones or yourself, and sometimes literally making yourself sick in the process. Or you may wear yourself into a frazzle trying to do everything for everyone.

> **The most important thing I've learned
> is that I am the only one
> who can take care of myself.**
> —*Participant in a financial seminar for women*

Are you giving too much of yourself to others?

Not long ago, the *Wall Street Journal* profiled a fifty-four-year-old woman whose accomplishments left us agape. In her twenties, she became one of the first female graduates of Harvard Business School. After working as a Wall Street investment banker for eight years, she decided to switch careers. She entered Harvard Medical School and became an eye surgeon. Marrying at thirty-nine, she had a daughter at forty-four and then founded a successful venture capital firm with her husband. Still, she felt her life was lacking. So in her fifties, she began fertility-drug treatments and at the age of fifty-three had twins, direct-ing the anesthesiologist during delivery.

After reading this, you may feel like lying down in a dark room with a damp washcloth over your eyes. But we know many women who struggle with the Superwoman syndrome, unwilling to give in on any front as they try heroically to measure up to an unattainable ideal.

Another example is thirty-eight-year-old Colleen, a former Peace Corps volunteer who married another volunteer she met overseas. Four children later, she tries to squeeze at least twenty-five hours into every day, tending her garden, preparing nutritious meals, play-ing with her preschooler, cheering on the older kids at T-ball and spelling bees. When her husband gets home from the clinic where he's a staff physician, she helps him with various projects on the new house they've built themselves. Generous and hospitable, she often invites friends and family to stay as houseguests. And several hours a week, she teaches adult education through a nearby univer-sity.

It sounds like the busy, productive life of an ideal wife and mother. But meeting all these priorities leaves little time for Colleen's own needs as an artist. Stealing a few minutes here and there for this cre-ative activity that invigorates her, she feels trapped by the many other demands she has willingly embraced. "Maybe it will finally be 'my time' when the kids are grown up," she says wistfully. As for planning her financial future, she flatly refuses to focus on this task when she already lacks time for herself.

This dilemma may be most agonizing for baby-boomer women, whose generation was caught in a cultural time warp. If you're in this group, you may feel stuck midway between the focus on individual fulfillment that began to pick up steam in the sixties and seventies, and your mothers' and grandmothers' dogma that the family comes first (which means that "good moms" should be content to be full-time cooks, gardeners, nest builders, and cheerleaders for their off-spring). You long to do your own thing but can't because you're too busy doing your mother's thing.

As a result, many women become frustrated and angry, often taking it out on their hapless partners as well as themselves: "If my inner needs aren't considered important enough for you to help me meet them, then I don't care what happens to me. Which means I'm not going to spend any time on retirement planning, dammit!" Thus, they end up sabotaging their own futures.

If you're strongly oriented toward giving everything to others, our advice to start taking better care of yourself may make you fear that you'll careen out of control and alienate people you care for. But we're not urging you to overspend, overeat, start smoking, drink too much, or otherwise wallow in wild self-indulgence. Nor are we insisting that you become a Scrooge with your loved ones in order to accumulate an enormous stash of money that won't see daylight for another thirty years.

> **When women come to me with selfishness issues, I try to help them see how taking better care of themselves will allow them to take better care of the people they love.**
> —AZRIELA JAFFE, *business coach, syndicated columnist, and author*

On the other hand, caring for yourself may mean stepping into new and unfamiliar territory. Where do you draw the line? For example, if you're like Colleen, the overcommitted mom, when is it okay to say to the kids, "No, I can't take you to the pool; it's my time to be by myself and paint"? When is it okay to say, "No, I'm not going to put that money in the college account; it should go into my IRA"?

The key, we think, is to acknowledge that an overstressed, overworked, depleted woman can't give her best to others. If painting is what makes you feel happy and fulfilled, taking that time will make you a much better mother than if you drop everything to chauffeur your kids everywhere they want to go. By the same token, a woman who's financially secure can be more loving and nurturing than one who faces the prospect of having to be supported by her children. Furthermore, caring for yourself in a healthy way teaches your children to take care of themselves. Your serenity and self-fulfillment are gifts you can pass on to them—gifts worth far more than indulging their every need and want.

Every person has to find her own right path, her own "middle road." If you think you've reached it, give it a try for a month. You'll know then whether you feel comfortable and at peace, or whether you need to move a bit more toward yourself or toward others.

How taking care of yourself can help others

It's both loving and prudent to make sure you won't be a burden on your family. In fact, what would be truly selfish would be to spend every dollar on transient pleasure for yourself and others now, leaving the responsibility for your future well-being in the hands of your children, your neighbors (whose taxes finance such government benefits as Medicaid and food stamps), and kind strangers who contribute to charitable organizations.

Take advantage of opportunities now, as Rebecca Adamson did, to put money aside for tomorrow. If it helps, tell yourself your savings are "for the kids." Or for your nieces and nephews, cousins, and friends who may otherwise have to support you in your later years.

In most cases, your loved ones will get the message—and they'll respect you for your prudence. For example, Arlynn Greenbaum told us of the influence her mother's example had on her. Arlynn is president of Authors Unlimited, a speakers bureau based in New York City, and recently headed the Women's Media Group, an organization of female top executives from the media and publishing industries. She said:

> Growing up, I hated it when my mother wouldn't overdo things for me. She would say, "Sorry, honey, but I've got to take care of myself."
>
> When I was in my twenties, my parents got divorced. My mother had alimony for ten years, then married again and was widowed after another twenty years. All this time she kept instilling in my two sisters and me, "Learn to support yourself." We've all taken her advice.
>
> My mother taught me that money should be part of your general level of self-confidence. Just as you take care of yourself physically and emotionally, in your relationships and in your profession, money should be an area that you take responsibility for with confidence.

Many other interviewees said that strong, independent mothers, aunts, or grandmothers had been role models in showing them how to take care of themselves financially. One of these fortunate younger women was Michelle Singletary.

If you read the *Washington Post*, you probably know Michelle, who writes a widely read syndicated column, "The Color of Money." The wife of a government engineer and mother of three children, Michelle originally came from a lower-income family in Baltimore. Along with her two sisters and two brothers, she was brought up by grandparents—a nurse's aide and a tow-truck driver. She explained how her loving grandmother's belief in self-care helped her develop her own sense of financial well-being.

> My grandmother was extremely good with saving and budgeting. She was very frugal and very strict. I didn't feel deprived in the sense that I wanted things I couldn't get; but she didn't want us to ask her for a lot of stuff, so she'd make it seem like we were one step away from living in the street—even though she would never be in that position.
>
> Later, I went to the University of Maryland on a full academic scholarship. I was a hoarder who never got into debt. If I had a balance on my credit card, I'd get nervous thinking I might go bankrupt, and pay it off as quick as I could.
>
> After I started working for the *Post*, I would talk about how "cheap" my grandmother was. In 1997 I got approval to write my own column about personal finance. Originally it was aimed toward African-Americans, but it was so popular that I began to write it for everyone.
>
> I still have bankruptcy fears. Being on the street is not an option. I know that I would go scrub floors in a hotel, whatever it would take. If I had to scale all the way down and live in one room with my kids, I could do it. My grandmother taught me that every job is important in its own right; you should never think you're too good for it. If that's what it takes to be secure, then so be it.

Motivated by her grandmother's example, Michelle has prepared well for her own retirement. And through her column, she has educated and inspired others to do the same.

Mary Quattlebaum, an author of children's books in Washington, D.C., learned financial responsibility from her mother. The oldest of seven children, Mary grew up with parents who handled money differently. "Although they both believed in saving, my dad sometimes would wreak havoc with the budget," she said. "He'd go off and buy a horse and an expensive saddle on a whim. It would really upset my

mother, who was buying hamburger and stretching it out with maca-
roni." She went on:

> My mom was a really good role model, at a time when women
> weren't empowered to think of themselves as being good with
> money. There are four of us girls; we're all good with money, and
> the three of us who are married have taken over our family's fi-
> nances. All four of us put ourselves through college.
>
> Now I'm working on how to empower our daughter, to help her
> learn about money as she grows. One aspect of that will be helping
> her learn about stocks so that she's not anxious about investing.

Doris Kiser, a Maryland homemaker, is another mother who's actively involved in helping her daughters learn to take care of themselves financially. She said that "money is an especially important
subject for women because they often control the family finances, so
it seems odd to me when they're afraid of learning. I'm trying to make
sure that doesn't happen with my daughters."

Doris began with the basics: "I started an in-house bank when they
were eight and eleven. They deposit money with me that they earn
from doing chores, I pay them interest, and when they want cash they
write out a check to me and I give it to them."

Women like Mary and Doris are to be applauded for passing on
their own financial awareness to their children. "We know that teaching their daughters about money is a priority for women," observes
Cathleen Stahl, who formerly managed the Women and Investing
program at OppenheimerFunds in New York. She says that when
women were polled about their experiences with money while growing up, they ranked money management as more important for their
daughters than computer skills or learning a second language.

One unexpected result of coaching your daughters is that they may
later turn the tables and encourage you to make better money decisions. For example, Melissa Moss, former CEO of the Women's Consumer Network, told us: "My mother kept bugging me about putting
money into an IRA. I finally did it. Then, at thirty-five, I bought my
own condo in Washington with tremendous anxiety and fear—not a
single woman in my family had ever bought her own home. I loved it!
Then I badgered my mother into buying her own home. She did it,
and was happy she did."

Most mothers would wholeheartedly approve of the idea of being a financial role model for their daughters (and sons, too). The hard part is living up to this ideal. To protect your own financial security, you may have to deny them some of the things they want, as well as other things they might seem to need—like an all-expense-paid, four-year college education.

Michelle Singletary, for one, feels it's shortsighted to put college for your children ahead of your own financial well-being.

> I have this big thing about parents mortgaging their retirement future on their kids. It's not good for them or you if you end up bankrupt. My grandmother wasn't gonna dip into her retirement savings for anything, even sending us to college. She knew that if you don't have enough saved and rely on your kids to take care of you, maybe they will and maybe they won't. You might end up in a little room in the back of their house, or in a terrible nursing home. Why risk it?
>
> I don't happen to think that we owe our kids everything. We just have to take care of them until they're launched. What kind of a person are you raising if you give them everything, and they don't have to work for it? They'll always expect you to give to them, and they won't learn how to get it for themselves.
>
> Look at all the kids moving back in with their parents to get Mom and Daddy to support them, because they want to live a lifestyle they can't really afford. But once they live with their parents, they can buy their nice car, fancy clothes, et cetera.

Michelle and her grandmother are right about the danger of overgiving to kids at your own expense. By continually putting their wants ahead of your own, you end up teaching them dependence and selfishness . . . the very opposite of what they truly need.

Getting started

To see where you are in taking care of yourself, look at the goals list you created in chapter 1. Is there at least one short-term and one long-term goal that might be considered self-caring?

If you don't see any on your list, think up some goals that are just for you. For example, a short-term goal might be learning to play a musical instrument, dance, or speak a new language; putting aside

$2,000 in the next year to invest in your own name; or taking a trip to a place you've always dreamed of. Make sure you have a self-caring long-term goal that will allay your anxiety about the future. (There's no shame in admitting to the bag lady fears that plague so many women. The only thing that's shameful is choosing to do nothing about them.)

Having Trouble Thinking of Goals?
Pretend You're Queen for a Day

The concept of "self-caring" is grounded in our ability to tolerate the pleasure of nurturing ourselves and treasuring ourselves deeply—a pleasure that many of us have been taught to repress. Even if we consciously tell ourselves it's okay to be good to ourselves, deep down we often resist letting go of the self-denial we're so familiar with.

To overcome this resistance, practice paying attention to your own needs and desires by describing your ideal day. How would you spend those twenty-four hours? When would you get up? Where would you be? What would you eat? Whom would you interact with? What would you do? What would the financial realities of your life be like? Write down all your thoughts (or dictate them into a tape recorder, if you prefer). New short-term and long-term goals may emerge from this exercise.

If thinking about your own desires and aspirations brings on a guilt attack ("No! It's too selfish! My kids'/parents'/partner's needs are more important!"), take a few moments to jot down your negative feelings about putting yourself first. Counter these prejudices with a positive statement such as "It's not selfish to take good care of myself."

Then go back to your "self-caring" list. Write down a step you'll take in the next two weeks to move closer to each of your goals. For example, if a short-term goal is to begin learning yoga, find out rates, schedules, and locations; then sign up. For a long-term goal of providing better for your financial future, you might take the step of opening an investment account and setting up automatic transfers to it from your bank account.

Remember, the purpose of writing down your dreams and goals is to remind yourself of your own needs. This reminder is all the more important because women are often conditioned to defer to other family members' wants—which can lead to sabotaging our own future security with misplaced priorities like these:

- "I've been reading about how important knowledge skills will be in getting a job. We've got to put every penny into making sure our kids get a really good education."
- "Dad's failing so, but I can't bear the thought of a nursing home. If we took the money out of our retirement savings, we could get him full-time home care."

> **The greatest gift we can give our children is our own financial independence. That's what my parents gave me, and I'm forever grateful for it.**
> —KATIE COURIC, *television anchor*

Candi Kaplan, a Certified Financial Planner who has headed her own financial planning firm for many years, told us of deferring her desire for financial independence to help her mother and father. She said frankly, "I thought being in service to my parents was what I was supposed to do." Growing up, Candi was overshadowed by financial insecurity.

When I was fourteen, my parents went bankrupt. We lost our home and the retail business they had been operating. After we moved to another town, they went into a similar business with my uncle. When I was twenty-five, they retired and I took over the business. I remodeled it and ran it for three years, and then found a buyer for it. When I went into business for myself at age twenty-nine, it was a clear act of taking care of myself.

Women are still led to believe that we have to nurture first. But I think more and more of us understand that if we don't put ourselves first, who the hell else is gonna do it?

My daughter said to me recently, "You know, if I go to a state university, I could save eighty thousand dollars. Then I could afford to go to business school anywhere I want." I think that's a sign of hope for the future.

Take a Look at What's Blocking You

If you're finding it hard to make self-care a priority, take some time to see what's standing in your way. Write down a list of all the bad things that might happen to others if you addressed your own needs.

For example, you might write, "If I spent more time in my garden each afternoon, I couldn't drive the kids to after-school activities." Or, "If I put too much money away for retirement, I might not be able to afford college for my son." Or, "If I went to investment club meetings on Wednesday evenings, I'd miss quality time with my partner."

Then, under each of these statements, jot down how you might deal with this problem. For instance, could you trade flowers or vegetables from your garden to another mom who might ferry your kids with her own? Could you lower your sights from the Ivy League to a state university, and rely on your son's ability to win grants or scholarships if he wants a pricier education? To compensate for your investment-club commitment, could you and your mate have a special date together on another evening every week?

If you're creative in brainstorming solutions, you may soon find that you can deal with your blocks without too much difficulty . . . leading the way to taking better care of yourself.

Preparing for your retirement

It's important enough to say again: Most women's first financial priority should be to max out the allowable contribution to a tax-favored retirement account. This simple step can help spare you a grim future of worrying whether your money will last as long as you do.

You can open an IRA or self-employed retirement plan through any bank, brokerage, or mutual fund company. It's your decision how to invest this money; your choices include traditional savings accounts or CDs (at banks), mutual funds, stocks, or bonds. With an employer-sponsored plan, you're usually limited to the options your employer has chosen.

If you aren't currently contributing to a retirement plan, which of these tax-favored arrangements are you eligible for?

IF YOU WORK FOR AN EMPLOYER

- *401(k)s.* These retirement savings plans can be sponsored by just about any employer, except government units. They typically offer you a smorgasbord of mutual funds, plus a fixed-rate choice and sometimes an opportunity to select other investments through a broker. You can contribute a percentage of each paycheck to your 401(k) account, up to a certain dollar amount (your employer will tell you the specifics, which differ from plan to plan). Many employers also match some or all of employee contributions, up to a fixed percentage of pay.

  Even if your company doesn't offer a match, don't pass up a 401(k). Contributions come out of your pretax income, which reduces your tax bill now. And as with all these plans, your earnings can grow faster because they're tax deferred. You pay the postponed tax on contributions and earnings when you take the money out.

- *403(b)s.* Similar to 401(k)s, these retirement savings plans for public schools and other tax-exempt organizations can invest only in annuities or mutual funds. (Some are called TSAs, short for "Tax-Sheltered Annuity" arrangements.) A drawback is that many 403(b)s aren't covered under ERISA (the Employee Retirement Income Security Act of 1974), which means there's less regulatory oversight and often less detail available about investment choices. Both employers and employees may contribute to employee accounts, and contribution limits are basically the same as for 401(k)s.

- *457 plans.* Also much like 401(k)s, these plans are available only to municipalities and other government units. When it comes to building up a nest egg by investing in their menu of mutual funds, you're on your own; employer matches aren't allowed.

- *ESOPs.* An Employee Stock Option Plan is a benefit plan to which a company contributes stock, cash to buy stock, or cash to pay back loans that help employees buy stock. Participants usually don't have to contribute any money of their own. When you leave the company, you can sell your stock or take it with you.

  Although stock ownership is a great way for employees to benefit from their hard work, it's smart not to make an ESOP your only retirement plan. After you've participated for ten years, you can diversify some of your holdings (25 percent at age fifty-five; 50 percent at age sixty) into other investments. But that still leaves you with 50 percent or more of your financial security tied up in one company's stock—a risk most investors would be wise to avoid.

- *SIMPLEs.* (See next section.)
- *Keogh plans.* (See next section.)

IF YOU HAVE SELF-EMPLOYMENT INCOME

It's possible to participate in an employer retirement plan *and* have your own self-employed plan *and* conceivably have an IRA, too. That's because you don't have to be self-employed full-time to open one of the plans listed below; you can be a part-time freelancer or have moonlighting income—even from your current employer.

- *SIMPLEs.* A SIMPLE (Savings Incentive Match Plan for Employees) will let you contribute as much as $6,500 a year, plus up to 3 percent more of your compensation as an "employer match"— all tax deductible.
- *Keogh plans.* There are two kinds of Keoghs: a profit-sharing plan (which allows you to contribute a varying percentage of your income from year to year) and a money-purchase plan (which requires you to contribute the same percentage each year). In either case, the most you can put in is 25 percent of your income up to a certain dollar amount (in 2000, it was $30,000). If you want to combine flexibility with discipline, you can piggyback a profit-sharing plan onto a money-purchase plan with a low ceiling—say, a 10 percent fixed annual contribution. However, the contribution units for a hybrid plan are the same as for the basic plans. The IRS requires you to report yearly on any Keogh worth more than $100,000.
- *SEP-IRAs.* These souped-up IRAs are solely for self-employed individuals. You can technically contribute up to 15 percent of your self-employment income a year to a SEP (Simplified Employee Pension), up to a certain maximum ($30,000 in 2000). The actual percentage works out to a tad over 13 percent, by the time you're done "adjusting" your income to the IRS's satisfac-

tion. If you're not able to stash away more than 13 percent a year, a SEP-IRA's lack of paperwork makes it a good choice. All you have to do is enter your annual contribution in the "Deductions" section of your Form 1040.

IF YOU HAVE ANY KIND OF COMPENSATION INCOME

IRAs are for nearly everyone who works, even just part-time. You can contribute up to $2,000 a year or the amount you earned, whichever is less, to any IRA or combination of IRAs. (This $2,000 limit doesn't apply to money you roll over into an IRA from a 401(k) or other company plan.) Which of the three types of personal IRAs do you qualify for?

- *Deductible traditional IRAs.* You're automatically eligible to deduct a contribution to a traditional IRA if you (and your husband, if you're married) aren't covered by a retirement plan at work.

  There are other ways to qualify for a deduction, depending on your household income. If one of you is covered by a retirement plan at work or through self-employment, the other can still qualify for a deductible IRA if your joint adjusted gross income is under $160,000. If you don't have earned income but your husband does, you can usually contribute $2,000 to an IRA of your own as long as he earned more than $4,000. Otherwise, your household income currently must be under $62,000 if married, $42,000 if single, to qualify for a full or partial deduction. And by the way, you must be under age 70½.
- *Roth IRAs.* Thank goodness, Roth rules are a lot simpler. To qualify, your household income must fall below a certain level (in 2000, the cap was $160,000 for couples and $110,000 for singles). Your annual contribution isn't tax deductible, but once your Roth is five years old, all withdrawals after age 59½ are completely tax-free! Also, you can keep contributing to a Roth at any age—a choice worth considering for older women who want to leave a tax-free legacy for beneficiaries.

  With joint or single household income of $100,000 or less, you also have the option of converting an existing traditional IRA to a Roth IRA. Although you'll have to ante up now for any deferred taxes, afterward your money can grow—and be available to you in retirement—completely free of federal income tax.

- *Nondeductible traditional IRAs.* If you're younger than 70½ and can't qualify for either of the two IRAs above, you're probably eligible for a nondeductible IRA. But before you get one, give it a mighty close look. Since it's a traditional IRA, you'll have a briar patch of tax rules to contend with at withdrawal time, without the solace of tax-deductible contributions to look back on. Given that freedom from hassle is worth something, you might prefer to put your money into taxable growth investments instead (which also qualify for lower capital-gains tax rates).

With Capitol Hill buzzing about more generous IRA rules and even Roth 401(k)s, the retirement-plan landscape may have changed by the time you read this. With this background, though, you'll be able to compare what's new with what's tried and true, making it easier to choose the plan that works best in your case. For more details, see IRS publications 590 ("Individual Retirement Arrangements"), 571 ("Tax-Sheltered Annuity Programs for Employees of Public Schools and Certain Tax-Exempt Organizations"), and/or 560 ("Retirement Plans for Small Business"). You can get them by calling 1-800-829-3676, or download them from www.irs.gov.

Socially conscious investing

Within the major investment categories (mutual funds, stocks, and bonds), socially responsible investments may provide a special emotional reward: the satisfaction of doing good while doing well (you hope) as you build your own financial security.

> **We need to help more women see that they can further their own interests at the same time that they are contributing to the social unit they care about.**
> —JUDITH JORDAN, Ph.D., coauthor of Women's Growth in Connection

This type of investing has special appeal to women. For First Nations founder Rebecca Adamson, choosing socially responsible investments for her 401(k) "makes investing more alive and meaningful." In a Morningstar.com interview in August 2000, Domini Social Investments founder Amy Domini noted that the socially conscious fund firm had slightly more women than men as shareholders—a significant difference, she felt, since mutual fund demographics ordinarily show the opposite.

Today, there are more than sixty mutual funds that use some kind of social screen in choosing investments, according to *Kiplinger's Personal Finance Magazine*. The drawback is that almost all of them measure positive social contributions differently —and their criteria may not match your own. For example, although you might agree with excluding companies involved in alcohol, tobacco, gambling, or pornography, what about screening out companies that profit from nuclear power or bioengineering, or that provide benefits to employees' unmarried partners? Some funds shun such potentially sound investments as Fannie Mae (the eminently respectable Federal National Mortgage Association, which buys residential mortgages and helps inner-city families buy homes) because it has contributed to Planned Parenthood.

If you do find a fund that suits your beliefs, make sure it's a good investment. Funds that seem to be on the side of the angels are perfectly capable of going to hell in a handbasket. For example, in one twelve-month span when the S&P 500 gained 22 percent, the socially conservative Timothy Plan A slid to a dismal –22 percent. Don't forget to check on fees, too; many ethical funds levy stiff sales charges. The Timothy Plan, for one, was dragged down by a hefty 5.5 percent front-end load.

But there are success stories, too. An example is the Domini Social Equity Fund, whose substantial weighting in socially and environmentally friendly high-tech firms led it to outperform the S&P 500 for the three-year and five-year periods ending June 30, 2000. And many socially conscious companies have proved to be a good investment for people who bought their individual stocks.

If you'd like to find out more about putting your money where your heart is, some good Web sites are the Social Investment Forum (www.socialinvest.org), Social Funds (www.social funds.com), and Green Money (www.greenmoney.com).

The joy of giving to others

When women are in the fortunate position of having wealth, they're more likely than men to want to share it. Asked in a 2000 *Money* poll what they would do with a $10,000 windfall, 17 percent of women said they'd help their children, compared to 11 percent of men. Some 13 percent of women (but only 6 percent of men) would help their parents or other relatives. And 11 percent of women (vs. 7 percent of men) said they'd give money to charity.

As you build your own wealth, one of its great benefits is that when you have "enough"—a point you must define yourself—you can use some of it to help others make their own dreams come true. One woman who has given to others in a big way is seventy-eight-year-old Deborah Szekely.

The Golden Door Spa near San Diego and Rancho La Puerta in Baja California have long been known as places where Hollywood stars and the wealthy go to tone up, slim down, and get a new lease on life. Both were founded by Deborah and her husband.

Divorced after thirty years of marriage, Deborah found herself at age fifty-nine deciding to pass the business to her children so that she could move on to something different. In explaining what prompted this life change, she said that during a get-together with friends, she imagined her life ten years in the future: "My friends' concerns and topics of conversation had not changed in years, and as I listened I realized that I was not ready to stay the same and wanted to make a change."

In short order she ran for Congress ("I was a Republican, a woman, a Jew, and pro-choice. None of these added up to a winning candidate"), then authored a management manual, reprinted half a dozen times, which is still the guidebook used by new members of Congress and their staffs. Named president of the Inter-American Foundation, an independent federal agency, she worked to help change people's lives in Latin America and the Caribbean.

Deborah then took a daring leap into philanthropy. She used her Szekely Foundation to provide over $1 million in seed money for a new enterprise, Eureka Communities, dedicated to developing, supporting, and networking the leadership of community-based nonprofit organizations around the country. Now supported by grants from other foundations, Eureka links nonprofit community leadership in most U.S. states.

Deborah told us, "There's a book I give to a lot of people by Andrew Carnegie. In it he writes, 'He who dies rich dies disgraced.' He felt that money belongs to the people whose labor made it possible, so he gave it back in the form of libraries to educate the poor in just about every city of the United States."

Her career change doesn't seem all that drastic to her. "The committed philanthropist needs to think of himself as an entrepreneur," she once said in an interview. "The goals are the same, but instead of making money for money's sake, you are making and using the money to affect the lives of people who have not had your good fortune."

Whether or not you're as financially fortunate as Deborah, you may feel the same inclination to give to those who have even less. If you have grandchildren, you may want to help make sure they get a good education; perhaps you tithe to your church or synagogue, make regular contributions to your college alumnae fund, or donate time and money to charitable causes in your community. But again: *Put on your own oxygen mask first*—don't sacrifice your own financial security out of altruism (or guilt).

If you're a serious philanthropist, there are many estate-planning strategies that can allow you to shelter income from taxes while benefiting your favorite cause. For example, a charitable remainder trust lets you receive the income from trust investments while leaving the remainder to charity; a charitable lead trust allows a charity to receive regular income during your lifetime while preserving the rest for your children. While these can be excellent ways to leave a legacy to others, they're complex to set up and irreversible thereafter, so consider them only as part of a carefully thought-out financial plan.

Providing for your child's education

One important cause dear to the hearts of many financially pinched parents is their child's college education. But the challenge of putting aside enough money to pay a youngster's way is daunting. Even after adjusting for inflation, college tuition more than doubled between 1981 and 1999 while median family income increased only 22 percent, according to the nonprofit College Board.

If you're not ready to bet that your children can surf through college solely on grants and loans, how can you provide for yourself and help them, too? Here's what we suggest:

- *Take care of yourself first.* If you postpone saving for retirement until after the kids have graduated from college, it will be virtually impossible to make up for lost time. That's because you'll have lost all the money that compounding could have made for you. For example, if you start saving $5,000 a year at age thirty-four and earn a hypothetical 10 percent a year, your portfolio would grow to an impressive $1,183,834 by age sixty-five. But if you wait until age forty-four to start the same program, you'd end up with only $378,031.

With the prospect of twenty-plus years in retirement ahead of you, this missing money could mean your children might end up having to support you financially—a burden you'd want to spare them if you can. So put on your own oxygen mask first, by making sure your retirement savings are on track before you set aside money for the kids.

> I see some of my friends being extravagant with their children, and I'm sure they have nothing saved for their own retirement. They say, "IRAs are for old people." "You're wrong," I tell them. "You need to start saving now. You're responsible for yourself."
>
> —DORIS KISER, a Germantown, Maryland, homemaker who manages her family's investments

If you can't put much aside, one option is not to set up a separate savings program for college. Instead, stash every possible penny in a 401(k) or other tax-deferred retirement plan. Unlike money in a taxable account, these savings won't be counted in calculating your child's eligibility for financial aid. And if push comes to shove, you may be able to borrow against your 401(k) assets to pay for college tuition. (Note: Borrowing from IRAs isn't allowed; you'd have to make a withdrawal.)

If you do have the wherewithal to establish an educational fund, here's how to start.

- *Estimate how much your kids will need for college.* To approximate what the cost will be when your children are ready to enroll, increase today's college tab by an inflation factor of 8 percent a year. (This is an average inflation rate based on past increases; the actual rate may be higher or lower.) A personal-finance program like Quicken can perform this compounding calculation for you. After determining this target amount (and picking yourself up off the floor), decide how much of it you can realistically expect to save without short-circuiting your own retirement savings.

- *Set up an automatic investment program.* Many mutual-fund companies allow you to set up automatic transfers of as little as $100 a month from your bank account.

- *Don't feel guilty if your college fund falls short.* Most parents will do well to save 30 to 50 percent of the total tab for college. Look to scholarships, grants, and/or loans to make up the rest.

Naturally, you hate to think of your kids starting their careers saddled with student loans. But education is an investment that should pay financial returns, and they'll have a long time to take care of this responsibility. By contrast, if you finance the shortfall out of your retirement savings, you're apt to have only a few short years to repay yourself before the paychecks stop coming in.

WHAT'S THE BEST WAY TO INVEST FOR COLLEGE?

Consider which of these options suits your situation:

- *State-sponsored college savings plans.* If your college-bound child or grandchild is still young, you may want to look into these plans (also known as 529 plans). You need not be a resident of a particular state to participate in its plan, and you can use your accumulated savings at any accredited postsecondary school in the country.

    State-sponsored 529 plans are run by professional money managers, like Fidelity Management & Research, who invest your money in a pool of securities. Your investment returns are subject to market ups and downs. The big advantage is that tax on earnings is deferred until withdrawal. At that point, earnings are taxed at the child's rate, as long as the money is used for higher-education costs.

If your child decides not to go to college or wins a boatload of financial aid, the plan account can be used by another family member. (Parents of only children: Make sure this pass-along privilege isn't available solely to siblings.)

In comparing state-sponsored college savings plans, check to make sure you like the investment style. The asset allocation should automatically become more conservative as college enrollment age draws closer. Also compare management fees, which tend to be higher than you'd pay to put together your own portfolio of no-load mutual funds.

- *Prepaid college tuition plans.* Many states offer these plans, which guarantee your child a four-year education in a participating in-state school when you prepay a certain amount, either in one lump sum or in regular payments while your child is growing up. In return for this guarantee, however, there are a couple of drawbacks: The rate of return on your investments (which is usually fixed) may be more modest than you could realize by investing in the market yourself. And if your child prefers to attend an out-of-state-school, the plan will provide you a lump sum equal to the average cost of an in-state education. If your kid's chosen college costs more, you'll have to come up with the difference yourself.

   For phone numbers and E-mail addresses of state-sponsored college savings plans and prepaid college tuition plans around the country, go on-line to www.collegesavings.org.

- A *self-managed investment plan.* If you decide to go for the potentially higher rewards (and accompanying risk) of managing your own plan, the first step is to structure your investments to suit your time frame. If your child is five or more years away from college, your education portfolio should be primarily or totally invested for growth. As he or she approaches college age, you'll want to shift some of the portfolio into more stable growth-and-income, income, and/or money market funds.

   Second, look for ways to give up less of your money to the IRS. To begin with, consider putting your college money in a Roth IRA. (You can't do this, though, if you're already using your annual IRA contribution for your own retirement savings.) Roth IRA contributions may be withdrawn tax-free at any time. Also, there's no IRS early-withdrawal penalty on earnings taken out to pay for higher education, provided the account has been open for five years (though you will owe income tax if you're under the age of fifty-nine and a half). In the meantime, your money can compound tax-free.

Kids with earned income also qualify to open a Roth IRA. In the 2000 tax year, for example, you, your husband, and a child could have put away a total of $6,000 a year in Roth IRAs, plus $500 more in an Education IRA (any of which can be withdrawn tax-free for college expenses).

Clearly, there are many ways to give your children the opportunity for a good education. Just be sure not to shortchange your own future while doing it.

Caring for parents who need your help

Someday most people may live to be over 100, robust and independent. But today, health-care advances have made longevity both a blessing and a curse. A blessing because fewer people now die in their prime of acute illness or infection, but a curse because we're more likely to survive until we become feeble physically and mentally, often needing the support and care of our loved ones. That puts many women today in the uncomfortable position of parenting their children *and* their parents or parents-in-law. (An estimated three-quarters of family caregivers are women.)

While we usually don't mind giving ourselves to our children, it doesn't feel quite as natural to take over this role with our parents. It often frightens and disturbs us when Mom and Dad begin to fail, because they stand between us and our own mortality. Yet as good daughters, we feel it's our responsibility to help them just as they helped us when we were young.

But many of us don't know where to draw the line. We feel guilty stinting on any emotional, physical, or financial support they may need. Some "good daughters" quit their jobs, deplete their savings, drop their friends, even ruin their marriages and alienate their children to care for their parents. In a 1999 survey, the National Alliance for Caregiving found that a caregiver's average financial toll in lost

> **Seeing my seventy-six-year-old mother struggle
> with limited income and a minimal Social Security
> benefit motivated me to begin investing, so I could
> have extra money to spend on her and her needs.**
> —*Participant in a financial workshop*

wages, pension benefits, and Social Security totaled nearly $660,000 over her lifetime.

If your parents need your help, deciding how much you can give is one of the hardest choices you may ever have to make in your life—and no one else can make it for you. We can only repeat: *Put on your own oxygen mask first.* Remember the effort your parents devoted to helping you become a strong and independent adult. Though their situation may seem now to demand everything you've got (and more), loving parents will always have your interests at heart. They don't want you to impoverish yourself for them, ruin your own health, or create an emotional wasteland out of the rest of your life.

The following tips may help.

- *Before providing financial support, be sure you understand your parents' situation.* What do they own, and what do they owe? If they don't have an inventory of their bank accounts, investments, loans, and insurance, you should help them create one. How much are their living expenses? Is their current lifestyle sustainable? Are they investing appropriately to keep their money growing? Could they weather a market downturn?

  If you were raised (as many of us were) with the idea that money is a taboo topic, it probably won't be easy to ask your father and mother or surviving parent about their money. You'll worry that they may think you're treating them like children or acting greedy about your inheritance. But the fact is, one of the most loving things you can do for parents in their sixties, seventies, or eighties is to help them feel more secure about their money. That's even more important if your parent is alone.

You might ease into the subject over lunch at a favorite restaurant by bringing up the latest news about Social Security or your own retirement preparations. Then say something like "I can't feel comfortable without knowing that you'll be all right. Would you be willing to take some time to tell me about your own plans and wishes?" (If this is too difficult to bring up in person, consider opening the discussion by writing them a letter along these lines. You might enclose an article about retirement security or estate planning, and ask if you can discuss their thoughts with them the next time you get together.)

- *Make sure they have up-to-date wills.* You don't have to know the provisions if your parents would rather not divulge them, but you should know who the executors are. It's especially important to be sure the will has been reviewed recently if your parents have moved to a different state, or if there have been family births, deaths, marriages, or divorces that might affect its terms.

Has each parent drawn up a power of attorney and a health-care proxy, in case they're unable to make decisions for themselves? Even a spouse needs a power of attorney to act legally for someone who's incapacitated. Otherwise, if your father were severely disabled by a stroke or Alzheimer's, your mother couldn't file a joint tax return or sell jointly held property without a court order. A health-care proxy grants similar authority to make health-care decisions if the grantor is unable to. A surviving parent should have a power of attorney and health-care proxy drawn up in your name, or that of someone else he or she trusts. (If desired, the power of attorney can be "springing"— designed to spring into effect only if the grantor is incapacitated.)

If your parents haven't taken these steps, steer them toward the family lawyer at the first opportunity. (For AARP members, simple wills are available from local attorneys for as little as $50. For details, go on-line to www.aarp.org/lsn or write Legal Services Network Fulfillment, P.O. Box 100084, Pittsburgh, PA 15290.)

Don't make the mistake of figuring that this is a morbid chore you can put off indefinitely. Once you've gone through with it, your parents will have the comfort of knowing they've arranged things just as they want them. And you'll avoid the potential nightmare of trying to guess their health-care wishes, or untangling a messy estate whose complications could disrupt family relationships for decades.

- *Look into long-term care insurance, if they're still in good health.* If your parents won't consider this insurance but don't have the resources to pay for extended care, you and your siblings may want to buy them a long-term care policy for your own peace of mind. (For more about long-term care, see page 181–86.)
- *If you live too far away to help a parent who's having trouble managing money, consider a custodial arrangement.* If your parents can't handle their bank accounts and investments any longer and you're not in a position to take over this responsibility, see if they would agree to appoint a local bank's trust department as custodian of their assets. The bank will pay bills and handle account chores, giving your parents spending money each month.

  Without such an arrangement, you could end up hearing some scary comments from your parents. For example: "I don't know where all the money went, dear. We're flat broke, and I don't know what to do!" Or: "Don't worry, honey. That nice neighbor says she'll take care of paying all our bills. We just went down to the bank and added her signature on our checking account." Or: "I just can't stop crying. The guardian the court appointed for me has put my lovely house up for sale, and he says I have to go into a nursing home! Can't you do something, dear?"
- *Don't hesitate to ask for help.* Some basic resources include your county Agency on Aging; the Eldercare Locator (1-800-677-1116), which lists state and local resources where you can get help with Medicare questions and other issues; and the National Association of Professional Geriatric Care Managers (1-520-881-8008 or www.caremanager.org), which provides local referrals. Also see the extensive list of national resources at www.sfgate.com/examiner/caregivers/resources/national.html.

It's hard when the child is parent to the man. But as a caregiver to an ailing mother or father, you have the responsibility to do what's right for yourself, as well as for those who depend on you.

Making contingency plans for your own family

An important part of being financially responsible is making sure your loved ones are taken care of when you're gone. Whether you're single or married, you may think your financial affairs are simple enough not to cause any problems for your heirs. But in these days of longer life expectancy, record-breaking stock market performance, and extended families that may include children and stepchildren by different marriages, it's more important than ever to make sure your assets go where you want them to go, without forfeiting too much to Uncle Sam.

How can you tell if you've done right by your loved ones? Stephan R. Leimberg, a consultant and retired professor of taxation and estate planning in Bryn Mawr, Pennsylvania, suggests conducting a "financial fire drill" every year (with your spouse, if you're married). Imagine you were to die tomorrow—and ask yourself these eight questions.

1. *"Would my loved ones know what to do?"* Prepare a contingency plan that summarizes your assets and debts, along with advice on the best choices for your survivors. (In the next chapter, we'll offer some suggestions on how partners can do this together.) Discuss the plan with your loved ones now, so you can answer any questions they may have. Also, be sure your spouse or executor knows where to locate important records: investments, bank accounts, loans, insurance, pensions, and so on. It can cost thousands of dollars in expenses if estate and financial documents are hard to find.

2. *"Have I left assets to the right people in the right way?"* If you die without a will, your state determines who gets everything you own (as well as who serves as legal guardian for your young children). Even if you hold everything jointly with your spouse and he's the beneficiary on your retirement plan, there are always other assets. And if you favor one child, or want money to go to specific relatives, you'd better have a will to communicate those instructions.

   Take care to bequeath those assets in the most appropriate way, too. For example, if you leave money outright to young children, the kids will receive everything when they reach legal age (eighteen in many states). At that age, it may be a big temptation to blow Mom's and Dad's hard-earned money on a Corvette, gifts for pals, and poorly chosen investments. If you set up a family trust instead, your trustee can dole out the money on a predetermined schedule or use his or her discretion in distributing it to the beneficiaries.

Don't forget to update your will to reflect changes in your family, new tax laws, or a move to another state whose different laws may affect your estate strategy.

3. *"Are my assets properly titled to minimize estate taxes?"* No one but a spouse can inherit unlimited assets free of estate tax (also gloomily known as death tax). But when you own everything jointly, the problem is making sure it doesn't all pile up in the second spouse's estate. For example, suppose John and Jane Doe jointly own $1 million in assets: a house, a retirement plan, life insurance, and an investment portfolio. When John dies, Jane will be sole owner of these assets, with no tax involved. But when Jane dies, her heirs would owe a huge amount of estate tax—close to $125,000 in 2000, for instance.

On the other hand, if your assets are split up and you write your will properly, you'll be able to leave up to $2 million by 2006 to your children or other heirs, free of estate tax. Here's how: When the first spouse dies (assume it's John), assets he owns individually go into a previously set-up trust, up to the currently available tax-free amount. Jane receives all the income from this "bypass" or "credit shelter" trust, and she can draw on the principal if needed. She also directly inherits, free of tax, any of his assets that didn't go into the trust. When she dies, her children receive the remaining funds in the trust and owe estate tax only on any portion of their mother's estate that's over the current exclusion amount.

The estate tax may be abolished someday. In the interim, many in Congress hope to liberalize the amount that can be passed tax free to children and other heirs. As of January 1, 2001, you're subject to the following limits.

Amount That May Be Given or Bequeathed
Free of Federal Estate and Gift Tax
(Lifetime Limit Per Person)

Year of Death or Gift	2001	2002	2003	2004	2005	2006
Tax-Free Amount	$675,000	$700,000	$700,000	$850,000	$950,000	$1 million

4. *"Who will inherit my retirement accounts and life insurance?"* No matter what your will says, the beneficiary will be whomever you've designated in your insurance and retirement plan documents—so make sure they're up to date.

5. *"Will my heirs know what to do with the money?"* Don't expect an inexperienced beneficiary to cope with a sizable investment portfolio, life insurance payout, or retirement plan distribution. If you can't arrange to have distributions made in installments, solutions might include educating your loved ones, leaving them detailed guidelines, or steering them to a financial advisor you trust. In the case of beneficiaries who can't or don't want to manage money, consider establishing a trust for their benefit, with a knowledgeable relative, friend, or financial advisor as trustee.

6. *"Will there be enough cash available to settle the estate, without having to sell assets?"* It can take close to a year to settle even a well-planned estate. If family squabbles or tax disputes complicate the picture, settlement can take four to five years or more. Since your family will need cash for living expenses, and your executor must pay your debts, taxes, and probate and administrative costs, your contingency plan should spell out where this money will come from. Should they cash in certain securities, tap your retirement plan or pension, or use life insurance proceeds?

7. *"Have I chosen an executor who will carry out my wishes fairly and diligently?"* Whom should you name to wind up your affairs and distribute your assets? Estate attorneys suggest choosing someone who's absolutely trustworthy, reasonably intelligent, good with details, and able to take the time to do things right. In other

words, your sister who works seventy hours a week, your uncle who travels all the time, or your ditzy former roommate are probably not good choices.

If you have someone in mind who's unwilling or unable to shoulder this big responsibility, consider asking if he or she would serve as coexecutor with an attorney or a bank or trust company. While this can add to estate costs (allowable executor fees vary by state but can total 5 percent or more of the estate's value), it may prevent family fights about executor bias, as well as expensive or time-consuming mistakes in settlement.

8. *"Have I provided for the unexpected?"* Do you have enough life insurance? Have you designated contingent beneficiaries in your will and in your life insurance and retirement plan documents, in case the primary beneficiary dies before you do? If you have minor children, have you named a guardian and set up a family trust in case you and your spouse are in an accident together? Keep saying to yourself, "What if . . ?" and you may head off big headaches for your heirs.

If your estate plan is simple, you may feel comfortable preparing your own will with a standard form available in stationery stores or with software such as Nolo's Willmaker. But as your finances become more complex, you'll want to have your will drafted by an attorney to be sure it expresses precisely what you want, minimizes income and estate taxes for your beneficiaries, and is legally binding in your state. If you have small children or an estate over the current tax-free amount, a professionally drawn will is a must.

You can expect to pay from $500 or less for a simple will to $2,000 to $4,000 for a more complicated estate plan. (If you're an AARP member, you may want to consider the low-cost option mentioned on page 169.) While your attorney is drawing up your will, it doesn't cost much more to add a power of attorney and a health-care proxy, so that someone you trust can act for you if you're incapacitated. And don't forget a living will, which expresses your wishes regarding life support if you become seriously ill.

This process takes some effort. But aside from the potential tax savings, it could save your loved ones a lot of frustration and anguish later on. And estate planning isn't just about what happens to your money. It's what happens with the people you love.

Insurance for your financial security—and your family's

There's one more extremely important precaution you can take to protect yourself and those you care about: ensuring that your disability or death won't destroy the financial security you've worked so hard to build. Consider this:

You may need life insurance if:
- You have loved ones who depend on you financially.
- It would be expensive to replace the contribution you make as a homemaker.
- Your family's lifestyle and financial plans would suffer drastically if you were gone.

You may need disability insurance if:
- You don't have enough financial resources to see you through three to twelve months of being unable to work.
- You don't have a way to support yourself if disability lasted more than a year.

You may need long-term care insurance if:
- You want to receive quality at-home or nursing-home care if you ever need it.
- You want to protect yourself and your family from the cost of care for a long-term illness or disability.

Admittedly, shopping for insurance isn't most people's idea of fun. Besides focusing on our least favorite subject—our own physical frailty—brochures and policies typically bristle with eye-glazing jargon. Fortunately, some insurers are beginning to catch on to the concept of consumer-friendly communications, but they're hampered by a thicket of regulations from fifty state governments. (By contrast, the mutual-fund industry and national banks are regulated at the federal level.)

Unless you enjoy sinking your teeth into such nitty-gritty stuff as mortality tables and tax rules, it's best to find a trustworthy insurance agent who can discuss your situation with you, then present an integrated solution and explain it thoroughly. Or seek a financial planner who is knowledgeable about insurance, so she or he can deal with your insurance needs (if any) in the context of your total financial picture.

In any case, make sure any insurance you buy is underwritten by a reputable company. All major insurance companies are rated by five independent firms: Standard & Poor's, Moody's, A.M. Best, Duff & Phelps, and Weiss. Your agent can show you these ratings, which measure the insurer's financial strength and potential ability to pay claims in the future. Since you hope it will be many years before the company has to pay out on you, don't choose any insurer rated below Excellent, Superior, or Very Strong.

> **There are two reasons to have life insurance: to create an estate, or protect an estate. But as to what kind you need, each situation has to be looked at individually.**
>
> —CANDI KAPLAN, CFP, head of a financial planning
> and benefits firm in Bethesda, Maryland

HOW TO SHOP FOR LIFE INSURANCE

To see if you really need life insurance (and if so, how much), ask yourself three basic questions.

1. *"Will there be enough cash available to take care of my obligations if I die unexpectedly?"* For a parent, these obligations might include paying off a mortgage as well as putting kids through college. For a business owner, it might mean paying off business debt or funding a buy/sell agreement as part of a succession plan. If these obligations won't otherwise be paid off after your death, a life insurance policy can fill the bill. A single woman with no dependents probably doesn't need any life insurance.

2. *"Will there be a way to replace the support I provide for my family?"* This may not be a problem if you have sufficient investments or other income-producing assets. If not, it makes sense to consider life insurance. For example, a death benefit of $1 million (after tax), invested to produce a 5 percent average rate of return, would generate $50,000 in annual income for your children or other beneficiaries.

Don't forget that caregivers may need life insurance just as much as breadwinners do, as financial planner Candi Kaplan points out. "If you're not around, how much would your husband have to pay to hire people who do what you do?" she asks clients.

3. *"Is my personal net worth (or my joint net worth with my spouse) enough to trigger estate-tax liability?"* Estate tax, charged on assets over a certain amount left to anyone other than a spouse (see chart on page 173), can claim up to 55 percent of your beneficiaries' inheritance. If you elect not to shelter these assets in a trust or give them away, there's an easy way to make sure your beneficiaries won't have to sell the family home or business to pay the IRS: buy an insurance policy to pay the estate tax for them.

Let's say you've decided you need life insurance. The next step is deciding which kind is best for you.

Term life covers you for a certain period—say, the next five, ten, or twenty years. If you die during that time, your beneficiary receives the full death benefit (your policy's face value). If you die a day after the term expires, your beneficiary gets nothing. In that respect, it's just like your car insurance, homeowner's insurance, or health insurance.

So choose term life if you want to be covered for a specific time period. For example:

- You want to be covered until you've paid off the mortgage.
- You want to be covered until your kids are through college.
- You want to be covered until you sell your business at age sixty.
- You want to be covered during your elderly parents' expected lifetimes.

Premiums on a term life policy are generally cheaper than on other kinds of life insurance, allowing you to buy more benefit for the buck. With *level term*, your premium payments stay the same until the term expires. You can usually renew for another term, often with a substantial increase in premiums, or convert to a permanent policy.

Permanent life is term life's big brother. Instead of going away after a certain period, it covers you for the rest of your life (as long the premiums are paid). Permanent life makes sense if:

- You're not sure how long you want to be covered, but it's more than fifteen or twenty years.
- You want to leave money to your beneficiaries, no matter how long you live.
- You want the option of being able to get money out of your policy while you're alive.

While term life works like car insurance, permanent life resembles an investment. As you pay premiums, your policy accumulates a "cash value" you can borrow against—much the same way you can borrow against your home equity with a home equity loan. If you choose not to repay a loan against your cash value, it reduces the amount your beneficiaries will get.

You're also free to cash in all or part of your policy's cash value and use the money for anything you want, including buying an annuity to provide yourself lifetime income. (a nice option if your retirement savings run dry sooner than you thought they would). Or, if you're terminally ill and need cash, you may be able to surrender your policy and receive a *viatical settlement*. This lump sum of cash will be less than the death benefit would have been; but on the other hand, you get to enjoy it during your lifetime.

Not to make things too simple, the insurance industry has thought up three ways to package permanent insurance.

1. *Whole life* is the simplest way to get coverage for a lifetime. The premiums are fixed, and once you've paid them for a certain length of time, the policy is all paid up and stays in effect until you die.
2. *Universal life* lets you change your premium by applying some of your accumulated cash value to it (a move you might make if you were unemployed and needed to conserve cash, for example). You can also modify the death benefit while the policy is in force. The rate of return on your cash value is set by the insurance company.
3. *Variable life* is a hybrid—half insurance, half investment. In this kind of permanent insurance, you get to decide where to invest your cash value, choosing from a selection the insurance company offers. At any given time, your policy's payout value depends on how well your investments are doing.

Our advice: Go with term life if it meets your objectives. If you need permanent life insurance, we like whole life because (a) it's cheaper and (b) you're not tempted to keep tinkering with it. With universal and variable life, you need to be constantly aware of how current market conditions may affect the payout scenario you originally envisioned. If you do buy either of these two forms of permanent coverage, it's a good idea to periodically ask your insurance company for a current projection of the policy's future performance. Then compare this projection against your anticipated needs, to see if you're underfunded. (If you'd rather not handle the evaluation yourself, take your policy projections to a financial planner or independent insurance advisor.)

If you have a life insurance policy whose purpose or potential payout is unclear to you, check it out. Because of potential changes in your needs, your policy's performance, or competitive pricing in the market, it's a good idea for *all* policyholders to review their life insurance every two to four years. But be sure not to switch without a good reason—especially if your agent is compensated for writing new policies. (If you work with a financial planner, she or he can monitor your insurance for you.)

Unfortunately, there's something that could devastate your family's finances even more than your unexpected demise. It's your unexpected disability.

> **If you can't afford to retire now,**
> **you can't afford not to have disability insurance.**
> —Peg Downey, CFP, *a fee-only financial advisor*
> *in Silver Spring, Maryland*

WHY EVERY WOMAN OUGHT TO CONSIDER DISABILITY INSURANCE

Do you provide most or all of your household income? If so, unless you already have disability insurance through your employer, make this coverage a number-one priority.

"If you haven't accumulated much savings, disability insurance may be more important than life insurance," says financial advisor Peg

Downey, "and it's far more pressing than long-term care insurance."
Planner Candi Kaplan agrees: "Disability insurance is critical. Any
woman who doesn't have it really needs to look into it." Here's why.

- If you're thirty-five now, you have a 50 percent chance of being
  disabled for three months or longer before you reach age sixty-
  five. If you're forty-five, the chance is still 44 percent.
- One out of every seven workers will be disabled for five years
  or more before age sixty-five.
- The older you are when you become disabled, the more likely
  it is that you'll remain disabled for five years or more.

Disability insurance replaces income you lose by not being able to
work. Typically, it pays 70 to 80 percent of what you used to earn.
Since it replaces only work income, it's not useful after you retire.
(That's why you may want long-term care insurance as well.)

When you meet with an insurance professional, ask the following
questions about disability insurance choices you're reviewing.

1. *"How is* disability *defined?"* Does it mean you can't perform your
    own job? ("Own occupation" coverage is more costly.) Or that
    you're unable to perform any kind of work?
2. *"Are both accidents and illnesses covered?"* Some policies cover only
    accidents. But the older you are, the more likely it is that any dis-
    ability would be caused by illness.
3. *"Would I be covered only for total disability?"* What if you're par-
    tially disabled?
4. *"Would a significant impairment trigger benefits, even if I can work?"*
    If you lost your sight, hearing, speech, or the use of your limbs,
    would you be paid full benefits?
5. *"What percentage of my income would the maximum benefit re-
    place?"* The more you earn now, the smaller a percentage would
    be replaced by a disability policy's flat monthly payment.
6. *"Would this benefit be adequate?"* Consider not only your present-
    day financial needs, but also your future obligations.
7. *"How long a waiting period can I afford?"* You can commit to wait
    for up to two years after your disability is confirmed before re-
    ceiving benefits. If your emergency fund can keep you afloat for
    a while, this is a way to hold down your premiums.

8. *"How long can (and should) I choose to receive benefits?"* A disability policy will pay only for a period you've specified, which could be from three months to life. While a short benefit period helps keep your premiums low, remember that the biggest threat to your financial security is a disability that lasts several years. Consider choosing to receive benefits until age sixty-five (or your target retirement age).

9. *"What are the policy's renewability rules?"* Noncancelable policies guarantee that your premiums and benefits will never change. Guaranteed renewable policies are automatically renewed with the same benefits, although the premium may increase for your entire class of policyholders. Conditionally renewable policies are renewed only if the insurance company agrees.

10. *"At what point would premiums be waived?"* If you do become disabled, you should be free of having to pay any more premiums after a certain waiting period.

11. *"Can I buy additional coverage later?"* If your income rises, do you have the option of increasing your coverage without having to provide new medical information?

12. *"Is there an inflation adjustment option?"* Without cost-of-living adjustments, the purchasing power of your monthly disability payment could shrink drastically over time. A COLA rider is an expensive option but could be crucial to your quality of life.

If you own a small business, ask about insurance that can pay for office overhead as well as disability benefits. Other options provide benefits while you recover your client base, or pay funds your partner can use to buy you out.

LONG-TERM CARE INSURANCE
CAN PROTECT YOUR SAVINGS IN RETIREMENT

As a woman, your chances of ever needing long-term care are greater than you may think. One out of two women (and one out of three men) will spend some time in a nursing home, according to a 1996 life insurance industry projection.

Long-term care insurance can be a good investment if you don't want your family to worry about taking care of you or your own life savings to be depleted by the cost of a nursing-home stay, at-home

Who Will Protect Your Independence, If You Don't?

If you ever face a long recovery, disability or long-term care insurance could help you stay financially independent—and protect the savings you've worked hard to build.

- *Medical insurance policies won't replace your working income or cover long-term care expenses.*
- *Workers' compensation covers you only if you're injured while working for a covered employer, and benefits are limited.*
- *Social Security disability benefits are modest and hard to get. More than 80 percent of applications are rejected the first time around.*
- *Medicare covers only about 5 percent of total costs for approved, skilled care—and provides no coverage for the custodial care most long-term care patients require. (Medicare Supplement plans, which generally pay only for the copayments and deductibles for Medicare's limited benefits, don't cover long-term care either.)*
- *Medicaid, essentially a health-care welfare program, doesn't take over until you've impoverished yourself—and then your choice of facilities may be severely limited.*
- *Your loved ones may not have the time, energy, or financial resources to care for you over a long period.*

If focusing on your own future makes you a little uncomfortable, remember Dr. Judith Jordan's comment earlier in this chapter: "What you're looking for is to find a balance: to take care of your needs and interests while still taking care of those you love." Insurance is only partly about you. To a greater extent, it's a way for you to look after others.

care, or other long-term health care. Many people also buy it to make sure they'll be able to afford long-term care if they ever need it, instead of being dependent on Medicaid. According to industry sources:

- The odds that you'll use your homeowners insurance are one in eighty-eight (about 1 percent).
- The odds that you'll use your auto insurance are one in forty-seven (about 2 percent).

- The odds that you'll use your long-term care insurance are two in five (40 percent).

The statistics are ominous, all right. A year in a nursing home currently costs about $40,000 (in some parts of the country, it can reach $70,000 or more). And the average stay is two and a half years—which means an average outlay of $100,000 to $175,000. Meanwhile, at-home care can cost $20,000 a year or more. Now the clincher: Health-care costs have historically risen as much as 6 percent faster than inflation, so these numbers could double by 2006! It's been said that long-term care is the single biggest threat to whatever wealth an older person has.

Many women are already aware of this challenge, but few feel prepared to cope with it. In a 2000 survey by the Employee Benefit Research Institute, just 18 percent of women said they were very confident about having enough money to take care of medical expenses in retirement, compared to 31 percent of men.

Different kinds of long-term care policies can cover you for different kinds of care, including home health care, community care (adult day-care facilities), assisted-living facility care, nursing-home care, care coordination services, hospice care, and caregiver training. Here are the ten major questions to ask as you compare policies (ideally with the help of a knowledgeable financial pro).

1. *"How much does it cost?"* The premium amount usually depends on your age (the younger you are when you buy the policy, the less it costs), the length of the benefit period (a policy paying lifetime benefits will be more expensive than one that provides benefits for a limited period), and policy options such as a higher daily benefit, inflation protection, or at-home coverage.

    At the time you buy your policy, you typically lock in your premium at the rate for the age group you're in. For example, if you buy your policy at age fifty-five, you'll continue to pay your insurer's current premium rate for fifty-five-year-olds, even as you get older. However, your premium could change if the rate for fifty-five-year-olds changes.

    You can get a rough idea of annual premium costs from the following chart, which uses information provided by the National

Advisory Council for Long-Term Care Insurance. *Minimal coverage* would pay up to $50 per day for two years at a licensed assisted-living or skilled-care facility, after a 90-day waiting period. No inflation adjustment is provided. *Generous coverage* would pay up to $140 per day in this kind of facility for your lifetime, after a 90-day waiting period. It also covers home health care, and includes a 5 percent annual increase in the daily benefit amount to keep pace with inflation.

Age	Annual Premium for Minimal Coverage	Annual Premium for Generous Coverage
40	$55	$1,300
45	$75	$1,400
50	$80	$1,500
55	$105	$1,700
60	$150	$2,600
65	$220	$3,400
70	$355	$5,000
80	$605	$7,900

For more information, ask your insurance agent for a free copy of *A Shopper's Guide to Long-Term Care Insurance*, published by the National Association of Insurance Commissioners, or call NAIC at 1-816-842-3600 (you may have to pay postage). The AARP Web site also has an excellent article on private long-term care insurance (go to www.aarp.org/confacts/health/privltc.html).

2. *"Is the daily benefit adequate for my anticipated needs?"* The answer depends on the level of nursing-home and other health-care costs in your area, and on how much you'd be able to pay from other resources, such as savings and investments.

3. *"How long would I have to wait before benefit payments start?"* The longer you can afford to pay costs out of your own pocket, the lower your premium will be. Waiting periods range from 0 to 100 days. Make sure you'll only have to go through this period once, even if you're treated for another unrelated problem later on.

4. *"Is renewability guaranteed?"* If so, you'll be able to keep your cov-

erage as long as you pay premiums on time, regardless of your health, age, or claims experience.

5. *"What are the benefit triggers?"* These are the events that cause benefits to start being paid. Make sure benefits will be triggered if you need assistance to perform a minimum of two of the activities of daily living (ADLs), which can include bathing, dressing, eating, toileting, continence, and transferring (that is, moving from a bed to a chair). Another trigger should be cognitive impairment, so that if you need substantial supervision because your awareness and judgment are impaired (as a result of Alzheimer's disease, for example), you'll receive benefits—even if you can take care of yourself physically.

6. *"How is* long-term care *defined?"* A flexible definition can ensure that you'll be covered regardless of the type of care you need—skilled, intermediate, or custodial.

7. *"Is at-home coverage included?"* If your long-term care policy pays only for nursing-home care, it may force you to be institutionalized in order to receive benefits when you could be cared for just as well at home.

8. *"How long can (and should) I receive benefits?"* Less expensive policies cover you for one or two years of care, while costlier policies pay for care as long as it's needed.

9. *"Is inflation protection available?"* This option boosts your daily benefit each year the policy is in effect, without increasing your premium. Many advisors think cost-of-living adjustments are vital if health-care costs continue to rise. If you can't afford an inflation rider, you may want to increase the daily benefit instead.

10. *"Does the policy qualify for tax advantages?"* If it's been designed to meet federal guidelines, you can deduct premiums (with some restrictions) and receive benefits tax-free. Premiums paid for nonqualified policies are not deductible, and benefits may be taxed as ordinary income. The catch is that tax-qualified policies can be more restrictive than nonqualified policies. For example, a doctor may have to certify that you'll be disabled for ninety days. If you recover faster from your illness or injury, you might not receive any benefits. It's best to compare costs and see just how important a tax break might be to you, compared to the risk of getting fewer benefits or none.

That's all we'll say about preparing for these uncomfortable possibilities. The good part is that once you've taken care of yourself in these ways (which means you've indirectly taken care of your loved ones), you'll experience an enormous amount of positive energy, which you can then share with others. You'll feel more solidly grounded, more secure, more peaceful and serene in the knowledge that no matter what happens in this unpredictable world of ours, you can survive and even flourish in the ups and downs of a changing landscape.

This is crucial work—choosing to put yourself first in the essential area of your own financial well-being. If you have children, you will be sending them the message that it's important to take good care of themselves, instead of "giving themselves away" to others in a way that undermines their own sense of security and self-worth. This message is particularly vital for daughters, since girls (especially in their teenage years) are often sorely tempted to give themselves away to boys who "need" them. As your children grow to adulthood, your attitude will also reassure them that you don't intend to cling to them in ways they might find financially and emotionally debilitating.

Be aware that if other people have grown to expect you to keep overgiving to them, they may well be disconcerted by your new practice of taking better care of yourself. In fact, women often worry that the conflict this may create with loved ones, coworkers, or bosses will lead to rejection and abandonment. In the next chapter, we'll address this myth and show you ways to protect your financial well-being in the context of relationships you value.

Two exercises for
guilt-free money management

1. *Find out if old money messages are keeping you down.* To see if you're being influenced by negative money messages you absorbed in your growing-up years, try this exercise. Write at the top of a blank piece of paper, "I need to take care of myself financially, even if it means I can't always give everybody else what they want."

   Under this statement, write down how influential individuals in your early life as well as important people in your life today might comment on it. For example, would your mother say, "Money isn't everything; your family is what's important"? How about Dad? Can you hear him saying, "Don't get obsessed with money—look what it did to Uncle Al and Aunt Martha"? Would your big brother tell you that no one will marry a woman who's pushy and selfish? Add comments from friends and family members (your partner, children, or grandchildren) who might have trouble dealing with this shift in your behavior.

When you identify these messages, write positive ones to counteract them. For instance: "My family benefits when I feel financially secure." Or "My uncle and aunt wanted money so they could lord it over everyone else. My goal is to give myself and my loved ones more peace of mind." As for the comment that guys don't like self-assertive women, you might write, "I don't want any man who's looking for a meek, mousy slave!"

Review these new messages every week during your regular money hour. If possible, read them out loud to encourage yourself to take more positive action with your money.

2. *Visualize yourself having achieved your self-care goals.* Carol Burnett once credited her success in becoming a comedienne to the fact that she could see herself performing on stage in front of an audience. Constantly visualizing this achievement made it possible for her to get there.

Take a few minutes right now to imagine your own success. Visualize yourself having achieved your goal of personal financial security. You're at peace, self-confident, and able to be generous with others without stinting yourself.

If you do this visualization exercise every day for two to four weeks to anchor the vision in your mind and body, you'll be paving the way to get there more quickly and effortlessly. This may sound like voodoo—but it does work!

Where are you now?

To debunk the myth that "it's selfish to put myself first. I'm supposed to take care of everybody else," make it a priority to complete the steps recommended in this chapter.

1. Consider whether you're focused so closely on taking care of other people's needs that you may be failing to look after yourself financially.

2. Determine whether you're a Money Monk, who thinks that paying too much attention to money will corrupt you. If so, look for positive role models who provide well for themselves as well as for society.

3. Explore whether you could apply what you've learned in taking care of others to take better care of yourself. Have you been sabotaging your own efforts because you haven't found the right balance between giving to others and taking care of yourself?

4. Make sure you have goals for yourself. If it's difficult to think of any, describe your ideal day and see what needs and desires emerge. Avoid postponing deeply felt dreams.

5. If you're finding it hard to make self-care a priority, jot down a list of the bad things that might happen if you addressed your own needs. Then see if you can think of creative solutions to these potential problems.

6. Commit to contributing the maximum amount allowed to a tax-favored retirement plan. If you don't have access to an employer-sponsored plan, set one up yourself.

7. Review the possibilities of socially responsible investing, and decide whether it's important to you. If so, find out more about suitable investments.

8. If you want to help relatives or favorite causes, be sure your gifts or strategies tie in with your overall financial plan or estate plan.

9. If you have children's college expenses to prepare for, decide how—and how much—you can save without putting your own future security at risk.

10. Help your parents prepare better for the future. If they need your assistance, be sure you understand their financial situation, and don't hesitate to get experienced help if necessary.

11. Make sure you've planned for your loved ones to be taken care of after you're gone. Prepare or update your will, and consider whether you need life insurance. If appropriate, see your financial advisor, attorney, or insurance agent.

12. Decide whether disability insurance and/or long-term care coverage could help you protect your financial security and prevent you from being a burden on your children. If so, consult a knowledgeable financial advisor to help you put together a plan that suits your goals.
13. If negative money messages are discouraging you, write down positive ones to counteract them. Visualize yourself being financially secure and generous to others.

Being responsible for yourself isn't selfish. It's the very best thing you can do for your own inner serenity. In fact, there's no more appropriate way to put this myth to rest than with the simple phrase you hear all the time: *Take care.*

> **I tell my women clients, "Your primary responsibility is to take care of yourself—and the people you're worried about are going to be most appreciative that you won't become dependent on them."**
>
> —PEG DOWNEY, CFP, *a fee-only financial advisor in Silver Spring, Maryland*

CHAPTER SIX

Myth 6:
"If I Take Charge of My Money, I'll Antagonize Others and Might End Up Alone"

I see women all the time who think that if they're good with handling money and have developed a net worth of their own, they won't be attractive to men.

—JJ JAMISON, *a CFP*
in Colorado Springs

* * *

A great number of women worry that if they seem too financially competent, they'll turn off the men in their lives—their husbands, boyfriends, fathers, bosses. Consciously or unconsciously, they often fear that becoming knowledgeable about money will lead to unresolvable conflict and eventually to being alone.

This fear affects how many of us interact with men about money, to the point where we may even sabotage our own potential for success. For example, a business coach told us that when she asks women who feel they've reached a plateau in their careers, "Why are you stuck? What's the payoff for you in being stuck?" she frequently hears them express vivid anxieties about advancing farther and making more money. For example:

- "I might lose my husband."
- "I might turn into a first-class bitch."
- "My husband might not be able to handle it."
- "I'm afraid I wouldn't like who I became if I got that successful."

The belief that financial competence and success will change us into someone unlovable is the most pervasive and powerful of the seven money myths, according to Marianne Walters, a renowned feminist family therapist and codirector of the Women's Project in Family Therapy. In fact, Walters believes that when women say "Money is too complicated for me to understand," it's often a smokescreen hiding their fear of this powerful and emotionally charged myth. According to Walters, "There is a terrible fear that if you appear too competent, you'll lose the opportunity to have a man take care of you."

The sad result is that for generations women have pretended not to be too competent with money, stayed powerless, and even ruined their own opportunities to become financially successful, in order to avoid threatening or scaring off men—or provoking their rage. As a result:

- *We downplay what we do know.* Women are only one-fourth as likely as men to see themselves as experts in financial matters, according to a study by the National Center for Women and Retirement Research.
- *To avoid doing the wrong thing, we often do nothing.* A Prudential study reports that women are much more likely than men to put off financial decisions due to fear of making a mistake, and to say that lack of knowledge keeps them from being more involved in financial planning.
- *We don't take credit for our successes—only our failures.* Financial planners tell us that if a woman investor loses money, she blames herself. If she makes money, she credits her advisor or good luck. By contrast, men take full credit for their own financial successes and blame their advisor or the market for their losses.

Connection with others is a primary value for women, says Judith Jordan, a codirector of the Jean Baker Miller Training Institute at Wellesley College and professor of psychiatry at Harvard University. Jordan notes that "individuation, autonomy, self-sufficiency are all values of the dominant group of our culture—men."

"What we women do really well in—the really important values like caring, nurturing, et cetera—are just not valued," agrees Martha Moyer, LCSW, BCD, a psychotherapist specializing in the psychology of money. But far from being an abnormality, both professionals say, the high priority women place on being connected is a wonderful quality. "It's a strength, something to be valued and celebrated," Jordan says. "And our culture needs this particular strength."

Women have internalized the belief that "if I get too good at taking charge of my money, I'll have more conflict or end up alone." Women who believe this are not "wrong" or deficient; it's the message they've gotten from our culture.

—JUDITH JORDAN, Ph.D., coauthor of Women's Growth in Connection

---

In fact, women's proven gifts for empathizing with customers and colleagues, facilitating discussion, and smoothing conflict are becoming sought-after qualities in the workplace. *Fortune* magazine predicts: "As peer-reviewed research affirms that female managers typically display these virtues more consistently than men, project team leadership will shift." And international human potential advocate Dr. Jean Houston remarked to us that in her travels, she's become accustomed to seeing women business leaders manage tasks and relationships on several levels at once—for example, simultaneously overseeing a budget discussion, noticing that someone has been left out and bringing that person back into the flow, and proposing trade-offs to make the numbers balance.

But in other parts of our society, Judith Jordan notes, "women are made to feel deviant for being more geared toward connection, more involved in caring about other people and developing growth-fostering relationships."

In fact, the threat of disconnection is one of the most terrible consequences we can imagine. And the signals we receive from men often suggest that if we challenge them by doing better than they do, they will avoid us or withdraw from us. Jordan concludes that the fear of being alone if we become too competent "is probably one of the most immobilizing myths of all!" because of its roots in reality.

We wholeheartedly agree that women's desire to feel connected to loved ones, family, coworkers, community, and larger causes is a necessary and positive quality. It definitely does *not* mean that women who prize connection (or need it) are too emotional, too needy, too dependent, or in any other way defective.

To help overcome the fear that financial competence will lead to disconnection and abandonment, you'll see in this chapter how to build on your strengths and enlist the support of those you care for. But let's be frank: For many women, learning to take care of yourself in this way may mean getting over a lifelong dread of conflict.

If your partner has always made and/or controlled most of the money, there's often no way to avoid rocking the boat when you begin to take on more financial responsibility. Says psychotherapist Harriet Lerner, author of *The Dance of Intimacy*, "You will begin to see yourself and your partner with greater clarity, and you'll be called upon to negotiate important differences regarding your values, wants, and beliefs. But money aside, this is the central challenge in marriage anyway. So it's better to jump in and get involved." As long as there's goodwill and open communication in your relationship, sharing money decisions can eventually make you feel closer to each other and more like true partners.

The Issue Isn't Just Empowerment. It's Financial Security

Fear of conflict keeps many women in the dark about their money—often to their great regret later on. One of the threads that ran through several of our interviews was the rude awakening many women encountered when they realized that their partners weren't as good a financial decision maker as they had thought or hoped.

At a therapy workshop, a woman we'll call Paula said ruefully, "It took me years to realize that my husband was a lousy money manager. Until we were nearly bankrupt, it was a struggle to get him to admit this and to let me handle our finances. Now I've been doing it for years, and we both acknowledge that I'm much better at it than he ever was.

"I could kick myself for staying in the dark about this for so long! If I'd woken up sooner, we'd have a lot more saved for retirement by now. But I know self-recrimination doesn't help, so I try to give it up and focus on the progress we've made since I took over keeping track of our money."

> **Any time one member of a couple gets more
> independent, self-sufficient, and autonomous, it breaks
> the pattern and makes waves—at least for a while.**
>
> —*Peg Downey, CFP, a fee-only financial advisor
> in Silver Spring, Maryland*

Eminent family therapist Betty Carter, author of *Love, Honor, and Negotiate,* often says that when it comes to relationships, money, and power, the "golden rule" prevails: "He who gets the gold makes the rules."

In most cases, this deck is already stacked in men's favor. On average, they're paid more than women for the same work; and even though more women today meet or exceed their partner's income, the husband still earns more than the wife in most couples households.

Complicating the picture is men's conditioning toward competitiveness and success. Both literally and figuratively, they're brought up to be on top. As sociolinguist Deborah Tannen has eloquently pointed out, this socialization makes many men see relationships as one-up/one-down—not the best prescription for a healthy and intimate marriage.

So in most relationships where a woman has previously surrendered money-management and investment decisions to her partner, any attempt to change this pattern is bound to shake things up. Initially, the partner may feel threatened by a request to give up some of his power in making major financial decisions. But once he weathers the storm of watching the relationship change in a way that is out of his control, he often experiences a profound sense of relief at no longer having to carry all the responsibility by himself. In many families, husbands actually feel burned out by years of shouldering the burden of money management. Once they adjust to the change, they welcome the opportunity to share it or even give it up for a while.

Even seemingly unlikely husbands may champion their wives' desire to learn more and share in financial decision making. For instance, Becky Berube and Robin Klee are both married to hockey players—guys who stereotypically enjoy such macho exploits as ramming into opponents with little or no provocation and knocking out defenders' bicuspids on the way to the goal. Certainly, no one would characterize professional hockey players Craig "Chief" Berube and Ken Klee (coincidentally, a finance major in college) as wimps. But on the home front, say Becky and Robin, both men are extremely supportive of their wives' interest, education, and empowerment. We hear there's even an investment club composed primarily of hockey wives. (You go, girls!)

In short, don't assume that your mate won't give up financial control simply because of what he does for a living. Whether he's a doctor, plumber, or truck driver, you need to look at your own dynamics to work out a way to share financial knowledge and power—a key ingredient for full, satisfying intimacy in a relationship.

> **I've never met a man who isn't threatened by a woman who makes more money than he does. I think they do exist, but the majority of men do feel it as a threat. Because the truth is, if women don't need men economically, then they have to be pretty great for us to want to be with them.**
>
> *—A female senior executive at a national financial firm*

One success story is that of emergency-room nurse Terry Forbes. When Terry was first married, she thought her husband, a doctor, knew much more about money than she did. But soon enough, she told us, "I discovered that neither of us knew very much. Money hadn't been talked about in our families."

This revelation prompted Terry to forge ahead. At first convinced that money matters were complicated and time-consuming, she was delighted by the ease of using money-management software. "I put our finances on Quicken three years ago while I was completing a family nurse practitioner degree and a master's in nursing," she explained. "I realized that I really enjoyed managing the money and learning more about it—and was better at it than he was."

Terry's software-based spending plan helps her feel comfortable about their finances: "Putting everything on Quicken makes it easy to track, and it's hard to deny where the money is going." With the income her new career is bringing in, she is out of credit-card debt and has extra money to invest.

> Since I'm already in my forties, I am concerned about retirement. But I feel confident about it. I have common sense and intuition, and will use all the available resources to thoroughly investigate my choices.
>
> At first, my husband was uncomfortable with the change. But I just stuck to the facts—we're out of debt, we're saving money, and we both feel better and more in control.
>
> Empowerment makes me feel freer, and I want to role-model this for my kids. Besides, I don't want to be dependent on anyone and run the risk of ending up divorced with nothing. In fact, I believe that for a wife *not* to manage the money is very stressful on her, her partner, and their marriage, especially since women are the major purchasers in most families.

What prompted Terry Forbes's transformation into a woman who is truly self-caring and confident in her financial competence? She just decided that she could do it. "I began to attend 'women empowerment' lectures and workshops, and read everything I could find," she said. "Once I believed I could do everything just as well as my husband, or anyone else, I began to do a better and better job of managing my family, home, and career. Even though I was naturally managing these things all along, until I believed I could do it well, I didn't take full responsibility or credit for my success and skills."

"The power relationship changed": Lynn Rivers's sobering story

Lynn Rivers, U.S. representative from Michigan, confessed that when she first ran for election she was warned that "getting more attention and making more money" might cause her husband to leave her. At the time, Rivers laughed it off. "I said, 'You don't know my husband. If I start making a hundred and thirty-seven thousand dollars a year, I couldn't get rid of him with dynamite!' I told that story over and over, and I believed it. Right up until he left me."

Rivers and her husband were high-school sweethearts. An auto worker, he supported her through law school and cared for her during bouts of manic-depressive illness. With her condition under control, Rivers made her successful bid for Congress, where she was publicly recognized for her integrity. Several years into this remarkable career, still thinking everything was fine, she found herself suddenly single.

"I think it's easy for women to assume that their accomplishments and success aren't affecting the relationship," Representative Rivers says now. "Most people spend the first part of their marriage hoping and planning for success. So they expect that when it comes, no matter who it happens to, it'll be wonderful. But that assumption could be wrong."

Ironically, one clue that things weren't right was her growing sense that she needed to give up financial power to her husband. "Even though he wasn't particularly good at money, I let him deal with it," she recalls. "Sometimes when the relationship gets shaky, women will give more and more financial decision-making authority to men, to pump them up."

After an "amicable" divorce, Rivers has started reclaiming her money power. "Retirement is something I'm finally beginning to plan for," she notes with satisfaction.

When a man feels threatened by his partner's success, is there a way to lessen the chance of such a drastic outcome? Representative Rivers advises: "My experience would say that as women become more and more successful, they need to deal with the potential problem. The minute the power relationship changed between us, we should have been in therapy. We needed to talk about it, deal with the feelings, and basically renegotiate our relationship."

How to turn potential conflict into cooperation

To make a shift in financial power less threatening to your mate, it's best to introduce change slowly, gently, and patiently. We recommend beginning with a suggestion that you take on one or two activities that your partner (or another family member or financial advisor) has handled on his own up to now. For example, you might propose taking turns in managing the checkbook and paying bills. Or if you're thinking of borrowing money for home improvements or debt consolidation, volunteer to do some research to find out the best rates and terms.

Here's how you might approach this important step:

First, identify one or two aspects of your moneylife that you'd like to begin taking charge of (or at least become more knowledgeable about). Figure out in advance exactly what you want to start doing and how.

Next, rehearse a conversation with your financial partner about the new actions you'd like to take. Make sure you communicate that you don't distrust him but simply need to empower and entrust yourself with more financial responsibility. You might tell him that since studies show most women live longer than men, you want to begin learning more about money now so you won't worry about being left helpless if something should happen to him. If you're anxious about how this discussion might go, write down (for yourself only) what you fear happening; then think through how you'll handle it if it does occur.

Last, set a time to have this conversation. Make it a time when you and your financial partner are fairly relaxed, not stressed over bill payments or other money issues. You might set the stage by saying something like this: "I've been realizing lately that it's not fair to make you carry the full burden of managing our money and planning for our future. So I'd like to come on board with you as a fuller partner where our money is concerned."

If your partner says, "It's no problem; I enjoy doing it," don't back down. Insist, "This is important to me for my own self-respect and sense of security, in case anything should happen to you. It will help me feel more competent about money and more confident in my ability to deal with it. And I do want to see if I can make things a little easier for you by sharing some of the responsibility. I'd like to set a time to talk about this together in the next few days."

Once the conversation actually takes place, begin with a "warm start" by sharing something you appreciate about your partner's financial ability (or his strength in another realm, if nothing comes to mind financially). Here's how this dialogue might go:

> You: *First of all, I want to tell you how much I appreciate all the time and effort you take to [provide for us/manage our investments/keep our retirement plan on track/etc.]. It's helped me feel secure enough to focus on [the children/my career/other aspects of our life together].*
>
> He: *Thanks. I don't mind doing it, but sometimes it's hard to stay on top of everything.*

> You: I can imagine. You know, it really opened my eyes re-
> cently to find out about the death of [a married male
> friend/celebrity/so many of my classmates' husbands/
> etc.]. I can't help thinking about what happens to
> women who are left totally in the dark about money, in-
> vesting, and insurance. They have to learn how to keep
> themselves financially secure at the same time that
> they're trying to deal with the shock of a dreadful loss. I
> don't want to be one of them! So I have some ideas
> about how I can start learning more and sharing the
> burden you've been carrying by yourself. I'm hoping
> you'll be open to this change and help me take on some
> of this responsibility. Will you?

If your partner is at all willing, then propose the actions you'd like to take. Don't flood him with too many suggested changes all at once; you don't want to bite off more than you can chew. One or two will be plenty to start with. Here's how you might introduce these suggestions (inserting your own desired activities, of course):

> You: Jane Smith, a financial planner here in town, is spon-
> soring a seminar next Tuesday evening on Women and
> Money. Would you mind looking after the kids so I can
> go?
> He: Uh, sure. I don't see why not.
> You: Great. I'm really looking forward to what I can learn
> from her. Also, I'd love to sit down with you for an hour
> or so every week or two and start finding out more about
> our money. How about Saturday mornings?
> He: Fine, I guess. But are you sure you want to get into all
> this?
> You: I know it's not smart to keep sticking my head in the
> sand. And I really want us to share more of the burden
> together.

Keep a notebook of questions and answers during this mentoring process. Your memory may not be reliable, especially if you subconsciously believe that forgetting will somehow ensure your partner's continued presence to steer you.

If you suspect your husband isn't doing a good job as a money manager, consider taking a somewhat different tack in this conversation. Since hitting the issue head-on will make him feel criticized, defensive, and inadequate, you'll need to be sensitive and gentle while suggesting an approach like the following:

> You: *I've been reading a lot about financial planners lately. There seem to be a lot of advantages in getting an overview of our situation from an expert who can address all our financial concerns, from soup to nuts, besides being up to date on tax laws and other issues.*
>
> He: *No way, honey. Those guys are always calling up with hot ideas—buy this, sell that. I can do it all for free.*
>
> You: *That's why I'd want to go to a planner who charges fees, not commissions. And they're more objective than we are. It really wouldn't hurt to have a second opinion on how we're doing versus our retirement goals—and discuss things you've been clipping articles about, like long-term care.*
>
> He: *Hmm. Well . . .*
>
> You: *There's another advantage, too. I really want to learn more about money management, and it could be easier to learn from somebody who does it all the time. I'd like to get the names of some good planners in our area and call on one or two. It shouldn't cost much, if anything, for a get-acquainted visit. Let's go together, okay?*

If your partner insists that he's been doing a great job and demands to know why you would need an expert when he's so good with finances, respond patiently along these lines: "This has nothing to do with how good you are. Even doctors consult other doctors, and therapists go to other therapists. It's important for my own comfort level and peace of mind to talk to somebody who's trained to look at the big picture. Won't you do this for both of us?"

If you're particularly concerned about upsetting your partner, consider a more vulnerable approach rather than an aggressive one. For example, you might say: "Honey, I'm anxious about something, and I need you to be patient and gentle in discussing it with me. Can you agree to try to do this?"

Sharing your fears upfront in this way makes it easier for your mate to be generous in defusing them. If you're fortunate, he'll be as loving, nurturing, and unthreatened as Anne Slepian's partner, Christopher Mogil. As we saw in chapter 1, Anne was initially overwhelmed and bored by the details of money management. But once Christopher took the lead in patiently coaching her, she got on board little by little. Now she finds learning about financial affairs worthwhile and more interesting than she ever expected.

But even with the most supportive mate in the world, it's a good idea to look around for other ways to polish your money skills. A seminar given by a financial planning firm may be a wonderful place to start. Consider adult education or community college courses, too. A women-only investment club can help build your confidence, and regular scanning of personal-finance magazines will keep you updated on new strategies and financial choices. (Also, see the appendix for our guide to some of the best books about money.)

The ideal solution is one that not only works for your particular relationship but also helps you take care of yourself. One woman we interviewed said that she gave her husband complete charge of their money so he would let her have total autonomy in her career. As she put it, "He respects my domain, and I respect his." Though not uncommon, this approach can be dangerous. Unless you're sure your partner has made the right financial moves, an impressive title on your business card won't guarantee your security if you're suddenly alone.

Instead, try to work out "domains" that allow you both to feel financially empowered, while still depending on each other. For example, Lori Smith, higher education operations director of Dell Computer, has a great idea: "I'm saving for my retirement now," she says, "so that if and when I marry and have children, I can stay at home and raise them while my husband works. He'll take care of our present needs, while I'll have taken care of the future." Even if she stops contributing later on, this smart woman's retirement savings will keep growing year after year, thanks to compound interest.

Financial writer and editor Grace Weinstein observes, "What happens with many couples is that the woman will do the day-to-day checkbook management, and the man will do the longer-term investment decisions." But it can be risky, she believes, for women to focus only on the "small stuff" and remain in the dark about bigger financial decisions. Both partners should sit down together and look over their entire financial picture monthly or quarterly, with an annual review to see how their situation has changed since last year.

Washington Post business columnist Michelle Singletary seems at first glance to take a traditional view about male/female roles. "In our family, he [her husband, Kevin] is the head of the household," she says. "I defer to him a lot about the little details, since there isn't a third person to break the tie." But when it comes to major choices, such as those involving money, her views are thoroughly modern and egalitarian. "We have a rule for important decisions: We both have to agree. If either one of us disagrees, we keep talking about it, working on it, and coming toward the middle until we both can say yes."

Among Michelle's guidelines for sharing financial power with her partner:

- *Talk to each other regularly.* "We constantly communicate," she says. "We don't store stuff up. Like any married couple, we have our issues, but we work them out."
- *Decide what's really worth fighting for.* She notes, "Professional women tend to fight over every little thing. We need to choose our battles more intelligently."
- *Don't belittle your mate.* "There's a way to discuss things that doesn't make him feel emasculated. Women need to be sensitive about this." For instance, instead of saying, "Listen, I've been researching this, so I know more about it than you do," phrase it this way: "I've been doing a lot of reading and thinking about this, and I'd like to get your viewpoint on what I've found."
- *What are important are core values, not behaviors.* Michelle's husband is more comfortable than she is with spending money. ("He's the one who has to start working on me when we need a new car," she says.) They're opposite personality types, too: "I sometimes laugh and cry at the drop of a hat, and he's patient and methodical and calm. But," she concludes, "when it comes to deeper values—to put our family first, save, and be secure in our future—we're definitely in sync."

So even if you're in a traditional relationship with a partner whose approach to money is quite different from yours, take heart. As Michelle's story makes clear, you can work it out if you're both open to making it work.

By the way, no matter how great your relationship is, your partner probably *does* have a different money personality than you do. One of Olivia's trademark sayings is "If opposites don't attract right off the bat—and they usually do—they'll end up in opposite places eventually." (Her workshop participants dubbed this adage *Mellan's Law.*)

In this dance of opposites, you have a big advantage: As a naturally empathetic woman, you're better prepared to take the lead in working toward mutual agreement. It's ironic that when women use subtle ways to get their men to take action, they're sometimes labeled "manipulative." The positive way to look at this is that a woman's emotional sensitivity to her mate often helps her know just how and when to talk to him to minimize defensiveness and create a climate for real progress.

> **I think the bigger issue is how men deal with powerful women, because money is a stand-in for power. Men and women have different comfort levels in handling power.**
> —KAREN GROSS, *a professor of law at New York Law School*

As you already know, what's at stake here isn't really money—it's who calls the financial shots. Research has shown that when men make most of the money, they typically feel they should make the decisions. Some men find it more difficult than others to accept their partner's right to financial equality, because it means giving up this power.

By contrast, women who make more than their partners usually share financial decision making, which tends to prevent ruffled feathers. Many men who could otherwise accept earning less can't handle being one-down when it comes to their "money power." For example, we heard of one husband who got so upset with his higher-paid wife for making all the financial decisions that he retaliated in a time-honored way . . . by withholding sex.

When you earn more than he does

In this progressive day and age, you might expect that when women earn more than their partners, it would be no big deal. Unfortunately, that's seldom the case.

Many women have a tremendous amount of inner turmoil about acknowledging their financial power and authority. Even women who consider themselves otherwise highly liberated are prone to this insecurity. In fact, one of our most bizarre discoveries was that many women who were willing to share with us that they earned more than their husbands (and insisted on how comfortable their spouses were with the imbalance) then asked us not to mention this fact in the book!

Journalist and author Linda Ellerbee explains that these women are reflecting society's increasingly outdated perceptions of a "normal" relationship: "If a woman marries a man who earns more money than she does and who is well known in his work, everyone congratulates her for making a good choice. But if she makes more money and is well known in her field, they ask him how he copes with it—which implies it's an unnatural situation. Even some really good men eventually start to think that it must be a problem."

Married four times, Ellerbee says, "In every case I made more money than he did." She is now CEO of a TV production company co-owned with her partner, Rolfe Tessem. One reason that their personal relationship works so well, she believes, is that Rolfe (who is younger by several years) grew up in "a different world" from her ex-spouses. "He wanted an equal partner," she explains, "because he was raised by an independent woman who worked."

Unfortunately, many men these days aren't so enlightened—which leaves many higher-earning women in an awkward position.

"Women are still expected to take care of men's egos," says Sharon Rich, president of a Boston-area financial planning firm specializing in women's issues. "Men feel good partly from feeling better than their partners. If a man is disappointed with how much money he makes compared to his peers, at least he can feel good that he's making more than his wife." She adds:

Many men in our culture use money to define masculinity. Because they can't prove themselves today by hunting, they need the financial proof of their manhood, which puts a lot of pressure on them. Men with less money often feel less masculine.

I work with several client couples where the woman is a highly successful professional and the man is pursuing his hobby, such as woodworking or trying to develop a business concept. These women are careful not to be critical of the man's pursuits, and their relationship is certainly more stressful and not as comfortable as when the roles are reversed.

Also, it's a rare husband who can feel comfortable taking care of the kids while Mom is out doing a traditional job. In most situations, couples have full-time child care, even though the man is available [to look after the children].

It can take maturity for both a wife and a husband to overcome their expectations of the man as primary provider, as Azriela Jaffe discovered. In addition to running her own firm as a business coach, Azriela is the prolific author of several books, a syndicated columnist, and the mother of three young children. She told us:

I thought I was liberated and mature enough to be the main breadwinner. So when my husband quit his job two weeks before our honeymoon to start his own business, leaving us to live on my fifty-thousand-dollar-a-year income, I figured I could adjust to it without feeling angry.

But it almost destroyed our marriage. He couldn't tolerate not bringing in money for a period of time, and I couldn't tolerate my anger and my fear that the man I had married was not able to care for me financially. I wanted him to be my knight.

I did *not* like that about me.

Now, several years later, both Azriela and her husband are a little older and wiser. "I'm now comfortable with saying that I'm willing to be the main breadwinner," she said. "My husband has *no* ego problems whatsoever with my becoming wildly famous, successful, and wealthy, so that he can quit work, retire, and garden full-time before the age of fifty. He feels secure enough that he doesn't have to prove himself to me or anyone else, and he's good at being home with our children."

Azriela ended her story by saying, "I want us both to be happy and fulfilled, and I want my husband to live a long life. I think that men's 'provider' burden compromises their health and longevity."

If you're outearning your partner, how do you feel about it? Like Azriela early in her marriage, many women who earn more than their mates feel uneasy—even guilty—about financially outshining them. Husbands in this position often feel humiliated or ashamed to be the lower wage earner. Sometimes both partners are uncomfortable with the disparity; but even if only one of you is troubled, you both need to address the issue.

> **Women are taught the rules: Don't be too smart, strong, powerful, successful. . . . I have clients in their late thirties and forties who are getting economically successful, and their mothers say to them, "This is really a problem for your marriage. You have to be careful how you deal with this. Don't put it right in your husband's face." It's a very, very powerful immobilizer and inhibitor.**
>
> —JUDITH JORDAN, PH.D., *coauthor of* Women's Growth in Connection

Let's say you're careful to make all major money decisions together with your partner. If it still bothers either of you that you earn more than he does, what can you do about it?

As Representative Lynn Rivers suggests, the first thing you need to do is discuss it. Be as tactful as you can in broaching the subject, remembering that your mate may find it humiliating to admit shame, resentment, or frustration about earning less. If you feel embarrassed or guilty about making more money than he does, a good way to begin is to share your own feelings in a vulnerable and nonattacking way, then gently ask how he feels about the disparity. For example, you might say something like "I feel bad about admitting this, but sometimes I feel uncomfortable that I make more than you do. Does it bother you sometimes, too?"

This discussion won't be easy, given the emotions that may be swirling around the issue. But avoiding it could cause negative feelings to fester and bubble up in unexpectedly nasty ways. For example, your partner may attack you one day for spending too much on gifts, instead of admitting how much it bothers him that he doesn't feel free to buy as lavishly. Or if he brings home a big-ticket item that he bought on his own, you may lash out at him for not consulting you, perhaps even blurting out that it's your hard-earned money he's spending without your approval. By talking things out, you can prevent a great deal of hostility from exploding somewhere down the line.

"WHY AREN'T YOU PRINCE CHARMING?"

The situation is more difficult when a woman resents her partner for making less than she does. In her view, he's shirking his responsibility to be the prime breadwinner, or at least to share the load equally with her. If you're in this situation, try to get past the traditional "I'm your wife, you should take care of me" stereotype to see if he's contributing as much as you are (or more) in other ways. For example, he might be a Mr. Mom, tending the kids so you can bring home the bacon, or a Mr. Fixit, happy to renovate the kitchen, tune up the cars, and build on the sunroom you wanted. Enumerate (for yourself at first) all the ways he enhances the quality of your life and your family's life.

Then, if you still feel the burden is unequal, continue talking with your mate about what bothers you. If you do this with sensitivity to his feelings, he may well be receptive to brainstorming some solutions that will help defuse your resentment—for example, taking over certain tasks to save you time or money. However, if you find you can't talk about this issue without getting into a heated and hurtful argument, you may want to visit a therapist or family counselor to help resolve your conflict.

"WHY CAN'T *I* STAY HOME AND WRITE POETRY?"

A woman may also resent a partner who pursues some low-paid dream or passion (e.g., painting or studying) while she slaves away at an unpleasant job in order to pay the bills. To put this in perspective, ask yourself how you'd feel if the roles were reversed. Would your partner be okay with supporting you? And if so, for how long?

If you feel your resentment is justified, a conversation with your mate is essential. Try to reach mutual agreement on how long you'll bankroll his dream before expecting him to start carrying his fair share of the financial load. Six months? One year? Two years? Knowing that there will be a limit to this inequality can go a long way toward resolving your difficulty with it.

In the meantime, if your partner is bringing home at least some money, you may feel less resentful if both of you pool a portion of your income to pay household costs, while keeping the rest in separate accounts that each of you can control. For example, one woman explained that to compensate for earning twice as much as her husband, she put twice as much as he did into a kitty for monthly expenses. "Once I put the money in, neither of us thinks about the disparity anymore," she told us. A woman in a similar situation added, "Contributing to a household 'pot' leaves me more money to spend on other things I feel are important."

Our grandmothers or mothers might have counseled, "If you earn more than he does, don't let him know." But we firmly believe that this kind of secrecy is unhealthy for a relationship. When there is goodwill, love, and open communication, it's usually possible to work out any underlying fears, myths, or frustrations, and arrive at a mutually respectful acceptance of the difference between your paychecks.

When you earn much less than your mate

If you bring in less than your spouse, proportional payment of household expenses can help both of you feel like equal partners. For ex-

---

Five Tips to Help Resolve Conflict
When You Earn More Than He Does

1. *Find an unpressured time to discuss how each of you feels about your income difference. Don't bring it up when you're upset or in a financial crisis.*
2. *Brainstorm creative ways to lessen the sting of the financial imbalance.*
3. *Consider contributing prorated amounts to a pot for household expenses, emergencies, and savings. Readjust your contribution ratios once a year, or more often if your financial circumstances change.*
4. *Commit to shared decision making, no matter who makes more money.*
5. *If you're supporting your spouse while he pursues a dream, agree on a specific date when the balance will begin to shift back.*

---

ample, Liz Lerman, founder and artistic director of the Liz Lerman Dance Exchange, told us:

> When I first met Jon, we kept all our money separate and paid into a joint account proportional to our incomes. Every year we rechecked those proportions. Jon made significantly more, and he was generous about this setup.
>
> Eight years later, when our daughter was born, we merged our money. I always pay for the groceries and her clothes and my own stuff; he pays for other household expenses. This year, I just started a private savings account for things I want to do for myself and my family.

Liz's strong relationship with her husband, Jon Spelman, made it easy to evolve this respectful, egalitarian money-management strategy. But without a feeling of equal partnership, it's easy for lower-paid women to feel powerless.

As therapy pioneer and author Olga Silverstein puts it, "Generosity is not the same as equality." (Silverstein herself earned a high-school diploma and college degree in her late forties to avoid feeling "beholden" to her husband, to whom she has now been married for over fifty-eight years.)

Family therapist Betty Carter says that whenever she was making much less than her husband, or vice versa, the lower earner would feel disenfranchised. It wasn't that the higher earner would treat the other one badly, she explains. Instead, the lower earner simply began denying himself or herself things, feeling that because he or she wasn't making enough money they were undeserved.

If you make less than your partner, this could be happening to you. Even though your mate may not care that you're contributing less income to the household, are you denying yourself the right to financial power because you think you don't deserve it? In particular, are you a mother who feels ashamed of not bringing home a paycheck because you stay home to raise your children—perhaps the most valuable job in *any* society?

If so, take some time to talk to other women who do acknowledge and value the contribution that they're making to their family and the larger community. And discuss with your partner the need for money of your own to reflect the worth of your efforts.

Getting Fair Compensation If You're a Stay-at-home Wife

In 1998, the world of company wives was forever shaken up by Lorna Wendt. After her thirty-two-year marriage to the CEO of GE Capital broke up, Wendt demanded half of her soon-to-be ex's estimated $100-million net worth, plus her fair share of the deferred compensation (stock options and pension benefits) he'd earned during their marriage.

At issue wasn't whether she "needed" all this money. She clearly could have maintained a comfortable lifestyle on much less. Her point was that money is a way of keeping score—the perspective endorsed by many high earners like her husband, Gary—and she felt her efforts in helping him rise to the top merited as high a score as his did.

"If marriage isn't a partnership between equals," she told Fortune magazine, "then why get married? If you knew that some husband or judge down the road was going to say, 'You're a 30% part of this marriage, and he's a 70% part,' would you get married?"

When the dust settled, Wendt didn't end up with half, but she did fare much better than if she'd accepted the modest settlement her spouse had originally offered. She also sent a signal to stay-at-home wives everywhere that the days are past when a divorcing husband would automatically keep most of the assets and the wife would get an alimony check—which would usually stop if she remarried, leaving nothing to show for the years invested in her first marriage.

"How did the two of you arrive at the decision that you would be the one to stay home and take care of the children?" asks therapist Betty Carter. "What skills and abilities made you the logical choice for this position?" And what's the monetary value of the cooking, cleaning, shopping, child care, entertaining, traveling, charity work, household management, and other chores you do while your partner brings home a paycheck?

You may be surprised. Only in nine states are the assets you've accumulated together considered to be owned equally by you and your spouse. (These nine "community property" states are Arizona, California, Idaho, Louisiana, Nevada, New Mexico, Texas, Washington, and Wisconsin.) If you were to split up, the other states would divide your marital property by equitable distribution, a term that allows courts to take into account the length of the marriage, the degree to which both spouses have contributed, and their ages and health.

The moral is not to wait for divorce court to decide what your contribution is worth. Assuming you and your partner currently have a healthy relationship, you may need to assert your right to fair compensation now.

We're speaking primarily of financial compensation here. Though other issues may belong on the table too—such as the amount of time your mate spends with you or the children—it's best to address money as a separate matter.

If you stay at home with the kids or keep house, you are contributing vitally to the household. That being the case, don't you deserve regular income of your own to meet your financial goals? We recommend sitting down with your partner and arriving at a fair salary for the work you do in helping your family thrive and prosper.

Harmony is a matter of attitude, not assets

Your success in taking charge of your money won't depend on how much you bring home compared to your partner, but on how well the two of you handle it. For example, one woman told us she knew two couples where the wife earned more than the husband. "One couple is doing very well," she said. "He used to have a prestige banking job, but now he loves staying home with the kids. The other couple were fine when their salaries were more even. Now there's tension, they fight, and it's hard to be around them."

The difference is the degree of inner security and self-esteem that both partners feel, allowing them to break out of stereotypical gender roles and do what works best for everyone in the family. You've heard Azriela Jaffe say that as her relationship with her husband grew more mature, they both became more open to the idea of his working part-time so he could stay home with their children while she pursued her career goals.

Doris Kiser, the Maryland homemaker who manages her family's investments, has worked out a good arrangement too. "The man I married is wonderful," she says. "He provides the money to get started, but as for the savings part, that's mine—that's my strength. When he tells other people what I do, he calls me our 'investment guru.'" Because Doris and her husband, John, claim their own strengths and cooperate for mutual benefit, she's developed a rela-

tionship that is conflict-free around issues of money and investment management, and doesn't hinge on who brings home a paycheck.

JJ Jamison, a financial planner in Colorado Springs, eloquently describes how she shares financial tasks with her husband, Larry, an engineer: "He's very comfortable with my handling the money. He
encouraged me to go back to school and get the education I wanted,
and his response to my good investment decisions is always enthusiastic." JJ adds, "He's a wonderful guy—strong enough to stand up to
me, but soft enough to be influenced by me."

Boston-area financial planner Sharon Rich observes that when a
woman takes on more financial responsibility, "it will rock the boat at
first, and some relationships won't survive. Any change in one person
changes the whole dynamic, the balance of power in the system." But
when there is trust, goodwill, and respectful communication in a relationship (three crucial aspects of any strong intimate bond), it's
possible to bring about this change gently but firmly in a way that ultimately benefits both you and your partner.

Should you merge the money?

Money merging is another potential area of conflict. While men in
committed relationships often believe that combining all the couple's
money is part of the deal, many women in the same situation feel
more comfortable having at least some money of their own. Participants in Olivia's workshops and seminars often disagree vociferously
on this topic. Husbands tend to protest: "Why do you want money of
your own? Don't you trust me? Are you thinking about getting a divorce?" Defensive wives respond: "Why do you want to put all our
money together? Are you trying to control me?"

In most cases, each partner is simply expressing a deep positive
need that she or he may not consciously understand. Men, for instance, often have difficulty in becoming and staying connected in
relationships. (Witness many men's withdrawal at the first signs of
tension or of emotional closeness.) A man who decides to merge
his money may be signaling his desire for merging and intimacy
with his life partner. If she pulls back, he feels rebuffed and
wounded.

On the other hand, women often tend to overmerge and lose their autonomy in a relationship, which means that their greatest challenge is maintaining a healthy sense of self. A woman's desire to control her own money may well reflect her need for a separate identity in the midst of intimacy. When her partner tries to deny her this independence, she may perceive that he is trying to keep her under his thumb.

If you and your partner are torn between wanting to merge all your money and keeping it separate, consider a compromise. Like Liz Lerman and Jon Spelman, you can merge some money for joint agreed-upon expenses and savings, including an emergency fund. We would recommend contributing in proportion to your respective incomes. After funding the household kitty, you should each have money left over to use as you see fit.

Two Kinds of Separate Money All Women Should Have

We think it's essential to have separate accounts in two areas: credit and retirement savings.

Every married woman should have at least one credit-card account in her own name, as opposed to sharing a card on an account in her spouse's name. You may even want to put your card in your maiden name. Needless to say, pay this bill faithfully! The object is to maintain a credit history of your own, so that if you're divorced or widowed you won't be in the position of being turned down for new credit.

If you don't have a card in your name at present, get one now. Your favorite banker will probably be glad to oblige. (Later, when you've established a good payment history, you can shop around for a better bargain if necessary.) Even a serious overspender should have a card in her name—but make it a "secured" card, which uses your own savings in the bank as collateral to make sure your spending doesn't get out of control.

It's also essential that funds earmarked for your retirement be held in your name only. Although they may still become part of the contested assets in a divorce, having them in your name makes it less likely that your ex could get his mitts on the money. With the exception of annuities, most tax-advantaged retirement vehicles are set up as individual (not joint) accounts.

What to do if your partner insists on keeping all the money power

Acquiring financial savvy is usually part of a general transformation that makes a woman more self-confident and independent-thinking, which often doesn't sit well with those men who like their wives meek and subservient. What if you're ready to claim your money power, but the idea of giving up control is totally unacceptable to him?

Ideally, you'll find this out before you tie the knot. One woman told us that she became increasingly uncomfortable as her fiancé grew more and more patriarchal, justifying his position with religious doctrine. One day, as he pontificated about the importance of a wife surrendering to her husband in all things, she asked him gently, "But what if I'm more knowledgeable about investing than you are?"

In dead earnest he answered, "Maybe we're intended to live simply and embrace poverty for a while."

That did it! She exited the relationship and is now seeking greener pastures with a more enlightened partner, while building her own investment portfolio.

> **Years ago, a woman came up to me at a workshop and whispered, "Can I buy your book? My husband would kill me if he knew I was doing this!" I was horrified. And I imagine there are still relationships today where these attitudes haven't changed.**
>
> —GRACE WEINSTEIN, *financial editor, author, and consultant*

What if you're married to a control freak who goes ballistic when you say you'd like to try managing the checkbook? You have several alternatives:

1. *Drop it.* Admit you goofed in pushing the issue, and go along with him. This is by far the worst option. "Staying silent and uninformed may keep the peace in the short run," says psychotherapist and author Harriet Lerner. "But as we know, what's most

comfortable in the short term can have disastrous long-term costs."

2. *Cheat.* Pretend to go along, but read *Money* magazine on the sly. Tell him you're going bowling with your friends when you're really sneaking off to your investment club. Keep a "secret stash" concealed from him. But secrets and deceptions aren't healthy for any relationship, so don't consider this option unless it's the only way you can have money of your own.

3. *Negotiate.* For example, you might both agree that you'll manage the household money while he continues taking care of the long-term investments (or vice versa) and that you'll compare notes on a regular basis.

4. *Get help.* If negotiation fails, consider going to a marital counselor or a couples therapist comfortable with money issues.

5. *Separate.* This is a painful and difficult choice, particularly if there are children involved. Only you can make the decision whether or not to remain in a financially oppressive marriage.

How to negotiate finances during a divorce

If you and your spouse do break up, for whatever reason, it's an immeasurable advantage to be knowledgeable about money.

One woman who told us she wasn't is Peggy Papp. Now a highly respected family therapist in New York City, Peggy was an actress during her marriage to Joseph Papp, an actor-director and founder of the Public Theater in New York. Neither cared much about financial matters during their long marriage. But when it ended, Peggy realized she knew too little about money to fight for a fair divorce settlement.

Like many other women in the same position, she was in danger of "giving away the store" for the sake of harmony and peace. Fortunately, a friend helped her connect with a suitably aggressive lawyer ("not the kind of person you'd want to invite to dinner," Peggy notes dryly) who saw that her interests were protected.

There isn't much you can do, unfortunately, to prepare for the emotional impact of splitting up. But you *can* take steps to ensure a divorce doesn't destroy your financial security. Here are some suggestions.

- *Open separate accounts* before *filing for divorce.* In some states, marital assets are frozen when divorce papers are served, so don't leave your cash sitting in a joint account. Besides opening a checking account in your own name, be sure to obtain a credit card of your own (even if it's a secured card) before closing joint accounts.

- *Collect your household financial documents.* To level the bargaining table, gather copies of recent tax returns, pay stubs, employee benefit summaries (including retirement plans), bank and brokerage statements, insurance policies, wills, loan documents, and a list of jointly owned valuables.

- *If possible, consider "divorce therapy" and mediation.* Though you may want to consult a lawyer upfront to find out what your rights are, divorcing should be done slowly and with emotional sensitivity for both parties. Divorce therapy (with a therapist or psychologist) is a way to give a respectful burial to a long-term relationship. Mediation—less adversarial than court proceedings—allows you to negotiate the division of assets and responsibilities with the help of an impartial mediator (often a psychologist, social worker, or clergyperson). This can help keep your breakup amicable . . . a big plus when you have children.

- *Know the property distribution law in your state.* Assets acquired during marriage are split evenly in community property states (Arizona, California, Idaho, Louisiana, Minnesota, Nevada, Texas, Washington, and Wisconsin); this means you might have to sell your house and share the proceeds fifty-fifty. In other states, the judge will try to divide assets fairly. Thus, if you want the house, your ex may receive cash or other assets instead.

- *Negotiate who gets the tax benefits of alimony, not just the amount.* The two of you can designate alimony (normally deductible by the payer and taxable to the recipient) as nondeductible and tax-free to the recipient. Child support is always tax-free and can't be deducted by the payer.

> **It's common for a woman to sabotage her own success, because becoming more successful than her husband is too threatening to both of them.**
>
> —AZRIELA JAFFE, *business coach, syndicated columnist, and author*

- *Obtain a QDRO.* A Qualified Domestic Relations Order entitles you to share your former spouse's 401(k) and/or pension benefits. Your lawyer should find out the plan's QDRO rules, then send the administrator a copy of the order as soon as it's issued by the court.
- *Find out more.* For a selection of financially focused books on divorce, see the appendix.

Sadly, some marriages aren't made in heaven. But if yours isn't working and needs to end, you can at least make sure the breakup won't leave you broke.

Is fear of conflict sabotaging your earning potential?

Sometimes, fear of endangering a relationship can lead women to suppress the talents, abilities, and drive that would have helped them become independent and financially secure. You may have heard female friends or colleagues make comments similar to these:

- "I got off the executive track because I didn't want to overshadow my husband."
- "He was having a hard time at work—I couldn't keep pushing for a promotion when he was so disappointed."
- "I knew that if my career took off, it would be a really big deal for me, but I was afraid I wouldn't be there for my family. I just couldn't risk it."

Whether single or in a relationship, these women often pay with their careers for their tendency to want everyone to be happy and their fear that conflict may lead to disconnection. Many others shoot themselves in the foot when a big job promotion gets near, or when they have the opportunity to succeed in money management and investing. In essence, these women create their own "glass ceiling."

What can you do if you sense you're sabotaging your own success? Since denial is often the companion of unconscious self-sabotage, the following telltale signs may help you know for sure.

- If you heard you might be in line for a raise, promotion, new responsibilities, or honors, would you feel a sense of high anxiety or dread?

- Have you more than once had an "almost got there but something happened at the last minute" disappointment about a promotion, raise, new job with more responsibility, or some professional accolade or honor?
- When practicing some pastime you love outside of work, have you almost achieved something you set out to do, only to feel it snatched away at the last minute?
- Before you accomplished something that no one in your family had ever done before (perhaps graduating from college, going to grad school, becoming a doctor or lawyer, or just leaving home for the big city), did you feel guilty, embarrassed, or ashamed, as if you were breaking a family tradition or taboo, or abandoning your loved ones?
- Whenever you're about to achieve or receive something really good, does a voice inside start saying things like "Who do you think you are, anyway?" or "What a show-off! Soon you'll think you're too good for everybody else" or "How long do you think you can keep this up before they find you out"?

If any of these sound familiar, there's a good chance self-sabotage is at work. Its roots may lie in your own beliefs about yourself—"I need to be perfect," "I'm not worth much." Or it may stem from messages you received from your family and other intimates, from your education or religious upbringing, or even from "survivor guilt." ("My dad only earned forty thousand dollars in his best year. If I make more, he might feel he's a failure or think I consider myself better than him—and I couldn't live with that!")

Wherever these tendencies originated, you can take these four steps to turn self-sabotaging messages around.

1. *Write down at least one powerful message giving yourself full permission to succeed, thrive, be happy and successful.* For example: "I am a good person, a talented woman with many gifts to give, and I choose to enjoy becoming totally successful in my personal life, my career, and my moneylife." Carry this message with you at all times, and read it often.

   If negative voices pop up in response, write out a dialogue between your guardian-angel voice (the positive one) and your demon voice. Make sure the positive voice prevails, educating the negative one and helping it lose its stranglehold on your success.

2. *Act as you wish to be.* Act as if you're confident, self-loving, and deserving of success and love in your life. If obstructionist voices pipe up as you move toward your goals and yearnings, write down a dialogue with them as in step 1.

3. *Overcome any negative parental messages by reminding yourself of the good stuff.* If old programming from parents has you stuck, visualize the goodness beneath your mother's and father's own wounds and anxieties—that positive parental spirit that wants only the best for you and hopes you will succeed and thrive in every way. If you can find a symbol of this unconditional love and support from your parents, a godparent or friend, or another mentor, keep it where you can see it, touch it, and connect with its life-affirming energy.

4. *Meditate on women you admire who are successful, powerful, happy, well-loved, and womanly in a way that integrates all parts of themselves.* Imagine borrowing a part of their spirit as you negotiate for a raise, work toward recognition and success, or pursue any deeply held goal toward achievement and excellence. Keep some reminder of these women around—a picture or description, or perhaps a tape of their voice—to turn to when you need to boost your energy or self-esteem.

To get what you want without conflict, learn to negotiate

Starting as a voice-over talent for TV and radio, Susan Berkley has developed her own business to teach and train others internationally. But on the way to becoming a seasoned business leader who now sells books and cassettes on the subject of voice-over and presentation skills, she went through a period when her naïveté about the ways of the world hampered her financial success.

For example, her attempt to seek suitable office space in Manhattan was a costly mistake. She exclaims, "I didn't know you were supposed to negotiate. I didn't know you *could* negotiate!" When high operating costs compounded the expense of upgrading her business premises, Susan soon realized she was in over her head. She backed up a few steps, enrolling herself in a course for women business owners at the

Fashion Institute of Technology, hiring a business coach, and learning how to keep books. The second time around, she bargained for an office lease in a suburb where rent was lower, parking was free, and air-conditioning didn't have to be retrofitted. Success came her way—aided, at least in part, by her willingness to negotiate for what she needed.

Women's fear of conflict often leads us to seek win-win solutions a little too quickly, hoping to keep the other side happy and friendly with us. Unfortunately, that can make us pushovers for anyone with a firm agenda and a loud voice. When conflict is necessary in order to look after our own interests, we must learn to make it work for us. As Dr. Judith Jordan puts it, women need to "see good anger and good conflict as a resource for connection." By learning to negotiate well, we can move through situations of conflict to arrive at win-win solutions that help us take much better care of ourselves.

> **I wonder how many decisions in my life that ended in self-erasure, compromise, or bulldozing over the needs of others might have been more creatively resolved by figuring how we could all be served at the same time.**
>
> —SALLY NASH, *dancer and choreographer*

NEGOTIATING FOR THE PAY YOU TRULY DESERVE

Part of self-caring is knowing the value of our own talents and abilities. Many women tend not to count among their strengths the ones that "come naturally," which in reality should count very strongly in their self-assessment. Only when we understand what our skills are worth are we really free to exchange them for fair compensation (or give them to others without personal reward if we choose).

In many industries and companies where women are still a minority, we're often not aggressive enough in asking for compensation equal to that of our male colleagues—even though we may be working much harder to prove ourselves. Brought up to be cooperators, not competitors, we tend to be loyal to employers who treat us

> **Unlike many men, I used to be uncomfortable selling my services. . . . I tended to underprice my talents or absorb certain costs out of my own pocket. I still prefer not to worry about how people are measuring me in economic terms.**
>
> —KAREN GROSS, *professor of law at New York Law School*

well, to the point of giving away our abilities in a lopsided exchange of value.

When we finally push ourselves into asking for what our services are worth, we sometimes make the mistake of assuming the boss already knows what we've done and are capable of doing. Or we couch our request for a raise in terms of needs and problems, instead of emphasizing our contributions and value to the company: "My car's quit, and I need to buy a new one," or "It's hard to get by with a kid in college."

Instead, we should use what is often described as women's greatest asset in managing others: our ability to empathize and build consensus. "Successful collaborative negotiation lies in finding out what the other side really wants and showing them a way to get it, while you get what you want," says Herb Cohen in *You Can Negotiate Anything*.

In negotiating pay with the boss, you need to take the following three steps. (If you're a stay-at-home wife, you can use similar tactics to seek compensation from your breadwinner spouse.)

1. *Figure out exactly what you want.* Well before your meeting, decide not only what you plan to ask for but what you'll settle for. If your boss balks at raising your pay, what trade-offs would you be willing to make? For example, would you accept another week of paid vacation or the use of a company car instead of a raise?

   Even if what you want is more time off, you might consider asking for money first. Then hint: "I know it hasn't been company policy to give employees at my level four weeks of vacation. But with the compensation increase I'm asking for, I could

afford to get away for more minivacations." Your boss will probably realize that giving you more time off could be easier on the
departmental budget.
2. *Figure out what your boss wants.* For example, is he or she focused
   on retaining clients and growing their business? On increasing
   sales by attracting more new customers? On making your division more efficient and productive? On developing a niche market and becoming a big player in it? You need to speak to your
   boss's needs and wants in order to get your own desires satisfied.
   Remember: *All progress is based on mutual satisfaction of interests.*
3. *Show that what you want will help achieve what the boss wants.* For
   instance, if you know that one of your boss's goals is to stimulate
   fresh thinking about customer needs, you might begin by saying
   that your hard work on the company's behalf has been paying
   off (mention a particular success story). With more vacation
   time, you'd be better able to renew your creativity.

Or if you know the boss is big on strong client relationships
to build business, you might do your homework so that you can
say something like this: "As you know, over the past year I've
been able to increase our sales to ABC Company by 20 percent
and to XYZ Company by 15 percent. I get along well with these
clients, and I think I can increase our business with them next
year by at least another 15 percent. But as I network with my
counterparts at other firms, I realize that my compensation level
is significantly lower than theirs. In fact, I've been getting some
calls from recruiters lately. Can I count on you to help make my
pay and benefits more competitive with my peers?"

Faced with such a carrot-and-stick request, almost any boss is
bound to say, "Er . . . how much did you have in mind?" (If you
take this tack, be sure to do your homework about competitive
salaries. Of course, if you're already being paid at a competitive
level, you'll need to demonstrate why you're worth more than
average.)

These three basics can work with other kinds of negotiating, too
. . . from buying a car to getting a discount on wall-to-wall carpeting. So what if some Neanderthal salesman grumbles that you're
"pushy" or "unfeminine." Is it "feminine" to be taken advantage of?

By the way, one word has probably jumped out at you in
these scenarios—*I*. Most women feel more comfortable saying

we, as in "we achieved this goal," or "the sales increase we forecast." You may need to accustom yourself (at least when it comes to asserting your worth) to saying *I*. Try it in front of a mirror. "I did this." "This is my contribution to the company." It can be very empowering!

Self-employed? Don't Sell Yourself Short

If you're self-employed and offer a superior product or service, don't be afraid to charge what your contribution is worth. Keep track of what your competitors are charging, so you know how to position yourself with your own pricing. Charging more than the other guys may lead some people to believe you're offering a superior service or product. (Keep developing your skills and talents so that you are!) It can be equally effective to underbid the big boys, but don't undercut them so hugely that people think you must be a rookie or skimping on quality.

When you decide to increase prices noticeably, turn this negative into a positive by explaining how it will help you give your customers what they want. For example, you might say, "The cost of materials and workmanship has gone up, but I'm still committed to providing the quality and durability that you, my customers, tell me you want." Or, "By investing in newer technology, I can improve the turnaround time on your orders." Your sensitivity to customers' concerns can help you build strong relationships that survive the assault of competitors selling solely on price.

Don't be afraid to stand up to Uncle Sam

Money behavior is often driven by fear of getting in hot water with the IRS. Awful blunders are made for this reason, such as having too much money withheld from your paycheck, or creating an estate that's promptly halved by a 55 percent estate tax.

It's beyond our scope in this book to arm you with a CliffsNotes version of the U.S. tax code. But there's a big difference between tax *evasion* (the crime of not paying taxes you legally owe) and tax *avoidance* (the perfectly legal practice of not paying any more tax than you have to). That's why we say it's okay to deny taxes to Uncle Sam that you're not obliged to pay.

If you don't do anything else, at least make sure your withholding allowance is correct (ask your payroll department for Employee's Withholding Allowance Form W-4, which includes a
worksheet), and know the rules about retirement investments so
you can take advantage of their associated tax breaks. Three more
rules of thumb:

1. *Never make an important financial decision solely for tax reasons.*
   Sure, it's nice to cut your tax bill in the short run. But be sure it
   makes sense in the long run, too. For example, if you sink all
   your money into tax-free bonds to reduce your current taxes, you
   could reach retirement age with a relatively puny portfolio, compared to what you'd have earned with taxable stocks. Part of a financial advisor's job is ensuring that you make the right tax
   moves for the right reasons.
2. *Don't assume you aren't capable of doing your own taxes.* Unless
   your financial situation is extremely complicated, all you need
   are good records (dig them out of the partitioned accordion file
   recommended in chapter 4) and good tax-prep software. The
   critics say there's not much difference between the two leading
   programs, TurboTax and Tax Cut; either one will ask you questions in plain English, automatically put the facts you provide
   into the right places, and alert you to errors or important omis-
   sions. If you'd rather delegate the task to a tax professional, ask
   lots of questions to be sure you understand what she or he has
   done.
3. *If you suspect something fishy in a tax return prepared for your signature, don't sign it.* Ask for an explanation, preferably in writing.
   When you sign your Joan Hancock on the back of that 1040,
   you're as responsible as whoever prepared the return. (While the
   so-called innocent spouse law has been liberalized, the IRS still
   doesn't accept the defense that "I thought my husband would
   get upset if I didn't sign.")

Singles and divorcées: learn about "prenups"

A prenuptial agreement is a serpent in the Eden of love—an admis-
sion that something dreadful might happen to poison your prospec-
tive bliss. Spousal debt, perhaps. Divorce. Or if you avoid those,

death. But in return for a little discomfort in setting it up, this agreement could save you a world of hurts later.

A "prenup" is a legally binding document between two marriage-bound individuals spelling out who gets which assets, and (sometimes) who pays for which debts. Usually triggered by divorce or death, it may include a sunset clause that terminates it after a certain number of years, although in many marriages the agreement simply fades into the background over time.

Most younger couples probably don't have enough financial assets worth protecting with a prenup. But there are several instances when it can make sense to draw up one of these agreements before heading to the altar:

- You have children from a previous marriage whose interests you want to protect.
- One or both of you have substantial assets, such as real estate or a closely held business.
- You're giving up a high-paying career and want to be compensated if the marriage fails.
- You want to be protected from your spouse's premarital (or postmarital) debts.

To hold up legally, a prenup needs to be more than a hasty scrawl on the back of a napkin. Each of you should retain a matrimonial lawyer. Acting as your respective advocates, these attorneys will hammer out the agreement together. It usually has to meet four conditions to be valid:

1. *Full disclosure.* Both parties must be completely open with each other about their financial situation.
2. *No pressure.* If your honey hauls out a prenup and insists you sign it as the church organist is launching into the Wedding March, it's apt to be thrown out of court later.
3. *Independent legal counsel.* When each of you has an attorney of your own, it's less likely that one party will take advantage of the other.
4. *Fair terms.* The agreement must be equitable. If either party would be impoverished as a result of enforcing it, a court may set it aside.

The process may take several months and cost close to $1,500 if you've paved the way by agreeing to the basic points ahead of time. Complications could boost the cost to $3,000 or more, depending on attorneys' rates in your area.

Introducing the subject of money into an idyllic romance can make you feel like a snake in the grass. You'll be branded unromantic at best, and possibly selfish, uncaring, distrustful, or cynical to boot. Reassure your soon-to-be-spouse that, as financial planners say, "once you prepare for the worst, then you can expect the best."

Although dealing with prenups is no bed of roses, don't give in if you think this protection is important. You may never have a better opportunity to see your partner's full financial situation. And if passing up a prenup were to cost you or your children the security an agreement could have provided, wouldn't that be a sin you'd really regret?

No conflict: enlightened guys
go for enlightened women

Alexandra Armstrong, chairman of a financial planning firm in Washington, D.C., and one of the nation's first Certified Financial Planners, cheerfully debunks the myth that "you're going to become some masculine person, or be a threat to men, because you understand finance." She explained to us: "Back in the sixties and seventies, I remember being at parties and meeting men who sought me out to talk about stocks, because they found out I was good at it. It even led to relationships.

"There's a certain type of man who's attracted to a knowledgeable woman who's good at investing and good with money. And isn't that the kind of man you'd want, anyway?"

Where are you now?

Check your emotional pulse right now. Do you feel empowered—or anxious about all the thorny issues that have been raised? If you're feeling a little nervous, write down your specific fears. Then think through and write down how you would handle each of them if it came true. If you feel more confident and empowered, write down two good things that will result from talking about money matters with your partner, parent, or employer. How will taking charge in this gentle and respectful way help you move toward greater financial well-being?

Here's a recap of recommended action steps to debunk the myth that "if I take charge of my money, I'll antagonize others and might end up alone."

1. Identify one or two financial activities you'd like to learn more about and take on as your responsibility.
2. If you're in a relationship, rehearse how you'll discuss this step with your partner. Some people find they gain confidence from rehearsing out loud in front of a mirror or with a supportive friend. If you're anxious about how the discussion might go, write down your fears and think through how you would react if they actually happened.
3. Schedule this talk with your partner, following the guidelines on pages 197–203.
4. If you earn more than your partner, explore how each of you feels about this, and eventually share your feelings gently and constructively. Is it a source of conflict? If so, sit down together and talk about how you could level the field between you in other ways.
5. If you earn less than your partner, see if that disparity is affecting your self-confidence regarding money. Review the case histories of other women who worked out equitable solutions with their partners.
6. Consider having at least some money of your own for emergencies. If you don't have a credit card in your own name, ask your banker or go on-line for an application and send it in within the next day or two. If you don't have retirement savings in your own name, make it a priority to at least fully fund an IRA by the end of this tax year.
7. Review pages 215–17 for what your options would be in case of serious conflict, so you're not anxious about the unknown.
8. Review the questions on pages 217–19 to see if you tend to sabotage your own empowerment. If so, follow the suggested steps to restore your confidence in yourself.
9. Practice negotiating in front of a mirror for something important to you, such as a raise or a big purchase. Anticipate

what the other party will want and say, and plan how you'll respond. Then negotiate in earnest using the suggestions on pages 219–23.

10. Think about how you're handling your tax matters. Are you avoiding conflict by letting your spouse do this, or refusing to make choices that could help you manage your money more productively? If so, take steps to become more knowledgeable.

11. If you're single or divorced, read the description of prenuptial agreements on pages 224–26. Know under what circumstances you might be likely to need one.

> **The solution is for both men and women**
> **to learn to do conflict better,**
> **while still staying connected.**
>
> —JUDITH JORDAN, PH.D.,
> coauthor of Women's Growth in Connection

With less fear of conflict, you may find it easier to resist letting someone else take over the thinking and decision-making process for you—a danger we'll address in the next chapter. In the meantime, congratulate yourself on learning to use a tool that can help you build solid relationships based on equality and mutual respect.

Myth 7:
"Someone Else Should Be Taking Care of All This for Me"

Even when women are making money, we often don't take ownership of it. Instead, we spend our energy trying to figure out who to give our financial power to—our partners, advisors, agents, even our fathers.
—EILEEN MICHAELS, *senior vice president of a major brokerage firm and author of* When Are You Entitled to New Underwear, and Other Major Financial Decisions

* * *

"What do you need to know about money? You're a girl. When you grow up and get married, your husband will take care of you."

It's politically correct to assume that girls aren't hearing this old message anymore, but our research shows that it's still being passed on from generation to generation (often at a subliminal level). These days, however, few women are willing to admit believing it. In fact, this myth elicits stronger emotional reactions than any of the others we've addressed so far.

Why?

One reason is the deep longing we all harbor for a kind of unconditional love and care that we hoped to get in childhood, but that virtually no one actually receives. Couple this yearning with women's traditional reliance on men as providers, and the result is that many of us grow up hoping to be taken care of by a benevolent authority figure (often male) as proof that we are truly lovable.

In past generations, women dependent on men to validate their financial choices might have expressed this myth as follows: "If I'm lucky, some man will take care of my money for me." Today, though, many of us are just as willing to hand over responsibility for our financial security to advisors who are female.

> **The belief that someone else should take care of us**
> **is almost ingrained from the cave-person days.**
> **I would tell women not to feel guilty about believing**
> **that—and that they can change it.**
> —CAROLYN CONGER, PH.D., *consultant and workshop leader*
> *in psychological growth and healing*

Victoria Collins, a financial planner and author who has a doctorate in psychology, believes that the power of this myth is waning as more women realize that they can take better care of themselves than anyone else will.

It's heartening to think of younger women growing up without this old message sapping their financial energies. "You have a whole new generation of women confronting the issue of managing their money for the first time in history," says Christine Stolba, director of economic projects for the Independent Women's Forum, a policy review organization. "I have a lot of friends, younger women in their twenties, who are just as savvy in the way they approach their finances as the men."

Yet children's book author Mary Quattlebaum observes: "I know a few single women in their late twenties and early thirties who still want a husband to come along and take care of them. Their job is sort of a stopgap. They make money, spend it, and don't think about saving or investing."

U.S. representative from California Lynn Woolsey, the mother of four grown children, agrees: "Way too many young women still think they'll be taken care of. I don't know where they get this idea, because they see their own moms working their fannies off. I think they must get it from TV and from romantic novels."

"I hear this all the time," adds Mary Hunt, author of *Debt-Proof Living*.

"They've just gotten out of college, they're twenty-six years old with forty thousand dollars in student debt and credit-card debt, and they say, 'I really thought by now I'd be married, and all of this would have gone away. Some rich Prince Charming would have saved me.' My feeling is, 'If Prince Charming does show up, he's probably going to be driving a Vega, and he'll keep right on going when he sees what condition you're in!'"

Clearly, this "obsolete" belief is still more common than we'd like to think. Some observers feel its prevalence varies with income, social class, and perhaps race. Psychologist Harriet Lerner asserts: "White women in particular grow up thinking we're going to be rescued like those fairytale heroines. We know better intellectually, but we may still harbor the belief that someone else will take care of us for the rest of our lives. Of course, this doesn't happen." Her view is echoed by pioneer family therapist Betty Carter, who says even more bluntly, "Middle-class white women are universally raised to expect to be taken care of for life by a man."

In other segments of society, young women may be more likely to expect that they will have to take care of themselves. For example, one African-American judge notes, "My impression is that more black women have grown up exposed to women having financial responsibility." She adds that, regardless of race, "if you grew up in a public-assistance household, I would speculate that your notions about sources of money, the ability to control the amount of money that you have, and who's responsible for providing for needs, as opposed to wants, are different from those who grew up in households relying on earned income."

Young or old, rich or poor, black or brown or white, if you believe that somebody else should take care of your money for you (a partner, a parent, an employer, Uncle Sam, or a financial advisor), you're far from alone. Take some time to review your expectations by asking yourself who this "somebody else" is and how likely this deliverance is to happen.

Forgive us if we bring out a bucket of cold water now to explain why you shouldn't count on Sir Galahad, regardless of whether he's in the guise of:

Your partner
- Can you be sure your mate is as smart about money as you think?

- Even decades-long relationships can end, leaving you on your own.
- New marriages break up even more frequently. And being more dependent on your spouse won't necessarily make the relationship better for either of you.
- If you're looking for Mr. Goodmoney, how long can you afford to wait?
- How many frogs will you have to kiss before you discover the prince?
- And what if the prince is unprincipled? (Gloria Steinem, author and founder of Ms. magazine, says, "I think women are *enormous* risk takers! What could be riskier than marrying a man whose financial abilities you know almost nothing about?")

Your parents
- You'll probably outlive them, so at some point you'll have to look after yourself.

An inheritance
- Wealthy Uncle Murgatroyd may live to a ripe old age, using up all his assets; or change his mind and leave everything he owns to a home for retired tuba players.

Your employer
- Even though your employer may currently offer good benefits to employees and retirees, companies have to think of the bottom line—not your personal welfare. For proof, just look at the corporate stampede from employer-paid pensions to employee-funded retirement savings plans. When you retire, the check that comes to you in Golden Acres will be (at least mostly) your own money, not your employer's.

The government
- Don't count on a rescue by Uncle Sam. After all, Social Security needs rescuing too; yet it still isn't fixed despite years of debate. And every attempt to "help" taxpayers simply makes the tax laws more complex. (That's why laughter so often greets the old one-liner: "Hi, I'm from the government, and I'm here to help you.")

However, once you decide to be responsible for your own financial security and independence, you can take advantage of almost all of these resources to make the task easier. Your partner or your parent may be willing to serve as a money mentor. Uncle Murgatroyd might be glad to share some wisdom with you about how he accumulated his wealth. Your employer probably offers a 401(k) for tax-deductible retirement savings and may even match some of your contributions. And Uncle Sam helps those who help themselves with a raft of tax breaks, from Roth IRAs' tax-free growth to a lower tax rate on investment gains.

> **My experience with men and their financial expertise tells me, if you think they're gonna rescue you, think again!**
> *—A financial planner in Maryland*

"My husband did all the money stuff": two cautionary tales

Often, women persist in believing this myth until bad experiences force reality on them. As financial planner-psychologist Collins puts it, *"Prince Charming gets lost on his horse."* It can be even worse if the prince actually arrives—and his inept attempts at money management turn you from a princess into a pauper.

In hopes of educating other women about the danger of trusting someone else to take care of their money, Eleanor Holmes Norton, the congressional representative for the District of Columbia, was courageous enough to tell us her sobering story. During her twenty-five-year marriage, Representative Norton says, "my husband did all of the money stuff" while she took care of their two children, one of whom has Down's syndrome. Both spouses were Ivy League–educated lawyers with active careers. "A natural division of labor developed, where he took care of the bill paying, tax filing, and so on," Norton explains. "He was a math whiz, and I thought everything was in control."

For years, Norton signed the joint tax returns he prepared without reading them. She knew they were paying "humongous federal income taxes" but was blindsided when a reporter revealed in the midst of her reelection campaign that her husband had failed to file their D.C. taxes for the past seven years. Her marriage ended not long after the reporter's story broke.

Representative Norton joins many other women in citing the "not enough time" myth to explain why she gave her husband free rein with their finances.

> I was a well-educated lawyer who always made a reasonable amount of money. In fact, I took a large pay cut to come to Congress. But like many professionals, I didn't have enough time to educate myself about money. I had two children and a busy career.
>
> Part of my problem is that money isn't important to me. I think capitalism is a good thing, but I've rebelled against money since I was a young person, and it's gotten me in trouble. I haven't tried to maximize money the way I should.

When we asked the congresswoman for hints that might help other women, she said, "You should never trust anyone 100 percent with your affairs. You need to retain oversight. I should have taken greater control of my own money."

Hollywood star Debbie Reynolds told a similar story at the 2000 Everywoman's Money Conference in Richmond, Virginia. Married three times, she said she lost millions of dollars by letting her husbands take care of her money. One was a gambler; another cleaned out their joint accounts and left her for another woman. Her message: Make sure you take charge of your money, and educate yourself about your choices.

On your own:
when financial independence is a necessity

Life traumas like Eleanor Holmes Norton's often motivate women to take charge of their finances for the first time. One medical professional told us that only when her husband's poor financial management drove the family into bankruptcy did she finally decide to learn how to do it herself. She later discovered, to her amazement and pride (and chagrin at having waited until crisis struck), that she was a much better money manager than he had been.

Along with sadder-but-wiser wives like these, many women have learned not to wait for a white knight by witnessing the painful experience of someone they loved—often their mothers or sisters.

> **I believed my father's philosophy: Turn all your money over to your husband, and he will always love and take care of you. . . . I was a dumb, darling, cute Victorian wife. . . . I never asked anything. Don't do what I did!**
> —*DEBBIE REYNOLDS, actress and entrepreneur*

Melissa Moss grew up deeply affected by the tragic events of her childhood. A week before her birth, her father had a massive stroke, which would leave him unable to function until his death twelve years later. Her mother was just thirty-two at the time, already caring for Melissa's two older sisters. The family had no insurance.

"My mom had no idea where the records were," Melissa told us. "She'd studied journalism at Northwestern but quit to get married." With courage and determination, Melissa's mother took over her husband's bookkeeping business, teaching herself accounting while raising three children on her own. Melissa and her sisters worked part-time jobs in high school and put themselves through college.

"Needing to work through school added to my fears," Melissa says now. "The notion of having no safety net was one thing that propelled me forward." In her impressive career, she has been an aide for San Francisco mayor Dianne Feinstein, finance director of the Democratic National Committee, an assistant secretary of resources of the state of California, and a staff member working with the late Ron Brown, U.S. secretary of commerce. In 1996, Melissa founded the Women's Consumer Network to help women obtain favorable pricing on commonly used products and services. Behind many of these accomplishments, she says, were her own bag lady fears.

I didn't marry until I was forty-one. By God, I was gonna keep working till I was financially secure! I was lucky and married someone who had a lot more money than I. But I insisted on having my own retirement accounts. He invests his money; I invest mine. We talk about life insurance, disability insurance, how to pay off the mortgage if anything should happen. I'm not worried. I know I'll be okay.

An interesting twist is that Melissa and her mother (her original role model) became money mentors for each other, as we reported in chapter 5. Melissa opened an IRA at her mother's prodding and then nagged her mother into buying a home of her own. The two of them are inspiring examples of women who transcended the myth that "someone else should be taking care of all this for me."

> **No matter what or where you are in your life, even if you're where you expected to be, it can all go away. And you'd better be prepared to take care of yourself.**
> —MELISSA MOSS, *former CEO of the Women's Consumer Network*

Childhood vow:
"I don't want to be controlled like my mom"

A different kind of childhood experience prompted another woman we'll call Sharon to take charge of her money as soon as she could. A former corporate marketing executive who is now a partner with her husband in a consulting firm, Sharon wrote us:

I grew up in a middle-class environment with Depression-era parents. My mother stayed home to raise four children. My father was determined to buy everything with cash. He made all money decisions, even those concerning my mother's personal needs or desires.

Over the years, I've watched both my mother and sister in marriage. The biggest conflicts they've faced stem from money issues because their husbands have controlled the family income. I learned quite young that "money is power." I guess that's the root of my lifetime determination never to allow anyone to dictate my money.

In fact, I believe a large part of what drove me to climb the corporate ladder years ago was my desire never to have to rely on a husband to take care of me. Because it appears that those who earn the gold not only control it—they also control anyone who relies on it.

Before Sharon's marriage at the age of thirty-five, she and her husband-to-be discussed who would be in charge of their finances. She persuaded him to turn the responsibility over to her by telling him "why it was so important for me to do it. Plus, I was better at it than he was." Fortunately, her entrepreneur fiancé was secure enough in himself not to be threatened by Sharon's determination, and he agreed to the arrangement.

After they sold their Pacific hillside home for a $300,000 profit, her interests expanded from basic money management to real estate, tax law, and investing. She earned a real estate license, acquired investment properties, and researched and chose a financial planner to handle her rollover IRA and their stock portfolio.

But even though she now relies on a financial professional, Sharon doesn't give up oversight. She reads financial publications and takes courses to keep well informed. And before accepting any advisor's recommendation, she told us, "I always have loads of questions to ensure that I understand exactly what they're advising and why. After all, if they were all that 'expert,' they'd be so filthy rich they wouldn't have to work at all!"

> **I'm shocked by the number of grown women who will say, "Let me check this out with my father, and I'll get back to you."**
>
> —SACHA MILLSTONE, *a financial planner in Washington, D.C.*

This assertive woman is evangelical in opposing women's willingness to give up control of their money: "Nonincome-producing wives
in particular seem to buy into this outdated belief system and allow
their husbands too much control. Don't they realize that this attitude
can affect not only their self-esteem but their independence?"

Echoing Sharon's observation, Washington, D.C., financial planner Sacha Millstone told us, "A lot of married women don't deal with
their money. They might do most of the buying and pay the bills, but
they don't have investments of their own. Their husbands do it for
them. I think it's ridiculous to give away that much power."

Well said. However, partners aren't the only men we tend to surrender our financial responsibility to. Often, it's dear old Dad.

Learning to let go of
"Father knows best" and other fantasies

"Often, Daddy is the first person women learn to rely on," says
Sharon Rich, president of a Boston-area financial planning firm specializing in women's needs.

Unfortunately, some dads don't see the need for their daughters to
be financially aware. Rich notes, "I've heard stories of fathers who tell
their daughter's fiancé what her assets are—something they've never
told the daughter herself!"

Barbara Stanny's father, one of the founders of H&R Block, was this
type of dad. Barbara, author of *Prince Charming Isn't Coming: How
Women Get Smart About Money*, recalls that after she and her two sisters were married, her father addressed his letters about money matters not to them but to their husbands. Sheltered from financial
knowledge, she was eventually forced to educate herself about money
after her spouse (now her ex-spouse) gambled away her wealth.

It's easy for many daughters to go along with the idea that Father
knows best. "Many women still hope that someone will take care of
the money for them or at least be a 60 percent partner in the process,"
observes financial planner Rich. She believes women are becoming
more aware that when someone else offers to look after their finances,
there's often a price to pay. "But that doesn't mean we give up our fantasy of being taken care of," she adds.

In time, some women learn to give up depending on their fathers to
rescue them financially, and take on the harder but ultimately more

fulfilling work of taking care of themselves. For instance, dancer-choreographer Liz Lerman told us about a time when she was hoping and waiting and worrying about financial support from her father, who had remarried after her mother's death. Finally her husband, Jon Spelman, opened her eyes by scolding her caringly, "Stop, Liz! It's not your money. It's your father's." This simple reminder, and the insight and growth it inspired, helped her move from dependence to becoming more autonomous and empowered about money. Liz says, "I mark that as the beginning of my adult relationship with my father."

> **Men have always understood how much power comes with the control of money.** It constantly amazes me that liberated, educated, "independent" women get married and give this power away. As much freedom of choice as women believe they have, why don't more of them stand up and demand complete equality with money?
>
> —SHARON, *an Ohio entrepreneur*

Many women have segued from dad to husband without ever standing on their own financial feet—not always willingly. One example was an older woman in one of Olivia's workshops, who said she had always been taken care of financially by her husband. "Whenever I try to learn more about our finances," she lamented, "he just hands me some money to play with and tells me not to worry my pretty head about it."

Don't misread us. We firmly believe marriage and financial independence can coexist. It's good to have someone you can rely on. And it's certainly not wrong to make your partner feel appreciated or to let Dad know that you value his advice on important matters.

But avoid the extremes. On one end, there's the Macho Man type of relationship where the man dominates all decisions, leaving the woman trailing meekly two steps behind. At the other extreme is the Scarlett O'Hara Kennedy syndrome, in which the woman pretends subservience to make her guy think he rules the roost, while actually manipulating him for her own purposes.

> As women, we need to learn how to take care of
> ourselves and not to be afraid. But that doesn't exclude
> having a good man at your side.
>
> —MICHELLE SINGLETARY, Washington Post columnist

Both of these situations are lopsided. Strong, solid relationships are based on respect, openness, and a sense of equality.

You may believe fervently that "I never want to answer to a man about money," like Broadway actress Faith Prince (who also praises her husband as "more logical about money than I am"). Or, like Michelle Singletary, you may be very comfortable sharing money-management responsibility with your partner. Find out whatever arrangement works for you, your loved one, and your relationship. But keep working toward the more financially confident, independent, savvy woman you know you can be.

Don't wait for a marital trauma
to make you financially free

When a marriage ends, financial empowerment can often rise from the ashes. A case in point is Betsy Downey, now education director of the Consumer Credit Counseling Service of Nebraska. Betsy's father, a retired Coast Guard officer, was "completely uninterested in money and the things it could buy." She went on to tell us:

My mother was an excellent penny-pincher who never looked farther than monthly bill paying and managing whatever income was available, leaving investing to "wiser heads than mine."

I loved and respected both my parents deeply, but when it came to money I found myself swaying wildly from being a carefree spender to being a strict penny-pincher. When I married, I became the daily money handler like my mother. Somehow I managed to find a man who was a lot like my dad in his monetary disinterest.

When Betsy and her husband divorced after fifteen years, she was left with three teenage children, two dogs, a car, and a house, "all needing monetary attention."

He left in a huff, predicting that I would sink like a rock alone. I was so angry I literally saw red and vowed that I would make it financially—and in good style, too!

I had thought that I was a good manager before, but now I really turned on the heat. I said no to myself and the kids so often I sounded like a broken record. I planned on being single and having to pay for everything myself, so I needed to conserve every penny.

As the children left home and I had more cash available, I started IRAs and other savings. I read a lot about investing and changed my investments to an all-stock portfolio to push my earnings as high as possible. Luckily the market cooperated. My confidence grew as time went on and my little empire didn't collapse.

As my wealth has grown along with my confidence, I find that my wild swings from spending a lot with guilt to pinching pennies like a miser have settled down. Most of all, I am accepting my financial self as I am and liking all of me. I am a great mix of Mom and Dad, and I'm proud that the best aspects of both live on in me.

I am a whole financial person and proud of it!

As painful as it may have been, divorce has proved to be a financially liberating experience for many women like Betsy Downey. Lynn Rivers, U.S. representative from Michigan, told us that her divorce resulted in "a shattering of my belief that I couldn't take care of myself. I found out that I very much could, and that has been wonderful." She added: "Money was always an issue; I gave my husband the money, he handled it, and we never seemed to have enough. Now that I'm in control of my own money, I'm finding that I do have enough."

California representative Lynn Woolsey is another believer. "I started investing my money when I got divorced and realized I would have to do it myself," she said. "I should have done it a long time ago. Being in control and having power over your own destiny is important. In order to do that, you really do have to have control over your own finances."

It's traumatic enough when a marriage ends, whether through di-

vorce or the death of a partner. With panic about your future intensi-
fying the pain of loss, this is a poor time to have to figure out how to
use and invest money wisely.

Someone to Watch over Me: A Cautionary Tale

*It was the sort of life your parents always hoped you'd have. There
was hard work, and love, and laughter, and enough money so you
didn't have to worry about paying the bills. Every year it just kept
getting better. And drifting contentedly from one day to the next,
you thought it would go on forever.*

*Then you lost him. The guy who was your best friend, your part-
ner, your anchor through the storms of life. That was hard enough
. . . but what made the pain even worse was the fear. Who would
look out for you now? Who would make sure you always had shelter, food, and care if you needed it? Who would keep tabs on the
spending and invest the money well, to make sure it would last you
the rest of your life?*

*He'd had substantial investments in a retirement plan, so you
weren't left too badly off. But not knowing what to do or where to
turn, you made some unwise decisions. With the choice of taking a
lump sum or annuity payments, you opted for the lump sum ("a
bird in the hand . . .") and converted most of the money into CDs,
where you knew it would be safe. And because debt felt risky, you
used the rest of it to pay off the mortgage.*

*But earnings from the CDs haven't come close to meeting your
needs, so every year now, your savings dwindle more. A little arithmetic could tell you how much longer they'll last, but you're scared
to find out. A friend of yours wants you to invest your money with
her son-in-law. Another friend says what you need is a reverse mortgage. But you've felt financially paralyzed ever since the humilia-
tion of being turned down for a credit card in your own name.
(They said you had no credit record.)*

*The kids are upset with you, but you pretend everything's all
right. You don't want to burden them. After all, they've got their
own families now.*

*You've cut way back on all your activities with your friends. The
house hasn't been painted in years, the carpeting is getting ratty,
and the plumbing in one of the bathrooms needs fixing, but you
don't think you can afford repairs.*

*Lately, too, you haven't been feeling well. Maybe it's just stress.
Your doctor could tell you for sure, but you won't go. It's so expen-*

sive, and what if you had to be admitted to the hospital? The cost would wipe you out.

So every night, you go to bed with your worries. Over and over, you hear yourself lament: If only he hadn't left me to look after myself.

And sometimes, in the dark of night, you're tormented by an even bitterer thought: If only I hadn't passed up so many opportunities to learn how.

Written by Sherry for Bank One. Copyright © 1997 Bank One Corporation. Reprinted by permission.

Develop a "surviving spouse" plan with your partner

You and your mate should put together a contingency plan so that if anything happens to either of you, the survivor will be better prepared to make sound financial choices.

As difficult as it may be to contemplate this, it's even harder to ask your partner to imagine a future in which the two of you won't be together. If you can't bring yourself to address the issue head-on, bookmark these pages for him—and know that if you can visit this painful place, you'll be creating greater peace of mind for both of you. No matter who survives, it will be easier to pull out the plan than to try to remember all the moves that seemed so obvious when your mind was unclouded by shock and grief.

A financial contingency plan isn't legally binding, of course, and can't replace a will or other components of a formal estate plan. If you have substantial assets or minor children, you still need to arrange your affairs with a financial advisor or estate attorney so that your beneficiaries will be provided for as you wish.

Although it can include some suggestions for the longer term, the primary purpose of a surviving spouse plan is to guide you through the first difficult year alone. Your plan could be as simple as a folder with a list of all your household accounts and assets. A more elaborate plan might call for a three-ring binder, allowing you to insert the latest quarterly or annual statements and policy declarations. To make sure you don't overlook important points, you might consider using a preprinted workbook. *Everything Your Heirs Need to Know* by David S. Magee features sections for family history, medical history, personal background, and final wishes.

Whatever form the plan takes, take time to discuss it thoroughly with your partner (and with your adult children, if desired). And be sure you know where to find it in case of need. It should include:

- *A cover letter.* Compose a personal message to help the survivor get through the first painful months.
- *A summary of what you both own and what you owe.* List all assets and loans, where they're held, their account numbers, and how they're titled. (If an asset is held jointly, the surviving spouse will be able to assert ownership immediately. However, your attorney may have advised you to own certain assets individually or as tenants in common, to facilitate estate planning.) Be sure to list all your insurance policies—health, disability, home, auto, travel, and credit life, as well as life insurance—and the location of important documents.
- *Names and phone numbers* of trusted advisors, as well as others who will have to be contacted, such as an employer, the executor or trustee of the estate (if someone other than you), insurance agents, creditors, and so on.

In addition, your plan may want to address these concerns:

- *Immediate cash.* Where to find money to cover funeral expenses and medical bills, as well as household costs.
- *Budgeting and saving.* Using current living expenses as a baseline, how much could you expect to need every month? Where will the money come from? Where should any surplus be saved or invested? Since it's difficult to anticipate possibly dramatic changes in your lifestyle and needs, this part of the plan will have to be flexible.
- *Investments.* Should you change investment strategies? Under what conditions should you consider selling any investments? How should you go about retitling assets? Who can give you objective investment advice?
- *Pension and insurance benefits.* What are your options in receiving your spouse's pension survivor benefits or the proceeds from his

IRA, company savings plan, or annuity? Which choice is best? Should you opt to receive Social Security survivor's benefits as early as age sixty? (Ask your local Social Security office for "Social Security—Survivors Benefits" or download this booklet from www.ssa.gov.) How should you handle a lump-sum payout from his life insurance?

- *Taxes.* Although you may need to consult a financial advisor on more complex tax-related issues, the plan can provide basic guidance. For example, widows are often tempted to cash in investments to pay off the mortgage—a move that could eliminate a tax deduction and lock up money that should be invested to protect their future purchasing power. Be sure the plan explains whether IRA contributions and earnings are both taxable, whether earnings only are taxable, or whether the IRA is a tax-free Roth. Last, include a reminder of what will be needed, and by when, to prepare the last joint return and the estate tax return.

Perhaps that's an appropriate way to end this section. For as the saying goes, few things in life are as certain as death and taxes. But with a well-thought-out contingency plan, you'll be better prepared for whatever may happen.

If your ship comes in, don't sink it

Many people think an inheritance, fruitful stock options, or a winning lottery ticket would solve all their financial problems. No need to learn how to manage money—after all, you'll have more than you know what to do with!

This is precisely the problem. When your financial skills are limited, a big windfall can just mean more money to manage badly.

Even though you shouldn't count on being rescued by sudden good fortune, the chances are fairly good that at some point in life you'll have a substantial sum of money to manage. Whether it's a life insurance payout, retirement plan distribution, divorce settlement, or severance check, the many choices it engenders may be mind-boggling. Should you pay off your credit cards and burn the mortgage? How about buying that vacation home or new car you've wanted? Maybe you ought to invest some (or all) of it for retirement, but what about other needs, like college for your children? Here's our advice:

- *Don't make a hasty decision.* Stash your new wealth in a money market fund or some other safe short-term investment, while you take time to think through your alternatives and figure out your real priorities.
- *Seek advice from experts.* Many people say they'd turn to a financial professional for help with a substantial sum. In fact, you may want to assemble a team consisting of a financial advisor, a CPA, and an attorney. Besides providing the tools to make planning easier, these advisors can help you evaluate your options objectively at a time when the emotional turmoil of losing a parent, partner, or job may make a solo decision difficult. Even if the windfall came to you through the sale of a home, a business, or investments, a sudden large sum of money can destabilize you and your thinking, making you prone to impulsive, fantasy-filled decision making. So objectivity can come in handy here, too.
- *Get a financial checkup.* How much money do you need for living expenses? What are your assets and your debts? Do you have adequate insurance?
- *Reexamine your goals.* How could the money bring the most value to your life? For example, might it make early retirement possible, allow you to set up a business you've dreamed of, or free you from debilitating debt? Remember to list your goals several times to see which ones emerge over and over again—they're the ones you can really trust.
- *Work out a plan based on your reassessed financial needs and goals.* This plan could include:

  - Investing strategies for moving into recommended portfolio allocations.
  - Disinvesting strategies for withdrawing cash, while minimizing taxes.
  - An estate plan that allows you to leave assets to your loved ones tax-efficiently.
  - A gifting plan that helps you support family members and your favorite causes, without putting your own financial security at risk.

Of course, not everyone is a candidate for a hefty windfall. But it's important to understand financial matters well enough that if this kind of money ever lands in your lap, you'll know how to put it to work toward your goals.

> **Learning how to handle money should be part of everyone's education, part of becoming an adult.**
> —SACHA MILLSTONE, *a financial planner in Washington, D.C.*

Ease your way into financial empowerment in four steps

Tony Award–winning musical star Faith Prince told us that even though she has a business manager and feels less logical about money than her husband she has "a contract" with herself to never give up control of her finances. "I have my own separate personal checking account," she said, "and I pay attention; I'm always looking for new ways to do better. I would like to be better with money." With a wry smile she summed up, "It's a work in progress."

This is a great way of looking at it. There are no grades for financial empowerment, no gold stars for becoming the best money manager in the family or on the block. It's enough to keep learning, bit by bit, so that bit by bit you can keep making your life better.

To make the move from "money shy" to "money sure" easier follow a few simple steps.

1. FIND THE RIGHT MONEY MENTOR

To have more fun while you're learning money skills, work with a money mentor. This could be a knowledgeable pal, partner, or parent who is patient and open. In fact, you're likely to find potential money mentors everywhere, once you start networking and looking for them in the same creative way that you seek help and connection in other areas of your life.

Psychological growth consultant Carolyn Conger asked her stockbroker to mentor her. "I called her every day and asked her to teach me something about investing," she says. "Like anything else, it's not so complicated if you break it down into tasks."

> **When it comes to money, we don't have to become
> better than, more than, or richer than anyone else. We
> just need to have this economic knowledge as one of
> the legs making our table steadier. But it's not the
> whole table.**
>
> —LIZ LERMAN, *founder and director of a national dance company*

In seeking a mentor of your own, she suggests, "look for someone who can bring the element of fun in finding new ways to be independent—financially and otherwise. Whether male or female, that person needs to be very patient."

2. SHARE YOUR KNOWLEDGE WITH OTHERS

The rewards of learning are tremendous—especially when they're reinforced by the satisfaction of coaching others who follow you later on the same journey. After learning from her first money mentor, a retired judge, Judy Robinett has mentored hundreds of other women as an investment club founder and business coach. Betsy Downey credits her divorce-inspired transformation into financial well-being with making it possible to "enjoy my present calling of helping others to manage their money and credit fearlessly. When I help others to learn, I can relive the great feelings of overcoming my own financial barriers."

Mary Hunt, author of *The Financially Confident Woman*, is another inspiring mentor. After digging out of $100,000 of debt through frugal living, Mary started *The Cheapskate Monthly* newsletter in 1992. She recalls: "Out of my fear, I started reading everything I could get my hands on about money. The more I read and understood, the more exciting it became. When someone asked me a question about investing, I would do all the research to answer the question." She and her husband put her new knowledge to good use. "We're now five years into our own investment portfolio," she reports. "Teaching teaches the teacher!"

3. IF YOU WANT ADVICE FROM A PRO,
DON'T HESITATE TO CONSULT ONE

Although we believe that any woman can learn to take care of her own money, we also realize that some won't want to. After all, there's only so much time in a twenty-four-hour day.

But it would be dangerous to simply wait around, hoping someone else will take charge of the "money stuff" for you. Instead, follow the example of the many women who have taken the bull by the horns and learned delegation without abdication. In other words, even after finding an advisor you trust (for search tips, see pages 125–31), it's important to continue learning about financial management and keep control of your money. Insist on asking questions till you understand your advisor's recommendations, and you're sure he or she understands your needs and goals clearly.

This ongoing search for knowledge and understanding is apparent in the relationship between Sally Nash, founder of the Workspace for Choreographers, and her financial advisor, Sacha Millstone. Sally departed from family tradition in seeking an advisor of her own—a good move for women who want to avoid an old family counselor's possible preconceptions. Millstone became her money mentor, helping Sally to develop her own financial knowledge ("combining my conservatism and her ability to take risks," Nash says) without taking over control from her.

Sacha Millstone belongs to the breed of financial advisors and planners we respect most—professionals who are committed to educating the women they serve, and who steadfastly refuse to let clients surrender their decision-making authority and control.

> **You take your clothes to the dry cleaner; you hire a baby-sitter when you can't be home. In the same way, if you don't have the time, interest, or expertise to manage your money, you're responsible for finding someone good to do it for you.**
> —MEGAN ROSENFELD, *reporter and writer for the Washington Post*

Sacha's attitude is shared by Peg Downey, a financial planner in Silver Spring, Maryland, and former chair of the fee-only National Association of Personal Financial Advisors. As you may remember from chapter 4, Peg believes that "ultimately, it's your responsibility. You fulfill part of your responsibility by finding a person you trust, and then the rest of your responsibility is to continue understanding what's going on with your finances."

We also applaud stockbrokers like Ellie Wotherspoon in Washington, D.C., who is committed to helping women investors get started, regardless of the size of their nest egg. Ellie has also made it her mission to help launch several women's investment clubs, and continues to attend meetings for the pleasure of seeing more women get involved in investing and excited about growing their money.

Another enthusiastic advisor of this caliber is Susan Freed, a fee-only planner who is president of her own Washington, D.C., firm, "I'm very lucky; I have wonderful clients," she says. "Many of the women I see want to be empowered. They understand that this represents their future, and they're smart enough to seek expert advice—but also smart enough not to give up total control to anyone."

Everyone Can Benefit from a Professional Financial Checkup

Consider consulting an advisor for a basic financial checkup early in your empowerment process. This will give you the opportunity to learn where you stand, review what you're doing right, and see which areas of your moneylife may need particular attention.

As we've mentioned, some financial advisors don't charge for a get-acquainted meeting, hoping to be compensated later through an annual asset management fee or by commissions on the investments you agree to make. But if all you want is an informal financial review or a formal plan that you'll carry out yourself, say so at the outset.

You may also want to check in with an advisor for an annual review after you get started. If the advisor is willing to work with you on this basis, expect to pay an hourly rate or a flat fee to benefit from his or her expertise.

---

4. DON'T BE ASHAMED TO SEEK THERAPEUTIC HELP

Because of the very deep roots of the old belief that "someone else should be taking care of all this for me," it can be hard to move past it to a healthier way of looking at the future. Some women who know they need to take on more responsibility, and feel stirred up when they think about it, just aren't able to take the steps they need to.

If this describes your situation, you may need to explore more fully why you feel this way and work on creative ways to free yourself. Consider seeing a psychotherapist or other mental health professional experienced with women and money issues.

To find a therapy professional who might help you resolve conflicts involving money and power, ask friends or your pastor, priest, or rabbi for recommendations. Try to gather the names of several therapists so you can interview each of them. Although there are very few designated "money therapists," people like Judy Barber in San Francisco, Arlene Modica Matthews in the New York area, and Martha Moyer in Torrance, California, are among the mental health professionals who are aware of, and knowledgeable about, the importance of helping clients deal with money.

For example, Moyer told us, "I would like women to understand that money is only legal tender—and my job is to help it become a less tender subject with them." She added that "it's a self-esteem issue. I'll know I'm doing well with a client by how much she starts caring about her own future."

Indeed, the root of money conflicts is *always* deeper than just money and may lead to exploring issues of dependency, power, love, control, and so on. But not all therapists are comfortable discussing

> **What you simply cannot do,**
> **or raise your daughters to do ever again,**
> **is to say that your financial security depends**
> **on anyone but yourself.**
>
> —LINDA ELLERBEE, *journalist, author, and TV producer*

money, so be sure you find someone who isn't reluctant to deal with this kind of problem.

Another avenue of self-exploration might be a spiritually oriented workshop that speaks to your hopes and longings. For instance, women's myths and empowerment are the focus of workshops given around the world by renowned creativity expert Jean Houston, author of *Jump Time: Shaping Your Future in a World of Radical Change* (for more information, visit www.jeanhouston.org or call 1-541-488-1200). Again, personal recommendations from friends and colleagues who know you well and whom you trust can be the best source of referrals. Just be sure to stay with this process of exploration until you reach closure, and your commitment is bound to bear fruit.

Real-World Views of This Common Money Myth

Have you ever thought that if you were lucky, some man would take care of your money for you? Here are some more realistic ways to view this myth.

- *"If you're unlucky, some man will take care of it for you" (author and feminist Gloria Steinem).*
- *"If you're unlucky, some man will pretend to be taking care of it for you" (family therapist Olga Silverstein, author of* The Courage to Raise Good Men*).*
- *"If I'm lucky, I'll learn how to take care of it myself!" (professor of law Karen Gross, an authority on women and bankruptcy).*

Nothing is more important to a woman's sense of self-respect and inner security than knowing she can truly take care of herself, no matter what happens.

Where are you now?

For those of you who already know that no one else can, will, or should take care of your money for you, congratulations! But if you're still plagued by the effects of the deeply ingrained belief that "somebody else should be taking care of all this for me," ask yourself the following questions to completely debunk this myth.

1. *Who do I hope will take care of it for me? And exactly how do I think this caretaking or rescuing will happen?* Once you have a clearer picture of your hopes and expectations, you can challenge beliefs that may be keeping you from moving toward independence and empowerment.

2. *What would I do if the person or organization I'm counting on didn't come through?* For example, if you were hoping for a large inheritance but your father remarried and began spending his money on his new family, how would you take care of yourself financially? Or what would you do if your employer changed your retirement options so that you ended up with less money than you expected? By thinking through the worst-case scenarios and figuring out how you would deal with them, you'll be able to move from dependency toward a more positive, self-reliant attitude.

> **Women's resourcefulness and resolve grow as things become more challenging.**
>
> —*JEAN HOUSTON, educator, author, and human potential specialist*

3. *Where will I find the help and support I need to manage my money well?* In our case histories, you've met women whose journey toward financial well-being has been aided by a variety of friends, mentors, and financial professionals. Who will provide this support, knowledge, and encouragement for you? Your life partner? A friend or colleague who can become a money mentor? A women's (or mixed-gender) investment club? Financial publications? Financial education or math-anxiety courses at your local community center or women's center? Perhaps you'll choose to consult a trustworthy financial advisor or maybe all or some combination of these.

With the information provided in these chapters, we hope you feel ready to proceed on this journey toward financial well-being with optimism, confidence, and a greater sense of self-worth. Considering the many helpful resources that are available, you can be sure you won't have to make the journey all alone.

Women, Myths, and Money

All over the world, women are challenging the way things are done, and slowly but surely building a new social order. It's the biggest revolution in human history. Women are embracing their power. At long last, their full creativity is being set free.

—JEAN HOUSTON, PH.D., *educator, author, and human potential specialist*

*   *   *

As you learn more about how to manage your money, you'll be rewarded with a greater sense of creativity, self-respect, and inner serenity than you may have believed possible.

That's why this book has no conclusion. Instead, it has an *envoi*—a send-off.

As you continue your journey toward financial well-being, be alert to self-sabotaging messages that are connected to the seven money myths we've discussed. As you've seen, what makes these myths so hard to conquer is that each one has at least a kernel of truth. In revisiting them now, do you have a better idea of what is and isn't true about each one?

Revisiting the seven money myths

MYTH 1: "MONEY IS TOO COMPLICATED
FOR ME TO UNDERSTAND"

- *It's true that* few people understand all the complexities of the constantly changing world of finance. Even professional financial planners need reference tools to develop a balanced strategy for a big portfolio, or a complicated estate plan.
- *But* the basics aren't that difficult. "I see women who have math anxiety or are afraid of the math involved," says planner Susan Freed. "But it doesn't get more complicated than stuff you can do with a calculator."

MYTH 2: "I DON'T HAVE ENOUGH MONEY
TO DO ANYTHING WITH"

- *It's true that* women tend to earn less than men and drop out of the workforce for child-rearing, often struggling with such modest income and so much debt that it can seem impossible to find any money to save.
- *But* if you save a little bit every week, whether it's $1 or $10 or $50, within a few weeks you'll feel a new sensation of being in greater control of your destiny. Then you can brainstorm ways to put even more aside. Most people who make their own wealth don't start with whopping amounts. They just *start*—and keep it up.

MYTH 3: "IF I TAKE RISKS WITH MY MONEY,
I'LL LOSE EVERYTHING"

- *It's true that* investing in stocks, bonds, or mutual funds is riskier than putting your money in safe, low-earning CDs.
- *But* with sensible diversification, you can reduce investment risk significantly. That's important because *not* investing is a far greater risk for women. By failing to accumulate a nest egg sizable enough to see you through a life span that's likely to be longer than a male partner's, you're taking an even bigger risk: that you may literally outlive your money.

MYTH 4: "I DON'T HAVE ENOUGH TIME
TO MANAGE MY MONEY"

- *It's true that* almost all women feel there isn't enough time to juggle all the important people and priorities in their lives.
- *But* if you keep putting money management last on the list, or even let it drop off the radar screen completely, your financial future will be seriously threatened. Wouldn't an hour a week be time well spent if it meant you could relax and feel financially secure in your later years?

MYTH 5: "IT'S SELFISH TO PUT MYSELF FIRST.
I'M SUPPOSED TO TAKE CARE OF EVERYBODY ELSE"

- *It's true that* if you spent all your time and energy caring for yourself, that would be selfish. Most women are oriented by nature and upbringing to nurture others.
- *But* the fact is that one of the *least* selfish things we can do is to take good care of ourselves—financially and in other ways as well. The rewards in self-esteem, peace of mind, general well-being, and happiness will spread to all those with whom we are connected. And from a financial standpoint, we'll be much less likely to have to depend on our children or charity later on. These are very real, unselfish gifts to give to those we love.

MYTH 6: "IF I TAKE CHARGE OF MY MONEY,
I'LL ANTAGONIZE OTHERS AND MIGHT END UP ALONE"

- *It's true that* some men are still threatened by financially powerful or competent women.
- *But* many others welcome a partner who can share the responsibility with them. And with empathetic communication, even men who initially feel intimidated may eventually welcome the easing of their burden as the perennial provider. As women gain a greater sense of self-worth and self-respect in this process, both partners can benefit enormously from the power, knowledge, and competence they will share.

MYTH 7: "SOMEONE ELSE SHOULD BE
TAKING CARE OF ALL THIS FOR ME"

- *It's true that* centuries of economic dependency on men have led women to hope that someone else will take care of money matters for them.
- *But* when women take charge of their own financial power, this shift in attitude can make full intimacy between two equal partners possible for the first time. Women who aren't in a relationship will gain pride in their expertise and feel more in control of their future.

To find financial well-being, consult your inner values

Misled by money myths, many of us make the wrong choices—to avoid investing, to spend as if there were no tomorrow, to give someone else the responsibility for our financial well-being. "Not enough women live out their values in how they spend their money and the life choices they make," says feminist author and editor Gloria Steinem.

Worse yet, we often pass the lessons of those misguided choices down to our daughters and sons. As Cecelia Morris, a New York judge, points out, "Your true legacy isn't money. It's the values you've given your kids."

If you're ever in doubt about whether a financial choice is the right one, ask yourself: "Where will this decision take me? Is it somewhere I want to go? Will I feel better about myself for having made this choice?"

Whether you have a little money or a lot, you'll begin to feel a sense of financial well-being when your money behavior mirrors your innermost values. To open the door to this well-being, the single most valuable step you can take is to begin saving for a purpose that's more important than everyday needs and wants. Once you start saving, you'll feel more in control of your moneylife. As your confidence grows, you'll feel more serene, because you're moving toward financial security and independence.

After you've begun taking good care of yourself financially, the next logical step in your evolution may be moving on to make positive changes in the world with your money. One woman who has succeeded admirably in putting her money to work in ways that reflect her values is Sarah Ban Breathnach. Today, she's the best-selling author of *Simple Abundance,* which focuses on the search for contentment and authenticity and, among other important themes, addresses the spiritual side of financial fulfillment. But money hasn't always been abundant for Sarah. She told us:

My parents weren't good money managers, but they always lived as though they had all the money in the world. This was a mixed blessing because on the one hand they gave me the priceless gift of abundance consciousness, but the gift came wrapped in financial ignorance. The reality of their situation hit hard when they didn't have the money to send me to college. They hadn't saved anything. So when the time came for my hardworking father to retire, he couldn't and continued working in a series of ever-diminishing menial jobs until the bitter end. After he died, my mother lived the next five years of her life riddled with fear, burdened with debt and guilt because she relied on the slender checks her children (who were all struggling on their own) sent every month to supplement her Social Security. After her funeral, when I was going through her papers, I discovered a slim red ledger in which she kept track of her "accounts." The pain evidenced in the penciled figures and erasures still haunts me.

Coming from a family of spenders, it was shocking (but not too surprising) that I married into a family of savers. My husband and I were the yin and yang of money handlers. At first I appreciated his frugality because it moved me toward a better balance. However, our different attitudes about money were a source of constant distress. But saving out of fear rather than prudence becomes hoarding, just as insidiously spending out of denial becomes irresponsibility. Living as if the wolf is banging at the door, even when the pantry is well stocked, is as soul crushing as spending as if you have all the money in the world when you don't.

The most difficult time of my marriage (which lasted 18 years) was when I was writing *Simple Abundance.* I'd received thirty rejections in two years, but was still determined to finish it and give birth to my dream. But my husband resented the fact that I wasn't holding down "a real job" and demonstrated his displeasure (perhaps unconsciously) by giving me a check every two weeks, which at times was very humiliating, especially if I had to ask him for it. I felt like a failure and was afraid for my daughter and afraid I'd end my life like my mother had.

The way I got over my fear was to truly live the values I was writing about. I gave thanks for every tiny blessing of each day and I began tithing, which had not been part of my spiritual background. But the moment I started giving back one-tenth of my grocery money to organizations doing God's work in the world, I began to experience financial serenity. You see, if I have ten percent to give away, it tells me that I have more than enough.

This was a transforming act in Sarah's life. Since her book was published, she has been able to take care of her daughter's college education, buy two houses (including her "dream" cottage in England), launch her own publishing imprint, and plan for the future with the assistance of a financial advisor, accountant, and attorney. She also founded The Simple Abundance Charitable Fund, a bridge group between the public and deserving nonprofit groups dedicated to increasing awareness that "doing good" and "living the good life" are soul mates. Over the last five years Sarah Ban Breathnach has given away more than $1 million. "Getting over the fear of money was the bravest thing I have ever done. But it is empowering," she says. "I'm having a ball."

We greatly admire Sarah Ban Breathnach for taking steps to be in harmony with her inner values. Think of the many other role models of empowerment you've read about in these pages—women who can testify to the power of giving to others and to society while taking good financial care of themselves. Ultimately, there's absolutely no conflict between the two. It's a question of timing and patience.

"Abundance has nothing to do with having a certain amount of money," Sarah emphasizes. "It's a shift in perception. By changing our attitudes, we can change anything."

Seven affirmations that can
lead you to financial well-being

To help change your own attitudes, become familiar with the following self-affirmations. Practice reading them, saying them out loud, and thinking about them. By the time you start putting the action phases into practice, you may be surprised to realize that the affirmations have become reality.

1. "Little by little, I am enjoying learning more about money and investing."
2. "No matter how much money I have, I am making my money grow."
3. "I am learning to take more intelligent risks. I'm confident that sensible risk taking will help me build my financial future."
4. "I am choosing to make the time to take charge of my money."
5. "It's not a bit selfish to take good care of myself financially. It's self-respecting and self-caring, and ultimately makes my relationship with others richer and more satisfying."
6. "My loved ones enjoy, respect, and appreciate my financial knowledge, power, and success."
7. "I enjoy taking care of myself financially. The more I do it, the more I feel supported by others in my life."

A wise Chinese proverb, "The journey of a thousand miles starts with a single step," contains the secret of success. Dream big! Dream thousand-mile dreams. Dare to set financial goals that will let you reach your dreams. Then break up these goals into bite-size pieces and commit to taking one step toward them every day (or at least every week).

Be prepared for the pace of your learning to seem slow at times. Progress is sometimes two steps forward, one step back. Don't beat yourself up for not knowing everything. What you don't know yet, you can always learn.

As you become more knowledgeable, share the wealth of your financial expertise and confidence. Make sure that the children who look up to you—especially your daughters or nieces—grow up financially savvy. Volunteer to mentor someone else who's following in your footsteps. And as you learn and do something new, let in the good feelings about your new learning.

Keep monitoring your progress

We'd like you to do one last exercise—in many ways, the most important one of all. It's something you can revisit every year or six months, as you move closer and closer to your goals. Just write down your answers to these three questions.

1. What three things connected to your financial well-being do you feel good about?
2. What are three things you still want to accomplish?
3. What steps will you take to transform your answers to question two into accomplishments you can list the next time you answer question one?

Once you've swept away the myths that limit your options and your sense of self-esteem, you'll be free to claim your financial power in the same way you exercise your skills and wisdom in other areas of life. This is a transformation worth working for—for each and every one of us to reach our true inner potential and feel at peace and serene about our future.

Total financial well-being is waiting for you. We hope you enjoy the journey.

APPENDIX

The right reference guides can be a big help in completing your journey from money-shy to money-sure. For our money, the following books are among the best.

Getting your finances in order

Financial adviser Karen McCall has been helping clients get through what she calls "financial recovery" for over thirteen years. She's translated this experience into a step-by-step emotional and financial workbook for readers who want to put their moneylives in order: *It's Your Money: Achieving Financial Well-Being: A Guide and Journal* (Chronicle Books, $19).

If you need a good way to monitor your own saving and spending, Judy Lawrence's *The Budget Kit: The Common Cents Money Management Workbook* (Dearborn Financial Publishing, $17) will guide you from goal setting through detailed expense tracking.

For a wider-angle view, try *Mary Hunt's Debt-Proof Living* (Broadman & Holman, $15). A recovered credit-card addict, Mary explains how to stay out of debt and put your life on sound financial footing. (She also publishes a newsletter called *The Cheapskate Monthly*, for those of you who want to embrace creative frugality.)

If you suspect that chronic overspending is at the root of your money problems, we recommend our own guide, *Overcoming Overspending: A Winning Plan for Spenders and Their Partners*, by Olivia Mellan with Sherry Christie (Walker & Company, $13), which helps you understand this behavior and offers tools and techniques for turning it around.

In *Slash Your Debt: Save Money and Secure Your Future* (Financial Literacy Center, $11), authors Gerri Detweiler, Marc Eisenson, and Nancy Castleman show how to develop a personalized dollars-and-cents strategy that will free up more money for savings.

Looking for ideas on how to pinch pennies that can add up to dollars? See *The Complete Tightwad Gazette: Promoting Thrift as a Viable Alternative Lifestyle* by Amy Dacyczyn (Random House, $20).

Changing the way you think about money

A fascinating (and very readable) reference on behavioral finance is *Why Smart People Make Big Money Mistakes—And How to Correct Them: Lessons from the New Science of Behavioral Economics*, by Gary Belsky and Thomas Gilovich (Fireside, $12).

George Kinder integrates emotional and spiritual perspectives with financial planning in a wonderful way in *Seven Stages of Money Maturity: Understanding the Spirit and Value of Money in Your Life* (Dell Books, $13).

General financial information

The *Wall Street Journal* paperback series by Kenneth M. Morris and Alan M. Siegel takes a "USA Today" approach to finance, with colorful graphics and bite-sized text. About $15 each, they're terrific for anyone (lots of financial professionals have them on their office shelves, too). If you buy only one, make it *The Wall Street Journal Guide to Understanding Personal Finance*, a primer on banking, borrowing, investing, and taxes. To expand your financial expertise, you may want your bookshelf to include the *Guide to Planning Your Financial Future* (retirement planning from A to Z), and *Guide to Understanding Money and Investing*, for the big picture (what the Federal Reserve does, how markets work, investments explained in depth).

For clear, friendly, in-depth information on a multitude of money topics, we like Jane Bryant Quinn's *Making the Most of Your Money* (Simon & Schuster, $30). While there are no cute graphics, you do get Jane's savvy opinions along with the facts—making this a superlative reference book for readers at any level of financial knowledge.

Sometimes, "getting" money concepts is just a matter of looking at them in a different way. Paula Ann Monroe's *Left-Brain Finance for Right-Brain People: A Money Guide for the Creatively Inclined* (Sourcebooks, $19) offers practical information in a format that allows you to skim, skip, and develop a plan in a nonlinear way.

For a reasonably confident reader who wants to improve her money skills, it's hard to beat *The Wall Street Journal Lifetime Guide to Money* by C. Frederic Wiegold and the *Journal's* personal finance staff ($16). It's full of clearly written advice on a wide range of financial subjects from accidental-death-and-dismemberment insurance to zero-coupon bonds.

Investing

No matter where you are on the investment learning curve, you'll find excellent reader-friendly guidance in *The Only Investment Guide You'll Ever Need* by Andrew Tobias (Harvest Books, $13).

Want to know more about building wealth by taking advantage of today's new ways to invest? Financial planner Victoria Collins offers commonsense advice in *Investbeyond.com: A New Look at Investing in Today's Changing Markets* (Dearborn, $19).

If you're in a high tax bracket, find out how to invest more tax-efficiently with *The Complete Idiot's Guide to Tax-Free Investing* by Grace W. Weinstein (Alpha Books, $19).

Money and relationships

Drawing on her credentials as a psychologist and a financial planner, Victoria Collins suggests excellent emotional and practical solutions for partners in *Couples and Money: A Couples' Guide Updated for the New Millennium* (Gabriel Books, $14).

Whether or not you're in a couple relationship, Olivia Mellan's *Money Harmony: Resolving Money Conflicts in Your Life and Relationships* (Walker & Company, $13) will help you understand the strengths and weaknesses of your own money personality. Valuable ideas, conversations, and exercises guide you toward true harmony with your money.

Divorce

For a comprehensive guide to protecting your financial interests during a breakup, see *Divorce and Money: How to Make the Best Financial Decisions During Divorce* (Nolo Press, $35) by Violet Woodhouse, who is both an attorney and a Certified Financial Planner.

Another good reference focusing specifically on women's needs and concerns is *Divorce: A Woman's Guide to Getting a Fair Share* by Patricia Phillips (Arco, $16).

Math anxiety

Besides Sheila Tobias's *Overcoming Math Anxiety* (W.W. Norton, $13), which we mention in chapter 1, two excellent references are *All the Math You'll Ever Need: A Self-Teaching Guide* by Steve Slavin (John Wiley & Sons, $16), and *Conquering Math Anxiety: A Self-Help Workbook* by Cynthia A. Arem (Wadsworth, $20).

Children and money

To learn ways of teaching your kids about money, Janet Bodnar's books are great. Her latest is *Dollars & Sense for Kids* (Kiplinger Books, $18). As "Dr. Tightwad," she also writes regularly for *Kiplinger's Personal Finance Magazine*. Another good choice is Elizabeth Lewin and Bernard Ryan's *Simple Ways to Help Your Kids Become Dollar-Smart* (Walker & Company, $8.95) If you like audio books, you can download *Mom, Can I Have That? Dr. Tightwad Answers Your Kids' Questions About Money* for $7 from Amazon.com.

No matter which resources you choose, the important thing is to keep learning. As you learn, periodically reassess your progress to make sure your money is working toward the goals and dreams you've defined. You'll know then that you're approaching the destination on your road map—the financial well-being that every one of us deserves.